NARRATOLOGY IN PRACTICE

MIEKE BAL

NARRATOLOGY IN PRACTICE

UNIVERSITY OF TORONTO PRESS
Toronto Buffalo London

ISBN 978-1-4426-5036-7 (cloth)   ISBN 978-1-4426-2292-0 (EPUB)
ISBN 978-1-4426-2837-3 (paper)   ISBN 978-1-4426-2291-3 (PDF)

Library and Archives Canada Cataloguing in Publication

Title: Narratology in practice / Mieke Bal.
Names: Bal, Mieke, 1946–, author.
Description: A companion to the fourth, revised edition of Narratology:
    introduction to the theory of narrative (2017). | Includes bibliographical
    references and indexes.
Identifiers: Canadiana (print) 20210221356 | Canadiana (ebook) 20210221437 |
    ISBN 9781442628373 (paper) | ISBN 9781442650367 (cloth) |
    ISBN 9781442622920 (EPUB) | ISBN 9781442622913 (PDF)
Subjects: LCSH: Narration (Rhetoric) | LCSH: Art. | LCSH: Motion pictures.
Classification: LCC PN212 .B25 2021 | DDC 808.5/43 – dc23

Artworks under copyright provided courtesy of the artists.

Figures 12 and 13: Louise Bourgeois, Cell XXVI, 2003 © The Easton
Foundation / VAGA at Artists Rights Society (ARS), New York / SOCAN,
Montreal (2021).

University of Toronto Press acknowledges the financial assistance to its
publishing program of the Canada Council for the Arts and the Ontario Arts
Council, an agency of the Government of Ontario.

 Canada Council   Conseil des Arts
for the Arts   du Canada

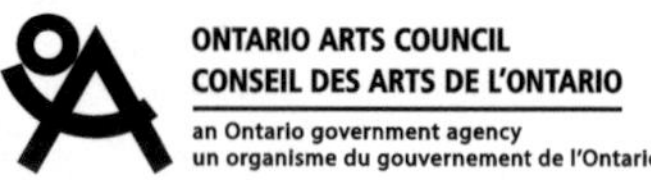 ONTARIO ARTS COUNCIL
CONSEIL DES ARTS DE L'ONTARIO
an Ontario government agency
un organisme du gouvernement de l'Ontario

Funded by the   Financé par le
Government   gouvernement
of Canada   du Canada 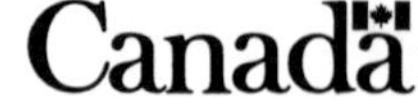 Canada

Contents

List of Figures   vii

Preface   ix

Introduction   3

1 Text: Signs   24

    1 Preliminary Remarks   24
    2 The Narrator   28
    3 Non-narrative Comments, Narrative Arguments   54
    4 Description   56
    5 Levels of Narration   63
    Remarks and Sources   70

2 Transition: Between Text and Society   74

    1 Preliminary Remarks   74
    2 Frame Narrative's Invisible Frame   76
    3 Con-fusing Meanings   82
    4 Between Narrative and Theatre   86
    5 Con-fusing Media   91

3 Story: Aspects   99

    1 Preliminary Remarks   99
    2 Temporality   100
    3 Characters   125
    4 Space   131
    5 Focalization   138

4 *Transition: Media in Dialogue*   145

1 Preliminary Remarks   145
2 Novel and Film, a Two-Way Street   146
3 Making and Thinking Images in Text   153
4 Image Making and Thinking in Images   156
5 Merging Everything   160
Remarks and Sources   164

5 *Fabula: Elements*   167

1 Preliminary Remarks   167
2 Events   168
3 Actors   176
4 Time   184
5 Location   189
No Conclusion   192
Remarks and Sources   195

References   197

Index of Names and Titles   207

Index of Terms and Concepts   213

Figures

1 *Ida*: Ida meets her aunt   9
2 *Ida*: The aunt returns to Ida   10
3 *Ida*: Aunt Wanda jumps out of the window   11
4 *Ida*: Lovemaking unrecognizable   12
5 *Ida*: Ida on her way to …?   13
6 Mary Longman, *Co-Dependents*   17
7 *Schindler's List*: Schindler watches   30
8 *Schindler's List*: Destruction of the ghetto   31
9 Nalini Malani, *In Search of Vanished Blood* (detail)   33
10 Don Quijote (Mathieu Montanier) in FID-focalization   39
11 Edvard Munch, *Red Virginia Creeper*   42
12 Louise Bourgeois, *Spider* (detail)   49
13 Louise Bourgeois, *Spider*   52
14 *Madame B*: "Broken House"   60
15 Ann Veronica Janssens, *Corps noir*   67
16 *A Thousand and One Days*: Who is speaking?   79
17 *A Thousand and One Days*: Tarek cannot believe the cops looked for him at his fiancée's house   80
18 *A Thousand and One Days*: Tarek always feels the hot breath of time   81
19 Ken Aptekar, *I'm Six Years Old and Hiding behind My Hands*   93
20 Ken Aptekar, *I'm Six Years Old and Hiding behind My Hands* (detail: shadows)   94
21 Ken Aptekar, *I'm Six Years Old and Hiding behind My Hands* (detail: envelope)   98
22 Fiona Tan, *Linnaeus Flower Clock*   104
23 Fiona Tan, *Facing Forward*   105
24 *Madame B*: Social cruelty, quoted from Maya Deren   115
25 *Madame B*: Emma gives up, quoted from Maya Deren   116

26 Roos Theuws, *Kitab al Manazir*   119
27 Roos Theuws, *Fences & Pools*   120
28 Jeannette Christensen, *Woman Interrupted* (detail: Razan)   122
29 Cronovizor (augmented reality)   135
30 Rembrandt, *Bathsheba at Her Bath*   157
31 Cassandra (Magdalena Żak) on her way to a new episode in her
    lessons in time-thinking   194

Preface

This book is a companion to the fourth, revised edition of my book *Narratology: Introduction to the Theory of Narrative* (2017). In that book I present conceptual tools, together forming a coherent theory of narrative, for the analysis of narrative texts and artefacts, or to put it differently: the analysis of the narrativity in a variety of texts and artefacts. The theory presented there is explained and briefly substantiated with succinct examples, mostly from literary narratives. In earlier editions I had progressively expanded the text with examples from other media than language, motivated by my own excursions into the visual domain. This, I was told, made it a bit confusing for students within literary studies. I listened to that criticism, as I tend to do. Since clarity had been my primary goal, I made a rigorous step: I eliminated practically all non-literary examples, with some regret, as well as some of the literary ones; and decided to set those aside for a companion volume. The resulting volume you now have in hands. In this book, therefore, I follow the opposite direction.

Here, I reduce the theory to simple definitions of the main concepts, included to enable reading this book independently from the companion volume if you so wish. I aim to offer more extensive analytical, interpretative bits and pieces. I do this to demonstrate the value of bringing to bear a coherent theory and a set of tools derived from it, on a variety of narratives or narrative aspects. To make the case for narrative's omnipresence in culture and the subsequent yield that a clear and systematic theory of narrative can offer, these include visual and cinematic narratives. This is a way of demonstrating that narrative is not bound to language and of making the theory useful for students and scholars in a variety of fields of the humanities and social sciences, and beyond. One case addresses medicine; another, the history of science, for example. And to foreground the dialogic nature of intellectual pursuits such as this one, I also include here and there a further interpretation not of a text but of a concept that, I will argue, harbours a narrative, without which the implications of the concept cannot be understood.

It is important to realize that the interpretations offered in the present volume do not form a coherent whole. Nor is any of them a "complete" analysis of a cultural text, if such a thing is possible at all. To emphasize this fundamental incompleteness of analysis, I conceived this book as a *mosaic* of theoretically fed reflections on and instances of the relevance of narratological analysis as a form of *cultural analysis*. This term I introduced in 1994 at the University of Amsterdam when (co-)founding a research institute that was to integrate the cultural-political perspective of "cultural studies" with the theoretical-analytical practices of semiotics and literary studies, visual analysis and anthropology. Primarily, these are nourished by the cultural text, the artwork, artefact; narrative, image, poem, or fragment, which are the concepts' interlocutors and primary centre of interest. An implied argument is also, however, to acknowledge the priority of the cultural object over the theory, which should not overrule it.

Instead, I seek to show how that object enriches our cultural environment, and also, conversely, how it can be used to manipulate. The small fragments of analyses together end up reconfiguring the theory as a whole, now made concrete and embedded in a framework of cultural analysis. The material, the collection of small case studies, can also be called a "constellation." Different from "mosaic," though, "constellation" suggests either a grouping without coherence or a pattern with its own logic. With the term *mosaic*, derived from a genre in visual art, I want to keep in sight both the fragmentary nature of the image, visible in the bits and pieces or shards out of which mosaics are made, and the tentative emergence of an image. That appearance of an image will not happen in the book but in the mind of the reader, who is hopefully being sensitized to the creative potential of the meeting between theory and practice. These images will be different in each case, as also converges with my argument about reading in general.

This book can be read in three different ways. The most likely mode of reading is in parallel with the other volume. It can also be read as a following volume for more detailed and deeper reflection. Or it can be read entirely independently from it. To facilitate the first mode of reading I indicate briefly and in brackets where in *Narratology* I have already written about a particular issue or text. For those who read this volume independently of the other one, these brief notes are skippable. The book must be able to stand on its own, with clarity. This goal of relative autonomy justifies the brief rehearsals of some key definitions, necessary for the independent coherence of this volume.

The primary goal of my writing, of my way of presenting, remains clarity, which I see as *intersubjectivity*: to give access and thus empower people, whether or not they are specialists in any of the fields from which the examples are drawn. Any reader should be enabled either by each of the two books or by the two together, to use the concepts as tools that assist them in probing narratives in the framework of the cultural analysis of narrative. To underline the systematic affiliation between the two books, the tables of contents of both are more or less similar. A difference of structure is that in the present volume, twice a section of "transition" has been added to reconnect what the theory has been compelled to distinguish. This goes to show that distinction is useful, but precisely because it does *not* equal separation. These two transitions are also meant to counter a possible tendency to rigidity in the understanding of theory. Between the first and the second part I have included a transitional section with a focus on the social relevance of narratology. Between the second and the third part, the transition focuses on intermediality: the dialogue between media such as literature and film or other forms of visual art.

As in the theory book, in order to avoid cluttering the text with references and footnotes, I have added a short section, "Remarks and Sources," after the three main sections. These explain the relevance of the sources listed in the reference list at the end. I apologize for what may seem an abundance of references to works of my own. This is necessary to avoid repetition as well as what is called "self-plagiarism," while also enabling further reading for those who wish to pursue a particular path in more depth.

The book focuses on the analytical and interpretive possibilities of the concepts on which the interpretations are based. They may sometimes strike readers at first sight as rather technical analyses. This is the ground of that intersubjectivity I mentioned. It facilitates discussion. But at the same time, my task is to demonstrate that something relevant for the understanding of the narrative in question can be derived from it; relevant for the world in which we all live, the cultures that make it understandable and enjoyable. It is to lighten the stricture of the structure that I insert between the parts those transitional sections, which connect the topics of the preceding one to what follows. These transitions consist of brief analyses of texts in different media, to give a taste of the wide possibilities the theory offers. But because they stand more or less on their own, they can be considered as more than fragments. Perhaps the term "case study," with some qualifications, would be appropriate. The combination of the technical analysis and the out-reaching interpretation is itself the *practice* that this book is meant to demonstrate and encourage.

The connection between technical analysis, socially relevant meanings, and interpretive freedom is the underlying issue on which the two books are based. This is also a plea for access to *dis*agreement. The technical part serves to make the procedure of interpretation as transparent as possible and accessible to those who might wish to contest an interpretation. This transparency is not a means to manipulate others to agree with one's interpretation. On the contrary: it is an attempt at opening it up for alternative possibilities while at the same time offering tools to come up with those in a reasonable and hence discussable manner. That is what intersubjectivity means: not that we all agree but that we can disagree, meaningfully and rationally. In this way, the procedure and the theory from which it is derived serve to enable an interpretive community to emerge.

A classroom is but one example of such a community; there are many others. While I am writing this preface during the 2020 coronavirus crisis, my hope is that the many colleagues who are struggling today with online teaching and the atomization of community this might risk entailing will find here ways of creating or strengthening a worldwide community within which disagreement, or (ex-)change of views, is always possible, and more than that: welcomed, so that difference can be respected. The primary aim of the two books is to offer clarity as a means of empowering people to participate meaningfully in the game of interpretation we are, unwittingly, constantly playing. Not only in study and in scholarly interpretative work, but also in everyday life, where disagreement is a crucial mode of practising freedom and of preventing disagreement from transforming into hostility. Instead, it can lead to intellectual friendship, of which criticism is an essential aspect.

Let me just briefly position my approach in relation to the discipline of narratology. (For more on this, see *Narratology* [esp. 150–3]). Most of the topics to be discussed in this book, especially in the second part, are known as parts of the traditional theory of the novel. In various countries, at various periods in the history of literary theory, and according to various principles, concepts have been developed, often independently of one another, that were presented under the heading "theory of the novel." This title is misleading for two reasons. The novel is probably the most heavily researched textual form of narrative. The concepts and distinctions that have emerged from this research usually have a more general scope. In so far as genre distinctions were considered, in these studies the novel was contrasted sometimes with drama, sometimes with poetry, and sometimes with the novella or short story. By using the term "theory of the novel" to indicate oftentimes (but not always) a much larger area of storytelling – a.k.a. narratology – critics unwittingly obscured the precise position of the novel with respect to other genres and types of text. Consequently, it is sometimes difficult to see to which area distinctions apply.

In the second place, the term "theory of the novel" is misleading because there can be no system as is presupposed by the term "theory." As I said, work was done in very different contexts on various components of the theory. For example, in Germany Günther Müller and his disciples concerned themselves with the temporal relationships in the novel, with what is here headed as "rhythm." In Anglo-Saxon countries work was done at another time, primarily on "point of view" theories. Müller worked with technical, quantitative criteria. The "point of view" theories were based mainly on psychological criteria. It seems difficult to imagine that these two groups of investigators were working on the same theory. Before reference could be made to a theory, all those different distinctions and concepts had to be brought together in one system.

One attempt to place all the traditional narratological distinctions together within one systematic, theoretical framework is formed by Genette's "Discours du récit," the larger part of his *Figures III* (1972). This has been a great inspiration for me in my wish to overcome the reductive approach of early structuralism, which was entirely concentrated on content: what is frequently called the *fabula*. Although I had taken this work as my point of departure and continue to take it as crucial, I have criticized it in depth. This author joins the different time aspects and focalization in one frame, in which he also places the narrative text. The highly different origins of the various aspects made it difficult to allot them all a place in a systematic theory of the story level. I have tried to solve this problem by retaining a clear point of departure: the question of how information about the fabula is shaped and presented to the reader, or the addressee, within the narrative. The more technical aspects within this framework, such as various time aspects, could be placed, but so could aspects such as the image of a character and space. Here the questions were specified: What kind of information do we get? How do we get it? How do the various elements and aspects function in relation to one another?

That last question as to how the elements and aspects function is determined by *focalization*. Focalization is a central concept in the second part. It has an overarching position with respect to the other aspects. The significance of certain aspects cannot be viewed unless they are linked to focalization. Moreover, focalization is, in my view, the most important, most penetrating, and most subtle means of manipulation. Analyses of newspaper reports that aim at revealing the hidden ideology embedded in such reports should involve focalization in their investigation and not restrict themselves to so-called content analysis (i.e., the semantic analysis of what the reports are about). I have written this book in the hope that the various readers it speaks to will experience, indeed feel, that they are being addressed.

In January 2020 I had the great pleasure of attending the inaugural lecture of William Marx, as a newly appointed professor of *littératures comparées* (mark the plural) at the Collège de France in Paris. Marx had himself defined and refined the mission he was going to conduct in this prestigious public institution. Both the plural form and the lack of geographical-cultural specification are fundamental to his conception of the (in-)discipline. Taking a poem by Cuban-French poet José-Maria de Heredia as his starting point, Marx circumscribes his field in terms that help me understand my own endeavour in this book better:

> Every text harbours an experience, every text confront us with an alterity. But that alterity is not a given; it must be conquered and understood painstakingly.

> [Chaque texte enclôt une expérience, chaque texte confronte à une altérité. Mais cette altérité ne se donne pas comme telle : elle doit être conquise et comprise de haute lutte.]

The poem by Heredia evokes stars as evidence of different worlds. This image made me consider the term "constellation" for a characterization of the ensemble this book offers. If I have chosen the other word, mosaic, for the reasons explained above, this is not because of the slightest disagreement with Marx; on the contrary. In addition to the argument given above, it is also my way of arguing that different words have different meanings, and that bringing everything to the same meaning would be a betrayal of the differences on which cultural practices are based and by which they can thrive.

NARRATOLOGY IN PRACTICE

Introduction

The central thesis of the theory of narrative demonstrated in this book is the usefulness of a provisional analytical division in three layers: text, story, and fabula. This division is not as self-evident as it may seem. For me it has primarily been an attempt to overcome the binary connotations of the older division in two – text and fabula, or story and plot. This older division is bound to a distinction, at risk of becoming a separation, of form and content. In addition to the explanation of the need for the three-partite division in *Narratology*, I hold that separation as untenable. Form shapes content and vice versa, inextricably. But for the purpose of analysis, merging it all poses a problem of clarity. Complicating the binary by distinguishing a layer in between those two makes a much subtler and more complex reading possible. But as said earlier, distinction does not entail separation. On the contrary: the connections between the three layers are the point of an analysis based on the distinction, which is by definition provisional.

Beginning In Medias Res

To set the intellectual tone for this book I begin "in medias res," with two examples, from different media; a novel and a film. They are both also "in medias res" in another sense: they demonstrate tight connections between narrative and the "real world," history, and other societal issues. With this I want to claim from the beginning that literature, film, and other forms of art are not frivolous beautiful things, but that they *matter*. Moreover, both are examples of narratives that seem to thematize the distinction that I am making only for analytical purposes. And thirdly, starting with a novel and a film and treating them strictly on a par is also a primary point of this demonstration of "practice." A key element of that idea of practice is "intermediality": the potential of a theory such as narratology to also help illuminate non-literary texts, such as paintings, films, and more.

Here is my first example. The popularly acclaimed Bengali writer Jhumpa Lahiri recently republished her earlier novel *The Namesake* from 2003. It is part of the growing number of novels on migration, recounting the difficulties of characters that are, either by their own volition or through their parents' earlier decisions, thrown into a world that is culturally foreign to them. The text is written in clear, almost plain prose. But this doesn't make language self-evident. Language and its uses are topics that come up with regularity. Relying on the definitions proposed in the other book, briefly reiterated here, I will give an example of each of the three layers of the narrative. *A narrative text* is a text in which an agent or subject conveys to an addressee ("tells" the reader, viewer, or listener) a story, in a medium, such as language, imagery, sound, buildings, or a combination thereof. *A story* is the content of that text and produces a particular manifestation, inflection, and "colouring" of a fabula. *A fabula is* a series of logically and chronologically related events that are caused or experienced by actors.

On the level of the text, these two examples clarify how the text inflects the story, and the story, the fabula. The novel's title suggests we begin with the name. Names: it couldn't be more textual. Also, the title *The Namesake* tells us that there is more than one person bearing the same name. Language and ambiguity: a good start. The main character of *The Namesake*, called Gogol for reasons he understands only much later, hates his name and in adulthood changes it to Nikhil. This name has the double advantage of sounding more Indian and of being easily Americanized to Nick. It provides more clarity, then, on both sides of the cultural divide that shapes the character's life. This is a textual element. However, there is something strange. When fully "Nikhiled," the narrator keeps calling the character Gogol, including when the text phrases the man's perception – his focalization. Initially, this puzzled me. It enticed me to read against the grain. Paying attention to perception, including its potential discrepancy from the text, what I call focalization has always been my primary tool for such reading. This is also the primary concept that justifies the distinction into three, not two layers.

Every single time I read the name in these passages, I felt slightly bothered. Calling the young man "Gogol" against his will seemed the act of a bossy narrator. Moreover, had the author been sensitive to the importance of focalization in the story, I thought, she would either have matched the character's decision and used the chosen name, or somehow differentiated between the two in ways readers could work with to make sense of the confusion of his identity that is obviously at the root of this name-game. Until late in the novel, on page 241 the two names cross swords. At a party, the following exchange occurs:

> "Hey there," Gogol says. "Need any help?"
> "Nikhil. Welcome." Donald hands over the parsley. "Be my guest."

Note that this short dialogue is an embedded text. The common English phrase "be my guest," meaning "do as you like" suddenly gets a slightly ironic inflection in which the notion of "guest" is taken literally for just a moment: Gogol does not belong. Not at the party, given by friends of his wife, nor in its very American YUP culture. The passage has no character that perceives the events. It is narrated in an objectifying tone. From then on, it dawned on me that the persistence of the name Gogol, in all its Russianness, stands for the persistently Indian misdirected longing of the character. Born in the US, he is unable to put down roots in either place, neither that of his parents nor his own. Due to that rootlessness, the Russian name turns out appropriate after all; precisely in its strangeness, its misfit.

The main character's mother, Ashima, is the actual immigrant. She is the one who is married off from India to an Indian-born man working in the US. Two key moments in her life set her in an intercultural, interlingual plight. The first is giving birth to her son (the one later to be called Gogol). When the doctor tells her that the delivery is going to take a lot more time because she is not yet fully dilated, she doesn't understand the key word and asks, "What does it mean, dilated?" (3) Clearly, the point is that we see that word anew as strange, somewhat threatening, and in need of explanation. The text is not so plain, after all. Then the text describes the gestures the doctor uses to communicate, and we are immersed in the story, in which "text" is under scrutiny. All we get is Ashima's vision-, hence, focalization-based understanding: "explaining the unimaginable thing her body must do in order for the baby to pass." This is a clear-cut instance of a narrator telling about a character perceiving. Ashima sees the gesture the doctor makes – the seeing an act of focalization, the gesture an event in the fabula – and she interprets it as "unimaginable."

Much later, when Gogol is an adult – hence, at least after twenty years of living and working in the US – Ashima is being told that her husband "has expired." Again, she doesn't get it, but this time, the lack of understanding is thickened:

> Expired. A word used for library cards, for magazine subscriptions. A
> word which, for several seconds, has no effect whatsoever on Ashima.
> "No, no, it must be a mistake," Ashima says calmly, shaking her head,
> a small laugh escaping from her throat. "My husband is not there for an
> emergency. Only for a stomachache." (168–9)

While the first lack of understanding might still be due to her relatively
recent arrival, the second one retrospectively explains the first. An implicit refusal to adapt to the new culture and language has informed her
life in the US all along those twenty years. But there is more to it.

In both cases, a form of denial is added to surprise, and to the awk-
wardness of talking about such intimately bodily things to a man (for
the birth) and through a telephone (for the death). Embarrassment, connected to cultural and sexual difference together, is at issue, rather than
linguistic ignorance. The frames within which these two linguistic mis-
haps occur, rather than the words as such, come together when Ashima,
reflecting on words, ponders, "For being a foreigner, Ashima is beginning
to realize, is a sort of life-long pregnancy – a perpetual wait, a constant
burden, a continuous feeling out of sorts" (49). The metaphor is doing
the telling, more than the very American phrase "feeling out of sorts."
It is in the equation foreignness–pregnancy that Ashima's perception is
expressed. But who, what subject, does this expressing, we may ask?

This, it turns out, is elaborated throughout the novel, especially in
the form of memories. The text tells the memories. The memories, as
aspects of the story, convey events from the characters' past, heavily
inflected by the characters' perception, imagination: in short, "focalization." These are "multitemporal" as well as "multidirectional" memories – two concepts that, like "focalization," will be discussed later.
Juxtaposing memories of the past, future memories, and acts of memory in the present, the narrator crosses the fine line between memory
and the imagination (62–3), all this negotiated through memories of
wishes that remain unfulfilled (127).

The key memory is of a trip Gogol made with his father, to the end of
a stretch of coast. The sentence that ends the chapter is an injunction by
the father, who tells his son:

> "Try to remember it always" … "Remember that you and I made this journey,
> that we went together to a place where there was nowhere left to go." (187)

Now that we have understood the way focalization functions to cross
the bridge and overcome the gaps migration has dug, including between father and son, the entire novel, it seems, unfolds to heed the

father's injunction. Keeping the attention on memory as a specific form of focalization, through systematic attention to focalization we can grasp how what I will call "multitemporality" and what has been called "multidirectionality" join forces in complicating the sense of history as a chronological series of events: in turning (factual) history into (subjective) memory.

Memory militates against a binary view of narrative as a text telling a story, or a story telling a plot. For the sake of this and the following example, I propose we consider the fabula a kind of history – but then, due to the story level, frequently imagined rather than necessarily having occurred in the past. Or both. The string of events we call history now turns from a line into a constellation from which rays go out in all directions. Futurality itself, then, is multidirectional, encompassing the past as well as the times of others. If subjectivity is porous, however, then memory and history are inseparable. In order to realize this intertwinement of memory, which is on story level, and history, which is on fabula level, it is important to first distinguish them. Only then can their interrelation and the misunderstandings it produces become clear.

Because narrative is not by definition linguistic, and the corpus narratology opens up is not confined to literature alone, many of the analytical fragments in this book propose a narratological analysis of artefacts in other media. I use the common term "text" to indicate artefacts in any medium. An obvious one is film, which is by definition narrative, due to the time-based sequence of images that constitute the moving images that are the substance of a film; its text. In film, a three-level structure is equally important, even though concepts can never simply be transferred from one medium to another without thinking through how they sit with the new medium. My second example again concerns history. This is a film, therefore, with a "text" of a different kind. How the concept of text can be transferred to film – or painting, photography, comics, and more – will become clear in the following account.

In *Ida*, a 2013 Polish film by Pawel Pawlikowski, set in 1962, the distinction between the three levels seems even a driving force. The film's beauty, a feature of the text, won it many awards and also some controversy. The issue of the controversy is whether the film's beauty counters, or distracts from, the affective impact of the sad historical theme. Let me say from the beginning that my opinion is a resounding no. On the contrary. Beauty helps affect. Knowing, not knowing, and discovering through perception is a key subtheme of the film. This entails a strong focus on the story, on focalization. Both text and story converge in the enigma of the fabula, which remains delayed or even unresolved. Key events are never mentioned. They can only be deduced from the text and story.

The text – which was characterized for *The Namesake* as ambiguous – is here characterized as "historical," a characterization that relies on many different features. The film text is made in black and white and with a 3:4 aspect ratio, thus inserting itself in the cinematic aesthetic of the 1960s, when the events of the primary fabula happen. The text's formal properties, thus, participate in the telling of the story. Moreover, it is composed of images shot without camera movement. Thanks to the converging of these formal features, the film also alludes to the very first bits of film in the late nineteenth century. Many images are shot outside, with the figures looking vertically forlorn in a low portion of a high landscape where the sky is always present. In view of the controversy mentioned, then, we can discuss the question of whether the resulting beauty is an anaesthetization of history – as opponents would claim – or, on the contrary, a withdrawal of the medium of film from its later aesthetic excess, as I tend to argue. One kind of beauty fights another. It is not beauty alone, however, that determines either affective effect or historical awareness, or the one through the other.

This is where the two examples join forces. Both narrative artworks foreground not only the narratological distinction but also and more crucially the importance of history in and for fiction, and vice versa. Thus, they counter the common assumption that fiction-making is an escapist manoeuvre. The novel *The Namesake* deploys plain prose, avoiding pathos, to highlight textual conflict between linguistic-cultural situations. Memory is central in these tensions. In a comparable mode, and also in relation to history, the film text of *Ida* feels like a refusal of everything cinema can do to make a strong impression on its viewers. The film narration uses none of the current cinema tricks that boast the medium's sheer-unlimited affordances. The unspectacular landscapes clearly show an avoidance of beauty for its own sake. The static nature of the camera work (by Łukasz Żal), a textual feature, suggests the idea that the characters are really inside history, trapped by it rather than having their own agency in it. They are not directing but undergoing history – their own moment in history and that which came before. This is where the specific work of the fabula impacts on the film.

As in *The Namesake*, in this film, storytelling is minimalist – bare, even. This is, however, not the same as neutral, indifferent, or objective. Refusal, avoidance, and rejection are just as much features of the narrative text as the positive features to which we usually attend. This film text feels like a refusal of everything cinema can do too easily. The static nature of the camera work, the long takes, the scarcity of changes of framing, light, and weather conditions tell us that the characters are immersed in history: not directing but undergoing it.

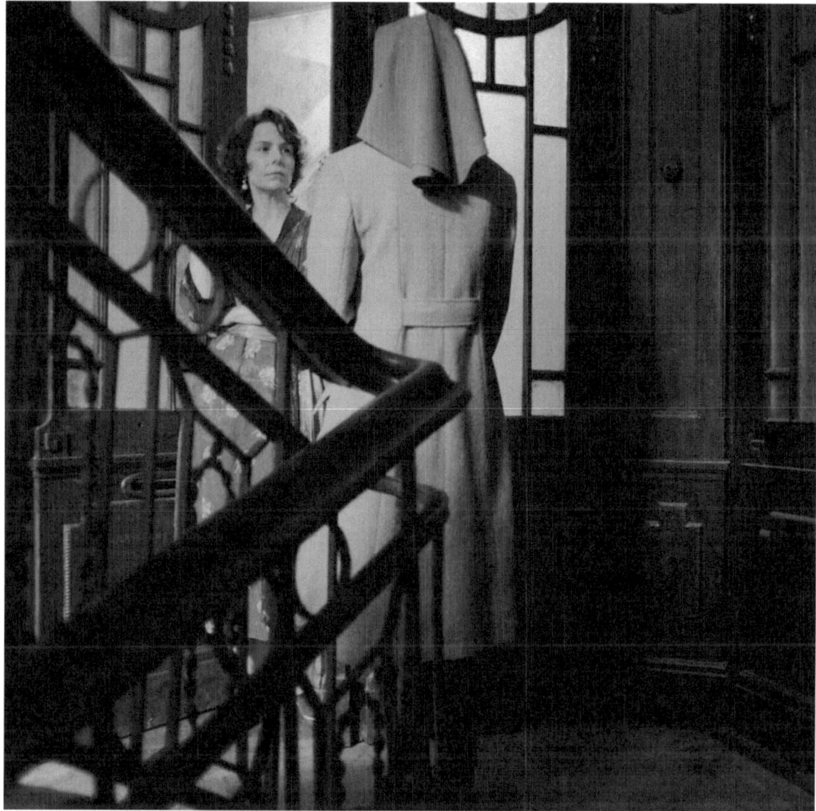

Figure 1. *Ida* (2013): Ida meets her aunt. Video still.

So far, my comments bear on the level of the text. Of the many aspects the story this text tells us that are equally based on the principle of omission, reduction, and a sparse use of cinematic means, I mention only a very few examples. First, when the main character's aunt, Wanda (Agata Kulesza), first meets her niece, Ida (Agata Trzebuchowska), she recognizes her immediately. But she is not very hospitable and soon dismisses her. Between the moments she lets her go, then a bit later, picks her up again in a café, no significant time lapse or a change in her look or behaviour helps us understand the change from dismissing to picking her up again (Figures 1 and 2). As a character she seems very different. The spaces of the two meetings may implicitly explain something: first the woman's home, then a public place. The situation of perception

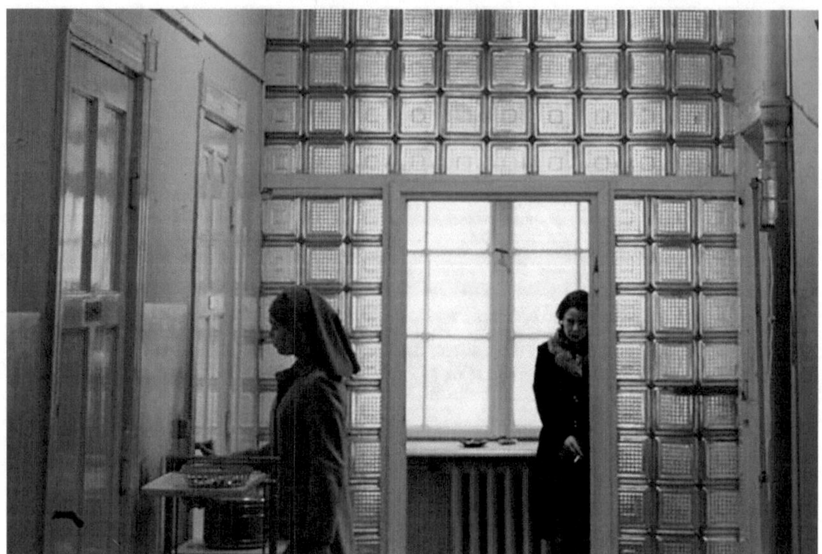

Figure 2.   *Ida* (2013): The aunt returns to Ida. Video still.

also differs. In the first, Ida rings the aunt's doorbell, and the aunt opens the door, recognizes her, and shows her in. In the second it is the aunt who peeps through the café window, sees (focalizes) Ida sitting somewhat dejectedly, and enters the café to resume her relationship with her niece, who is a novice, about to take her vows in a convent.

Second, there is a significant embedded instance of perception and omission. When the aunt shows Ida a photo of her with her parents, there is also a little boy in the picture. Ida asks if she has had a brother. No, says the aunt, you were an only child. No explanation of the identity of the little boy is given. Note that this confrontation of ignorance and knowledge constitutes an event that brings together an image – an embedded text – and the perception of it. Later, the aunt tells Ida she had entrusted her own little son to Ida's mother for safekeeping. She never saw him again. It is left to the viewer to contribute to the story by remembering the photo and making the link between these two moments.

Third, towards the end, the aunt is in her large apartment, framed as primarily that: a large space. The aunt quietly walks around in it and equally quietly goes to the window, opens it, and steps out (Figure 3). Due to the undramatic image sequence and the absence of dramatic sound, that this is a suicide is not clear at the moment.

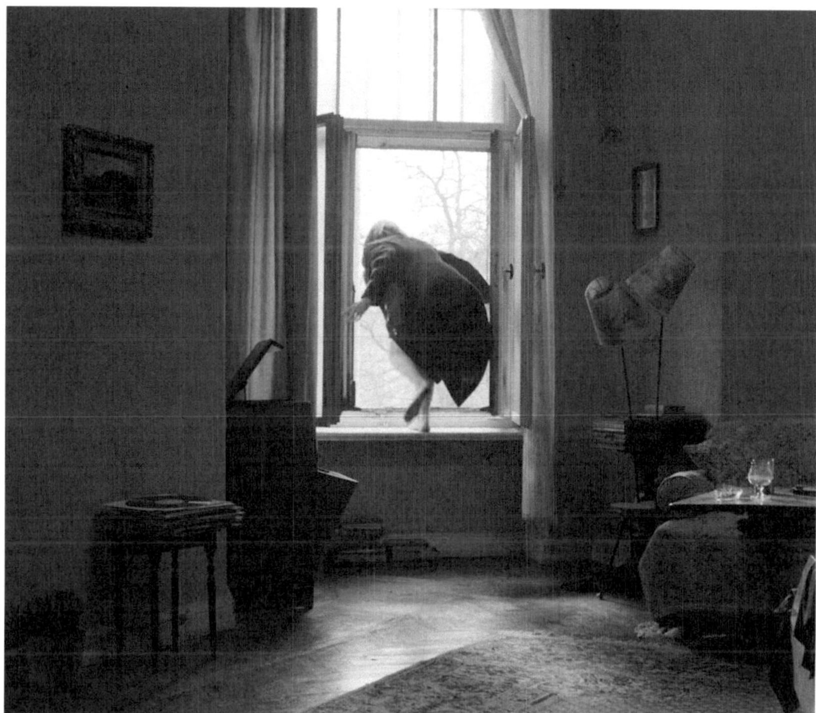

Figure 3. *Ida* (2013): Aunt Wanda jumps out of the window. Video still.

Only later, when Ida attends her aunt's funeral, do we retrospectively understand the silent act. Among the effects of this de-dramatization of the suicide is that it is making us viewers confront the important question of the tension between modesty as the opposite of voyeuristically and sentimentally looking in, and witnessing, in order to refuse letting the horrors of history remain invisible. By declining to show the act as a suicide, the story raises an issue that is characteristic of the cinematic story level. For it is on the story level that perception is opened up for reflection, for the characters as well as for readers and viewers. Isn't there a potential voyeurism in attending to the ultimate decision of someone who has lost everything? That such avoidance of voyeurism is a consistent aspect of this film also shows in the images – barely readable, confusing close-ups – of the moment after the funeral. Ida spends the night with a musician she had met earlier and who offers her a life of love and togetherness. The scene of lovemaking is not

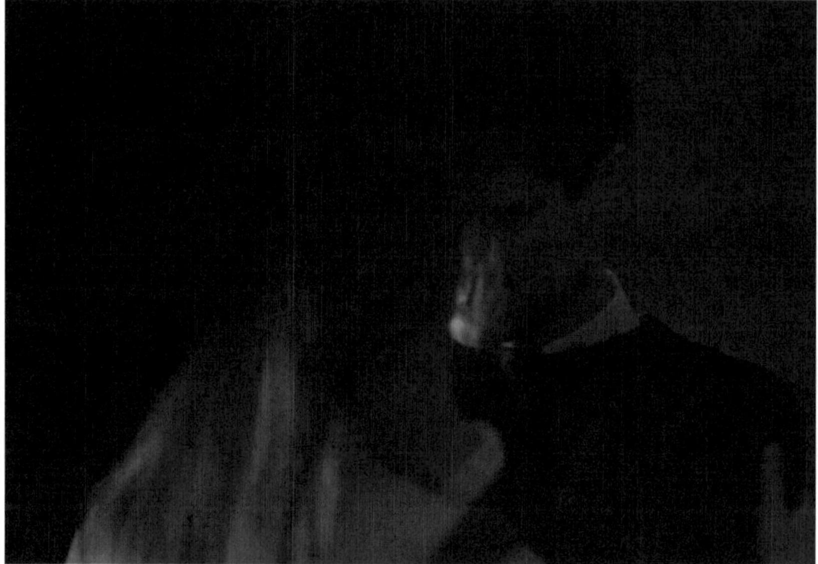

Figure 4. *Ida* (2013): Lovemaking unrecognizable. Video still.

visible (Figure 4). So far, the story level, where focalization is ambiguous, sometimes blurry.

In reviews of films, the fabula is the first thing mentioned, but in my narratological framework it comes last. What strikes most in *Ida* is the omission of many explanatory elements that would constitute the links among the causally related events. A standard summary of the fabula goes like this. Ostensibly set in 1962 in Poland, Catholic-raised war orphan Anna, destined to become a nun, uses her final days before confirmation to visit her only living relative, her aunt Wanda. This woman doesn't give her much, other than revealing that she is Jewish and that her real name is Ida, not Anna. After showing a photograph of her and her parents, the aunt dismisses her with the harsh words, "Family reunion is over." When Anna/Ida sits in a café waiting for the bus to return to the convent, the aunt looks through the window and seems struck by her resemblance to her mother, which sets in motion a retrospective fondness she transfers from mother (her sister) to daughter. They start all over, and together they begin the search for Ida's parents' grave. After finding the bones in a forest, they bury them in a proper cemetery. Then Wanda kills herself.

After her burial, Ida does not accept the proposal of her one-night lover to accompany him, and instead we see her walk with her suitcase

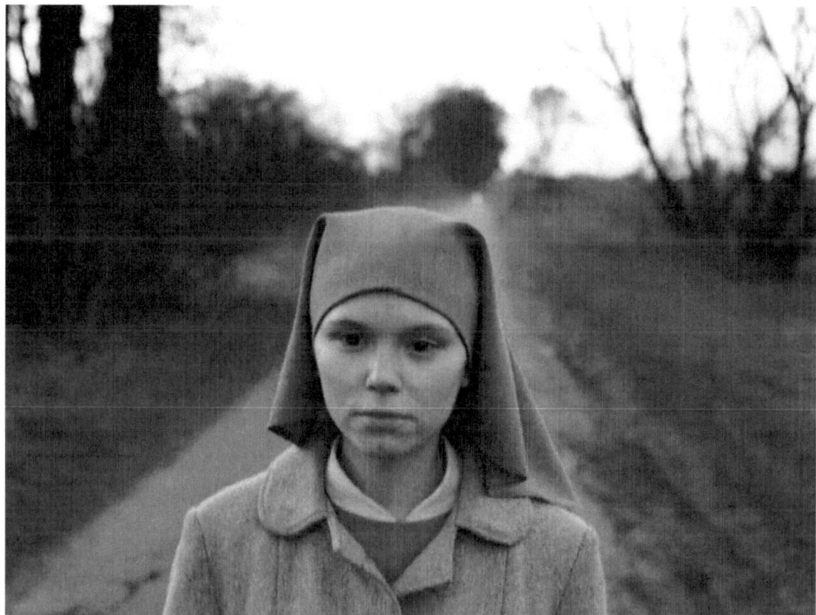

Figure 5.   *Ida* (2013): Ida on her way to …? Video still.

on a straight, empty country road, alone (Figure 5). Where she is going is not made explicit. Most likely, we tend to fill in: back to the convent. But this is only an assumption, compelled by the desire for an ending we as viewers tend to bring to our reading. Nothing indicates where she goes, only towards the picture plane, towards us viewers. But she doesn't come close. This ambiguous ending in aloneness moving towards our time and company is only one of many fabula elements that are not fleshed out.

These two short presentations of narratives of the kind we can all have access to show not only how the three layers I distinguish gain their momentum from their distinction and the ways they interact. They also intimate that history "outside," the history of the world, is of great relevance, whether the narratives are fictional or not. I propose to suspend that distinction, and surely don't want to make it an essential difference. They complement each other. The bits and pieces in the rest of this book will show time and again that fiction is a useful tool precisely to make the realities at stake tangible, so that they can be experienced on a profound level where cognition, understanding, empathy, and other forms of affect merge.

In presenting examples from visual as well as linguistic narratives, I do not deny differences between media. Especially in relation to focalization, that aspect of the story-level that most forcefully suggests visuality, confusion lurks. It may be useful to consider the following differences between focalization in linguistic and in visual texts. First of all, the focalization is the direct content of the text. If the text consists of lines, dots, light and dark, and composition, the focalization is already a subjectivized, interpreted content. In linguistic narrative, there is an external focalizer, distinguished in function, not identity, from the external narrator. This external focalizer can embed an internal narrator-focalizer, or just an internal focalizer. In visual narrative, such internal focalizers are usually depicted, or figured. The reality status of what they see differs according to the imagined vision of the external focalizer who embeds them. The same object or event can be differently interpreted according to different focalizers. If we didn't understand right away that Wanda committed suicide, it is because Ida didn't understand it either. Her focalization guides us.In literary narratives, an identification between the external focalizer with an internal one, if linguistically configured, can lead to "free indirect discourse." This merging can occur also in visual texts. There, too, it can be noticed in the visual means deployed for the narrative presentation. In the analyses that follow I will point these differences out, not to essentialize the media but to assist the work of analysis and avoid unwarranted conflations.

"Intership": Narratology between Disciplines

Many of the analytical bits and pieces in this mosaic-volume come from different academic fields or disciplines. Probing how narratology can serve the purpose of understanding how relations between disciplines can work responsibly has been my goal in the work through which I sought to expand narratology from literature into what I have been calling "cultural analysis." This is for the benefit of all participating disciplines between which relationships can be established without erasing the specificity of each. This is why I call this interaction interdisciplinarity, not transdisciplinarity, as is more common these days. "Trans" means going through, without being influenced by the itinerary; "inter" means connection, encounter. To insinuate the many other uses of that preposition "inter," I have termed the attitude towards the disciplines that are involved in this encounter "intership." The two narratives I have just considered in order to justify and make sense of the distinction between three layers on which my narrative theory is based belong to two different disciplinary fields: the studies of literature and film respectively. But even if these disciplines can easily be distinguished, neither of the two texts can be considered strictly monodisciplinary. Both reach out to other disciplines: the issue of immigration in *The Namesake* connects to sociology and (colonial) history; *Ida* addresses (post-)holocaust history and its repulsion for fiction. They are both deeply involved with history and using fiction to shape that involvement.

My brief presentation of a few instances where they not only present the three levels that I have distinguished for the sake of analysis but even focus on or thematize the distinction between them is my way of arguing for the relevance of this distinction, whether or not a narrative is primarily fictional or historical, and whatever the medium is in which it appears. Behind this refusal to make a firm distinction between fiction and history lies a conviction that neither one can do without the other. This issue will return throughout the book. I do not mean to suggest they can be collapsed into one, however. In the same vein, the differences between media are substantial and often material but not absolute. This will help me make sense of films based on literary novels, for example.

The fragments of analysis presented so far are attempts to clarify the way form and content are intertwined. Having been asked about this, I contend that such an analysis is *not* formalistic. It considers form, but it is not formalistic in the pejorative sense this term has been given with the onset of social criticism. On the contrary, it supports an awareness of the responsibility of readers for the meanings they produce, even if thinking they just get these from the text. The old idea that the proponents of close reading advanced, that the text speaks for itself, is not what I am proposing to retrieve. In contrast, I want to keep present the procedures of and responsibility for meaning in dialogue with philosophies of language that insist on the diversity of provenance (Bakhtin) and ambiguous meanings (Derrida) of any utterance. Far from rejecting such philosophies, I find them useful to avoid over- as well as under-estimating the freedom of readerly agency.

I claim that the analytical distinctions and concepts presented in these companion books help us to account for subjectivity in reading, for the cultural processes that brings such subjectivity into an intersubjective framework, and for ambiguity as a forceful, productive element therein. In a culture that functions within such complex forms of meaning-making, it is all the more important to take and assign responsibility for the choices we make. Cognitive and reception-oriented theories of language and narrative have persuasively argued that it is the reader who makes the meaning. But in doing so, the reader is in dialogue with the text. And to have such a dialogue, conceptual precision is effective. It is only once we know how a text is structured that the reader's share and responsibility for acting within those constraints can be assessed. Then the reader can become a co-author.

The mode of analysis presented based on this assumption is also deployed in visual criticism, even of rather abstract or non-figurative works that seem to yield little narrativity. As a third introductory example, then, Mary Longman's 1996 sculpture *Co-Dependents*, reminds the viewer of bones (Figure 6). This is a metaphor; it should not be taken to mean that the work is only a skeleton. On the contrary, the bonelike texture provides the wooden "bones" with a patina that shines with age. The sculpture is suggestive of, in Gerald McMaster's (1996, 24) words, "a sexual edge, giving rise to sensuous relationships." If the two parts that the slingshot-type connection binds together can be seen as anthropomorphic actors, the relationship between them is so full of tension, of desire and hostility, push and pull, that they instil a perpetual narrativity based on a delicate balance. The figure on the right, especially, barely touches the platform on which they stand, as if ballet dancing.

This delicate balance can be narratively fleshed out – turned into a story – with all the references that the material and formal aspects of the work bring along. The allusion to Aboriginal culture in the bones, slingshot, and earth-colour base provides a charged backdrop for an implicit argument in favour of close relationship. The bones connote death, but the figuration brings them to life, emphasizing that Aboriginal cultures are not dead. The patina of age provides the soft-polished wood with claims to a longevity that entitles the actors and the people they stand for to a future. McMaster interprets the relational quality of this work to shape an ecological ethics that reaches beyond the political issue of Aboriginality alone. And whatever the further story one wishes to read in this sculpture, it can only be effective in such a way if the anthropomorphism is allowed to enter the visual field.

The point of doing all this is not so self-evident, however. Instead, I would like to foreground, in this introductory section in particular, the difference between the presentation of tools and the demonstration of what they are for, and what they help us do. This difference is that between an intellectual loyalty to a disabused and adjusted structuralism, and an equally strong conviction that I, too, must make clear what purposes, other than intellectual rigour for its own sake, narratology can serve beyond itself and beyond literary studies alone. Here is an example, then, to set this slightly different stage for the concepts that follow. As a fourth, multiple example I will make an argument about interdisciplinarity; in this case, the interaction – not conflation – between narratology and anthropology.

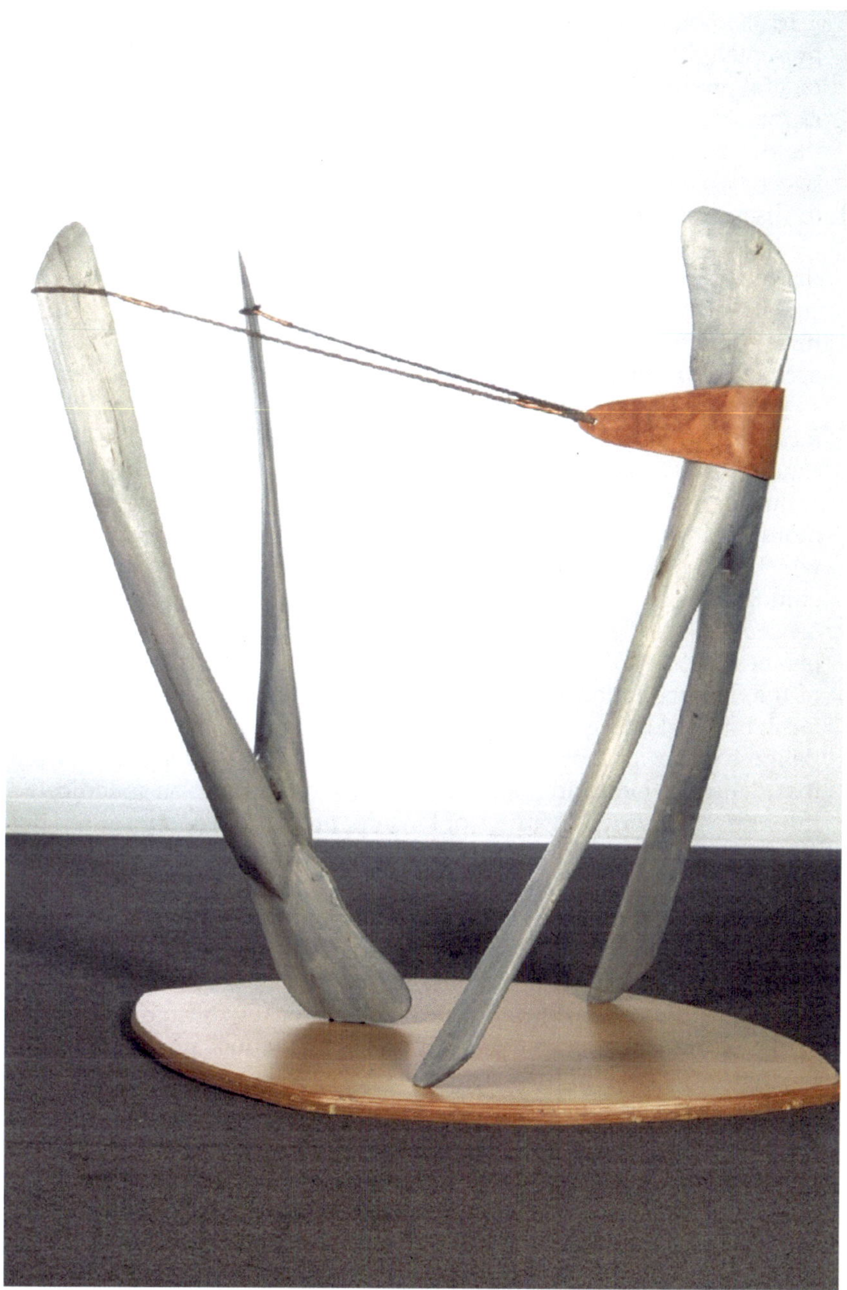

Figure 6.   Mary Longman, *Co-Dependents* (1996).

In a famous article in his book *Local Knowledge* (1983), Clifford Geertz presented a few case studies meant to provide insight into the fundamental problem of anthropology, that of the relations between ethnographer and ("native," "autochthonic") subject. Importantly, this is not the distinction between general – even universal – and local but between two local subjects of knowledge. The issue Geertz chose in order to discuss this problem is precisely the concept that lies at the heart of that problem as well as at the heart of narratology: the concept of the subject. As Geertz demonstrates, both the content of the concept of subject – what defines an individual in a given society – and the structural properties of the system of interpersonal reference vary greatly according to different cultures. Hence, the very notion of subjectivity, so central in narratological considerations of, for example, narration, focalization, description, but also of actors, the agents in the fabula, cannot be given a fixed, universal meaning.

But the different concepts of the subject that Geertz described are more clearly demonstrated in the person-to-person interaction in which he perceived them, in (social) drama if you wish, than in the ethnographic narrative itself. For there, while exposing the different conceptions of the subject, Geertz constantly doubles up the Balinese, Javanese, and Moroccan voices with his own, which for the purpose of the demonstration he leaves blatantly ethnocentric; hence, equally local, but pertaining to a different locality. Thus, he explains how the Balinese widower represses his grief and derives his subjecthood from that denial of mourning, and how the Moroccan person is indicated through a network of features of kinship, profession, and location. But he does so in a structure built on the Western concepts of person, the ethnographic "third-person" narrative.

A subtle narratological analysis of anthropological material can go a bit further, precisely because such an analysis temporarily brackets both ends of the embedding reality, the reality of the events "out there" and the reality of the ethnocentric reporter; for the duration of a prior analysis, the narratologist presupposes that the narrative is structurally self-sufficient and thus, fictional. I have experienced the usefulness of such an integration of anthropological eagerness for understanding real otherness and a narratological discipline of structural textual analysis in my studies of the Hebrew Bible, particularly the Book of Judges, which poses a number of acute problems of alterity, if only the reader is willing to see it.

I was particularly struck by the fact that three concepts referring to women seemed inadequately rendered, in translations and commentaries, by modern Western concepts: virgin, concubine, prostitute; not a haphazard series. The problem with virgin was that the immediate contexts of its occurrences systematically overdetermine the concept, adding apparently redundant phrases like "who have not known a man" (e.g., Judges 11); or the opposite, as with concubine, where no primary wife is ever mentioned, although in the current Western sense, the concubine would be a secondary wife (e.g., Judges 19). And with prostitute, it seemed strange that the certainty of paternity – that Jephthah, the alleged son of a prostitute, knows who his father is – seems to contradict the very idea of prostitution (again, Judges 11 and 19). Moreover, the word for prostitute, *zonah*, also occurs in the masculine form, and then it has a very different meaning. Then it means "stranger" or "foreigner." These three concepts indicating figures of women have a predominant role in the Book of Judges. In each of these cases, the fabula seemed determined by precisely these opaque figures.

My first response to these problems was, let's say, anthropological. Just as Geertz became particularly suspicious in the face of the generality of a concept that is so central in Western culture – the individual subject – so I became suspicious in the face of the concurrence of these three concepts indicating female status in a culture from the (non-European) past, translated into modern patriarchal terms. In other words, these translations seemed too smoothly to endorse the notion that patriarchy is a monolithic, transhistorical social form. But how to deal with that problem? Well, narratology may be able to help. My second response, my attempt to solve the enigmas the first response had produced, was narratological. A close analysis of the narratives in which these figures were so prominent suggested a different structural context – a different type of fabula – for "virgin" on the one hand, for "concubine" and "prostitute" on the other. Once that distinction had become clear, things got even more complicated. "Virgin" became continuous with two other terms referring to young women, according to age or life phase. "Concubine" and "prostitute" became synonyms, of which the projected features of "secondariness" and "harlotry" had to be suspended, since no element whatsoever of the fabulas had any relation to such notions. This is the kind of exciting alterity that William Marx had in mind in his inaugural lecture, mentioned in the Preface. These decisions were motivated by structural properties of the narratives. For example, the noun rendered as "virgin" is both hilariously overdetermined in Judges and then spoken by a male voice who seems obsessed by it, and not connected to a fabula about what we consider to be virginity at all, and then spoken by a female or ungendered voice.

Compare, for example, two passages from Judges. Judges 21:12: "found ... four hundred young girls, virgins, that had not known man by lying with him," where the external narrator speaks and the focalization also remains external so that the women do not focalize their own status. I would like to foreground here the addition "young girls." Compare this to 11:37: "leave me alone two months, that I may depart and wander upon [towards] the mountains, and lament [until] my 'virginity' [?]." There the "virgin" herself, Jephthah's doomed daughter, expresses her view of self. Virginity has no connection here to what we would call deflowering. It is more likely she will lament her death sentence at such a young age. The one juxtaposition of "virgin" and "concubine" in 19:24 ("Behold, my daughter the 'virgin' and his 'concubine'") is revealing in favour of the earlier separation as well as of a different interpretation of "virgin." I considered the word as referring to a life phase – sexually mature, but not yet married young women – rather than to a state – bodily integrity. The speaker and focalizer ("behold") in this case is the man who is the father of the one woman and host of the other.

The issue in the fabula is to protect the male guest from gang rape by offering a more attractive alternative: two young women to be swapped for one older man. Now, if being a virgin in the now-common sense were a recommendation to the rapists, then being a concubine in the common sense would not be. The host would have been well advised to leave the women's status unspecified. Unless the terms refer to life phase or age: two mature women, sexually usable, hence, rapeable, but still pretty fresh. Incidentally, it is necessary to keep in mind who is doing the focalizing.

The two other concepts also change their meaning according to story and fabula. Here the usefulness of the provisional suspension of both contemporary and modern reality becomes visible. Suspending moral views of sexual lasciviousness as well as assumptions about ancient Hebrew life often based on projection, and looking at the fabulas for which these terms are used, reveals a structurally recurrent combination, in which the terms referring to female status are linked up with the father's house, inheritance, and displacement – mostly literally, travel. The key is the *location* of marital life; this was the idea I came up with. In all cases where these terms occur in Judges, the status of the female partner is at stake, and that status is related to her not living or not staying in the house of the husband, but staying or going back to the house of her father. In that sense, for readers used to "virilocal" cultural contexts (where the husband's home is the marital place), such patrilocal habits make the women cultural strangers or foreigners.

The terms, then, must not be related to a moralistically loaded concept such as prostitution or a class-bound, condescending concept like concubinage. The apparent display of the father's wealth, in Judges 19, hardly imposes the view that this woman has been sold by her poor relatives to serve as a secondary wife. Instead, the original question of translation, through narratological analysis, is turned back to anthropology. The terms must be related to the issue of marriage forms. Judges displays other symptoms of a violent transition from one culturally sanctioned form of marriage to another, from what I have indicated above as patrilocal marriage, to what I call virilocal marriage (e.g., Judges 15). The hypothesis that this tension underlies the narratives as well as the uses of the problematic terms helps explain the most obscure passages, in particular of the book's final section. There, the most horrific violence against a woman in the entire Hebrew Bible suggests more than a gang rape and the cutting up of a woman's body by her husband as a call to war. It suggests that this civil war over the woman's dead body is about an intolerable cultural alterity.

What is the interdisciplinary interaction going on here? Let us assume that I learned from Geertz to suspend the content of the category of the subject, for he suggested we take apparent incongruities as evidence of otherness, not of stupidity. Thus, anthropology came first. As a result, I refrained from wondering what Jephthah's daughter may have thought of her imminent death, as a modern realistic psychologism would entice one to do, and instead took her words as indicators of some sort of ritual behaviour. Through considerations of fabula, the meaning of the term could then be related to phase rather than state. But I could do this only because, in a second move, I had related the detached term to narrative structure. This second move is the one Geertz does not make; instead, he narrates in the double voice I have pointed out.

In the second case – regarding concubine and prostitute – the transaction between the two disciplines is slightly different. Now, narratological analysis of the fabula came first. The structural property found – systematic connection between female status and marriage location, inheritance, and property – again covers an anthropological topic. But that background is a matter of established knowledge, not of method. The methodological issue is in the suspension that narratological structural analysis entails, of what we take to be or know as reality. That suspension, paradoxically, is necessary in order for the less ethnocentric view of reality – of otherness – to emerge. In other words, narratology and anthropology, here, are constantly and polemically intertwined.

This kind of interaction between narratology and anthropology is the more relevant as it addresses implicitly the major challenge posed to narratology: that of, precisely, the social embedding of narrative – in other words, its relationship to reality. Paradoxically, perhaps, privileging structural analysis over a reflection theory of language has in fact helped to reach reality more precisely, by a detour that made it more rather than less accessible. What is at stake is the intertwining of three ideologies and their influence on real lives: the ancient male ideologies according to which women's value is derived from bodily integrity, and where the location of married life inflects the power of men across generations; the ancient, perhaps male and female ideology according to which shifts in life phases are crucially important moments; and the modern ideology which projects sexual exclusivity as the major issue of an ancient narrative, perhaps as a pretext for its own continuation of that form of possessiveness. Narratological analysis helped disentangle these. Thus, it helped to do justice to otherness. It also, albeit implicitly, makes it easier to see the nature of the otherness in sameness: that is, to what extent these modern translations are informed by an ideology that is masculinist and thus represses female concerns. Interdisciplinarity, here, helps to disentangle confusions and, subsequently, to connect the strands anew.

In what follows, I will go through the main concepts of the narrative theory presented in *Narratology* by means of analytical fragments, some brief, some a bit longer, but never comprehensive. These are meant to make the case for the four points raised above:

- the usefulness of distinctions, especially the one in three layers;
- the relevance of what seems a technical analysis for the understanding of socially significant issues, and the patient, sometimes painstakingly meticulous concentration on the text that this requires;
- the importance of history, in fiction as much as in non-fiction – the latter a distinction that in itself has dubious connotations; and
- interdisciplinarity as the grounding for the theory presented in the two companion books.

Concepts that bridge between the technical analysis and the assessment of relevance, and which have remained implicit or ignored in *Narratology*, will be brought in contact, in "intership" encounters, with the more technical tools. Examples of this are, for example, trauma, the imagination, and the political. It is not always clear how "the political" can be understood in cultural analysis. The term "the political" as I use it here is understandable in distinction from "politics." Although both belong to the domain where social life is structured and to which it is subjected, these two terms are each other's opposite. In a concise book about this distinction, Belgian political theorist Chantal Mouffe defines the two terms as follows:

> … by "the political" I mean the dimension of antagonism which I take to be constitutive of human societies, while by "politics" I mean the set of practices and institutions through which an order is created, organizing human coexistence in the context of conflictuality provided by the political. (2005, 9)

"The dimension of antagonism": at first sight, that does not sound very nice. In this distinction, politics is the organization that settles conflict; the political is where conflict happens. Yet it is through the political that social life is possible. It can thrive, be alive, and also be dangerous. No wonder, then, that we usually seek to avoid conflict by means of consensus. Politics comes in to avert the potential of danger. Politics, which responds to it, constantly attempts to dampen the political.

This positive view of conflict might sound counter-intuitive, since most of us love to hate politics as domineering and menacing. We tend to attribute the negativity of conflict to politics rather than to its counterpart, yearning to be reassured by political leaders that conflict can be eradicated. Yet, as Mouffe cogently argues, the culture of consensus resulting from politics does not at all eliminate conflict; it suppresses it, and thus leaves it to its own underground and, consequently, potentially volcanic devices. Politics is in fact highly exclusivist and lives by "the negation of the ineradicable character of antagonism" (10). It is also in blatant contradiction to the lived social reality, in which conflict is generally present. Whenever in this book I write "the political" it is meant in this, Mouffe's sense.

Emerging from the mosaic of analyses, these concepts will build a more explicit bridge between narratology as a specialized theoretical framework and cultural analysis as the broader framework within which the narratological one earns its relevance, not in spite of but thanks to its technical precision. This is what I advanced above as intersubjectivity.

1

Text: Signs

1: Preliminary Remarks

A narrative text is a text in which a narrative agent tells a story. The first question this definition raises is that of the narrative status and identity of the narrative agent. Who is doing the telling? And in the wake of that question, we ask why that matters. Here, I first place this concept in relation to some neighbouring, although different concepts. When, in this part, I discuss the narrative agent, or narrator, I mean the (linguistic, visual, cinematic) subject that "utters" the text; that is its technical, medium-bound *source*. This is a function, and not a person, that gains expression in the unit of language or images that constitutes the text. This agent is not the (biographical) author of the narrative. The narrator of *Emma* is not Jane Austen. The historical person Jane Austen is not without importance for literary history, but the circumstances of her life are of no consequence to the specific discipline of narratology nor the analyses of Austen's work achieved within that discipline. This is more obvious with instances in which the author seems far removed, in terms of identity, from the main character. Just think of Flaubert and his Emma. In spite of the often-quoted (but undocumented, apocryphal) statement "Madame Bovary, c'est moi," the author's biography does not substantiate that claim at all. Far from it. Yet it makes total sense of the novel and the affective bond the narrator produces by means of ambiguous focalization. In order to keep this distinction in mind, I shall here and there refer to the narrator as "it," however odd this may seem. For an understanding of the importance of this distance between author and narrator, we have learned from French philosopher Michel Foucault and literary and cultural critic Roland Barthes half a century ago.

Barthes (1967) declared the "death of the author," a phrase so strong that it triggered a lot of discussion and controversy; Foucault (1979) came up with the arguments. In his famous attack in "What Is an Author?" on the concept and, especially, the authority of the author, Foucault banishes four different concepts of authorship. Not only does he question the psychological idea of the author, of the authorial intention, and of the historical author as origin of the work, but he also jettisons the last stronghold of the concept of the author, the author-function as the centring of meaning. He does this by demonstrating it to be a projection of a reader who needs semantic centrality to deal with the work. Foucault's alternative is a radical proliferation of meaning, where the author/work relation becomes a fluctuating function always interacting with other functions in the larger discursive field.

So far so good; but then, on behalf of the intersubjectivity, or discussability, of interpretation, the question arises, Is there a limit to these fluctuations? Or are we thus bound to an anything-goes attitude, which flaunts the reader's freedom but hampers meaningful discussion? This way of putting the dilemma is wrong; it demonstrates, incidentally, the damage done to thought by binary thinking. If we wish to make the interpretation of texts a worthwhile activity, we must resist this boundlessness. There is a limit, because if not, the alleged freedom of the boundlessness makes any future shift in power relations within the culture invisible, unarguable, and hence, virtually impossible; and it makes discussion futile. My position here is that there are limits, but these are not limits that can be authenticated through an appeal to the author, even when interpreting "author" in the widest sense of the historical context. Instead, those limits are strategic, yet of fundamental importance.

They are fundamental, because any position that does not assess the political basis of the status quo cannot challenge the established cultural powers. This is so, simply, since these powers were established on political grounds. But once shifting, strategic limits are accepted as replacement for both those limits that appear as natural because we have always alleged them, as well as for Foucauldian "anti-limits": where authorship and authority become one. Then, the new boundaries will offer a new starting point. From that point on it becomes possible to develop a politics of reading that draws its legitimacy from explicit political positions, not from any "real" knowledge – always at least partly fictitious – let alone alleged neutrality. And once we acknowledge both the necessity and the strategic nature of limits to interpretation, we move from the question of the author back to the question of interpretation. And the material object of interpretation is the (narrative) text, with its agent, the narrator. The limits are there where the text protests against projection-based interpretations.

This is not to deny the importance of the author or artist as the historical subject who made the text. My concern to make this distinction is not to deny authorship but to emancipate both author and reader from the stronghold of a misconceived authorial or interpretive authority. In his essay Foucault rightly foregrounds the link between authorship and authority. This authority ultimately entails a problem of censorship. Censorship of art, be it overtly political or subliminally social, is confirmed, strengthened, and perpetuated by censoring forms of interpretation. In a world where access to writing and other forms of artistic expression is made difficult – by the institutional censors of art – for all individuals not conforming to a self-asserting mainstream, making interpretation a privileged form of art processing risks subjugating it to the same mechanisms of exclusion. In such a context, authenticating an interpretation through appeal to the author is potentially oppressive.

But there is more to it. True, the academic practice of interpretation, linked with journalism and other more popular forms of interpretation through a common ideology and often even through shared personnel, can be a form of censorship in itself. Nevertheless, the margins built within art and the reigning concepts of beauty leave some space for the production of works that cannot be exhausted by mainstream responses. Smart interpreters can bring those qualities to the fore. But the exclusions operating within the very activity of interpretation as a practice taught and learned can easily subsume all interpretations that might enhance the unsettling aspects of these not-so-mainstream works; of interpretations that make the works appear as threatening to the established order. Masterful interpretations based on invisible assumptions can thus be given an authority that censors other views. But for the same reason, censorship *of* interpretation can be used to cover up censorship *by* interpretation. Appeal to an unverifiable authorial intention or biography assists such censoring.

A final issue must be kept in mind regarding the author. In what is now generally called neoliberal (late capitalist) culture, the author has become a marketable commodity. This constitutes a trap for readers seeking to translate their intimate experience of narratives into a discussable, intersubjective proposal. The commodified author is as fictitious as any character in a narrative and must be subjected to analytical criticism, lest the interpreter be already locked up in a specific partiality from the beginning. The result of such a position is a disempowerment, a political position that puts a strain on interpretive creativity and produces blindness to alternative possibilities.

A more open critical, academic, and educational policy can make room to include the views of those who respond to art from a less dominant social position. Such an opening up is an indispensable next step towards a better, more diverse and complex understanding of culture. In spite of its challenging and persuasive logic, we must place the authority of authorship within this dynamic. To put it overly simply: as soon as women began to speak, the subject of speech was no longer considered relevant; but also, as soon as more women began to interpret, many declared that there was no more need for interpretation. In other words, the same threat is acutely present as the one that the "death of the author" poses. This demonstrates how the problematic of interpretation and the challenge to the authorial authority are related. The distinction between author and narrator, once a structuralist reification of textual agency and frequently dismissed for that reason, continues to carry strategic weight in this sense. It helps to disentangle the different voices that speak in a text so as to make room for the reader's input in judging the relative persuasiveness of each of those voices.

Another widespread concept needs to be bracketed. In speaking of the narrator, I do not mean the so-called "implied author," either. This term was introduced by Wayne C. Booth (1961) to discuss and analyse the ideological and moral stances of a narrative text without having to refer directly to a biographical author, which was at that time still quite commonly done; it preceded the generalized use of the term "narrator." There are three problems with Booth's term, which I reiterate here because they are so tenaciously ignored.

First, in Booth's use of the term, it denotes the totality of meanings that can be inferred from a text. Thus, the implied author is the result of the investigation of the meaning of a text and not the source of that meaning.

Second, therefore, the term mystifies and overwrites the reader's input and is easily recuperated to grant the interpretation of one person – for example, a teacher or critic – the authority of knowing "what the author meant to say." This circles back to Foucault's warning about the author-authority conflation. Thereby the concept relegates the other readers again to the margins. This disempowers students, whereas empowering them is the primary goal of narratology.

Third, the notion of an implied author is, in this sense, not limited to narrative texts but can be applied to any text. This is why the notion is not specific to narratology, which has as its object narrative texts or the narrative aspects of a text. So, even if the two first-mentioned objections are not accepted, the more practical third one suffices to eliminate the implied author from narratology. These objections also hold, then, for

Seymour Chatman's 1990 comparative study of narration in fiction and film. Chatman relies entirely on the implied author as the basis for his concepts and distinctions.

The notion of the narrator needs still further positioning, however. It does not denote a storyteller, a visible fictive "I" who interferes in his or her account as much as they like or even participates as an actor in the action of the fabula. Such an explicit narrator is a specific version of the narrator, one of several different possibilities of its manifestation. The idea that a narrative text is uttered by a narrator is inferred from the communicative nature of the text: if a text can be conveyed, some agent does the conveying. In this discussion, I shall rigorously keep to the definition of the narrator as the agent that utters the (linguistic, visual, or other) signs that constitute the text. Only if we confine ourselves to this definition can we avoid confusions that ultimately lead to an appropriation of authority, a blurring of textual nuances, and an invisibility of the power inequalities involved. In the end, the term is not a personification but an indication of where the responsibility for the narration can be placed. The fragmentary analyses that follow will hopefully demonstrate the relevance of that distinction. These analyses will also clarify, as we go along, how the narratological concepts derived from primarily textual narratives can be useful brought to bear on non-linguistic narrative works.

One final note for this preliminary comment. According to what I wrote about it in the Introduction, the use of "political" in this discussion does not imply a particular political choice; this remains entirely up to the reader. I just mean to alert the reader to the presence of political pressures everywhere in cultural practices. This is where my insistence on intersubjectivity belongs; not in order to agree but to freely disagree, with a mutual understanding and without the authority Foucault rightly wished to bracket.

2: The Narrator

Distinguishing layers as I have proposed it also leads to the idea that seeing and other forms of perception of the events and characters constitute the object, or content, of narrating. What the narrator – seen as an agent, in order to specify where the narration comes from – tells about is the direct content or object. On that middle layer I situate other agents: most influential, the agent of perception. Precisely when the connection between these two activities is not self-evidently attributable to the same agent, it becomes easier to gain insight into the complexity of the relationship between the three agents that function in the three layers – the narrator, the focalizer, the actor – and those moments at which they do or do not overlap in the shape of a single identity or person. The word "person" here is not meant as an anthropocentric nor an anthropomorphic subject, but as an instance from which the text emanates. Here is another example of a film, this time a widely known one, through which the status of the agent of narration in mixed-media such as cinema will hopefully become clearer.

In Steven Spielberg's controversial 1993 film *Schindler's List* the distinction between narration and focalization turns out to be important. In the beginning, the actor Schindler is just one of the Nazis, socializing with them, taking economic advantage of the war and of the depletion of the Jews. But to do that he must deal with – that is, *see* – an individual Jew, the man named Stern. The filmic narrator has to *show* – cinema's major form of narration – what Schindler *sees* and what that seeing does to him, so that it makes him *act* differently. I didn't know the story when I went to see the film; I didn't know this awful man was going to change into a good man. There was no explication, no moment it happened inside him, but at some point, he just was a different man. How was this transformation, which occurred on the fabula level, narrated? Was there a conversion? If so, that is a Christian concept. True, culturally Schindler was a Christian, although a cynical enough one to be using the church to do business. Yet the reduction of conversion to a Christian meaning would obscure the narrative as well as the (inter) cultural importance of that moment.

The distinction between narrator and focalizer is crucial here. The "conversion" scene implies an important statement on vision: as distinct from the Christian concept, conversion is defined as a transformation caused by seeing, not in a positivistic or in a psychological but in a narratological sense; seeing differently, seeing difference, as a consequence of what the filmic narration shows. And seeing difference turns the fabula around, makes the character different. In Jewish culture, as many biblical passages demonstrate, seeing primarily equals insight. The turn-around is, for Schindler, to see individuals instead of the devastating, dehumanizing bureaucracy of numbers. Schindler's moment of insight happens – as is visually told – when the filmic text tells – shows, that is, through a suturing of two images (Figures 7 and 8) – how he watches the destruction of the ghetto from the top of a hill and from horseback, sutured to what he sees. This demonstrates the filmic narrator.

The visual text of the scene emphasizes the character's act of seeing from top down, which in the visual discourse of Western culture is usually a mastering, colonizing gaze. Here, the combination of a place,

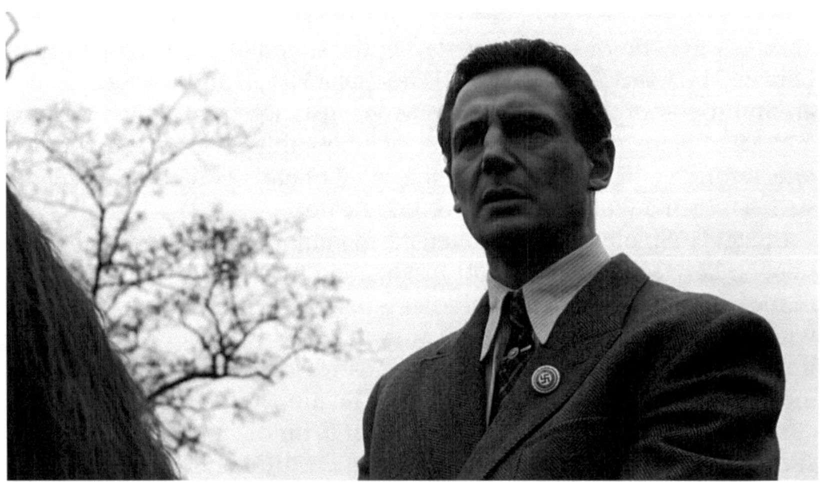

Figure 7. *Schindler's List* (1993): Schindler watches. Video still.

moment, and action that we call topos is deployed to suture that powerful position to what is actually visible, turning the overseeing of domination into insight. Later on, by another intervention of the narrator, this gaze is echoed in the gaze of Schindler's evil twin, Amon Goeth. Goeth oversees the camp from the balcony of his villa, which gives him the impulse to shoot inmates randomly. His gaze is steeped in power and the thrill of omnipotence, with killing for pleasure as its consequence. No insight emerges here.

These are two opposite extremes of what a top-down gaze can produce. It takes an agent of narration to (visually) tell these two opposed reactions to a similar visual event. During his conversion scene, Schindler sees the horror of what he has so far participated in when he sees a little girl, whose red coat is the only element of colour in the film (after the introductory credit sequence and up to the ending). Both colour elements are outside the primary fabula. That scarce use of colour is a stylistic mark of the narration; the fact that Schindler sees it and acts on that perception is an issue of focalization. That we see him seeing it results from (cinematic) narration. Later, at the holocaust, one of the bodies on a cart is also coloured in this red; and again, Schindler's look follows it, probably her. Thus, the narrator marries Schindler's spiritual itinerary from evil to good with the girl's itinerary from life to death. This matching is an act of narration. Only through analysing this narration can we see that this film,

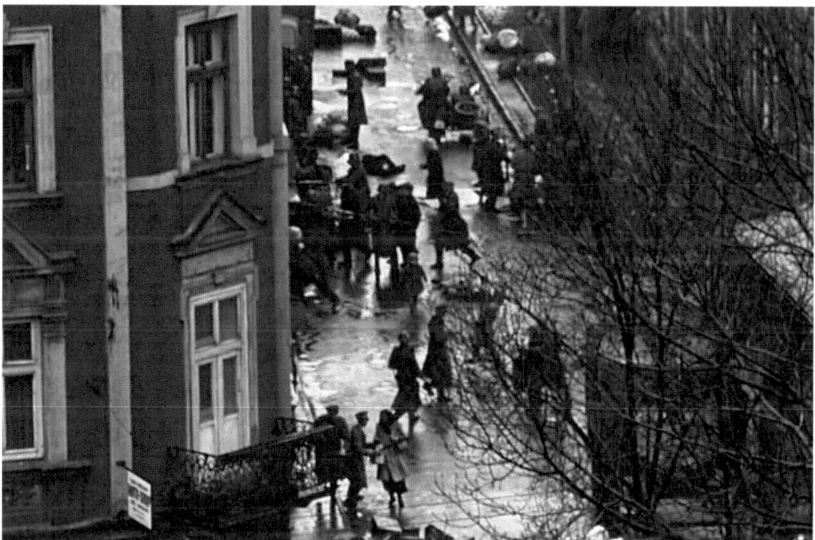

Figure 8. *Schindler's List* (1993): Destruction of the ghetto (Danka in red coat at the centre). Video still.

at least in these moments, does not glorify the former profiteer but marks the fatal fact that his conversion is always-already too late; that sacrifice accompanies it.

The narrator's visual language works out this conjunction between Schindler and the little girl in complex detail. Schindler's look becomes an engaging look instead of a mastering gaze at the precise moment when it detaches an individual from the machinery of massacre. The little girl who runs around is detached from her parents – she seems lost – and visually detached from the masses, from hell as backdrop. Schindler's visual connection to her is her only place in the narrative. Looking becomes in itself a way of saving – although, because of the narrative's avoiding of individualism as anecdotal, this girl will not survive and never enters Schindler's factory; his list.

The current academic tendency to dismiss the concept of the narrator could easily be brought in here. For it is the film's author, Steven Spielberg, who must have designed and determined this subtle play with the directions of looks, suture, colour, and the distinctions between mass and individual, wide shots and close-ups. However, having become a filmmaker myself, I resist this. It would be an individualistic privileging of authorial authority over the much more relevant attention to collective creation that filmmaking is. The acting, the editing, the sound design, and much more: it all is part of what I here indicate as the text. It is uttered or, if you wish, created by a considerable group of people. This plurality of authorship fits well with Foucault's insistence on this plurality. Even if Spielberg signs for the authorship and has the rights over its commercial success, as well as the responsibility for the political implications, the text, here, is collectively made. A technical term such as "narrator" makes it possible to recognize this and analyse the various streams of meaning-making involved.

Forms of Narration

The distinction between a narrator that tells about itself, or him- or herself (which I propose to abbreviate as CN – character-narrator; such a narrator is personified) and a narrator that remains external to the fabula (an EN) entails a difference in the narrative rhetoric of truth. But that difference remains a rhetorical one. The basis of the theory of narrative I have proposed in *Narratology* and am expounding in this book is that no utterance can escape the responsibility of its subject. As a consequence, even the strictest, most objective-sounding narrative utterance is the doing of an agential, indeed subjective function I have termed "narrator." Behind the invisible, neutral, objectifying narration there is also a subject. And that subject is plural, since no one is alone when thinking about what to tell and how to do it. This plurality is also crucial for a concept of the narrator that is neither anthropomorphically individualistic, nor just a mechanical machine. There is no better way to substantiate this claim than by calling on an artist who combines painting, video, literature, and installation in her multimedia video-shadow plays that are mostly, sometimes implicitly and sometimes overtly, narrative. I am referring to Indian artist Nalini Malani (b. 1946), most widely known for her complex, brilliant *video-shadow-plays*.

In her best-known shadow play, *In Search of Vanished Blood* (Figure 9), made for dOCUMENTA (13) in 2012, Malani presents us with a multiple narrator that confuses all assumptions of identity and subjective uniqueness we may hold concerning the narrator. Its soundtrack begins with abstract sound. The sound is neither calming nor threatening. It is no illustrative music; it is not music at all. It is hard to say what it means; that seems to be its point. Sound to which we cannot give meaning becomes meaningful when after a while we hear the words "This is Cassandra speaking." This is where CN narration begins. These words present a CN. But it is Malani's voice, distorted and, importantly, pluralized by means of making it "out of sync," that speaks these words

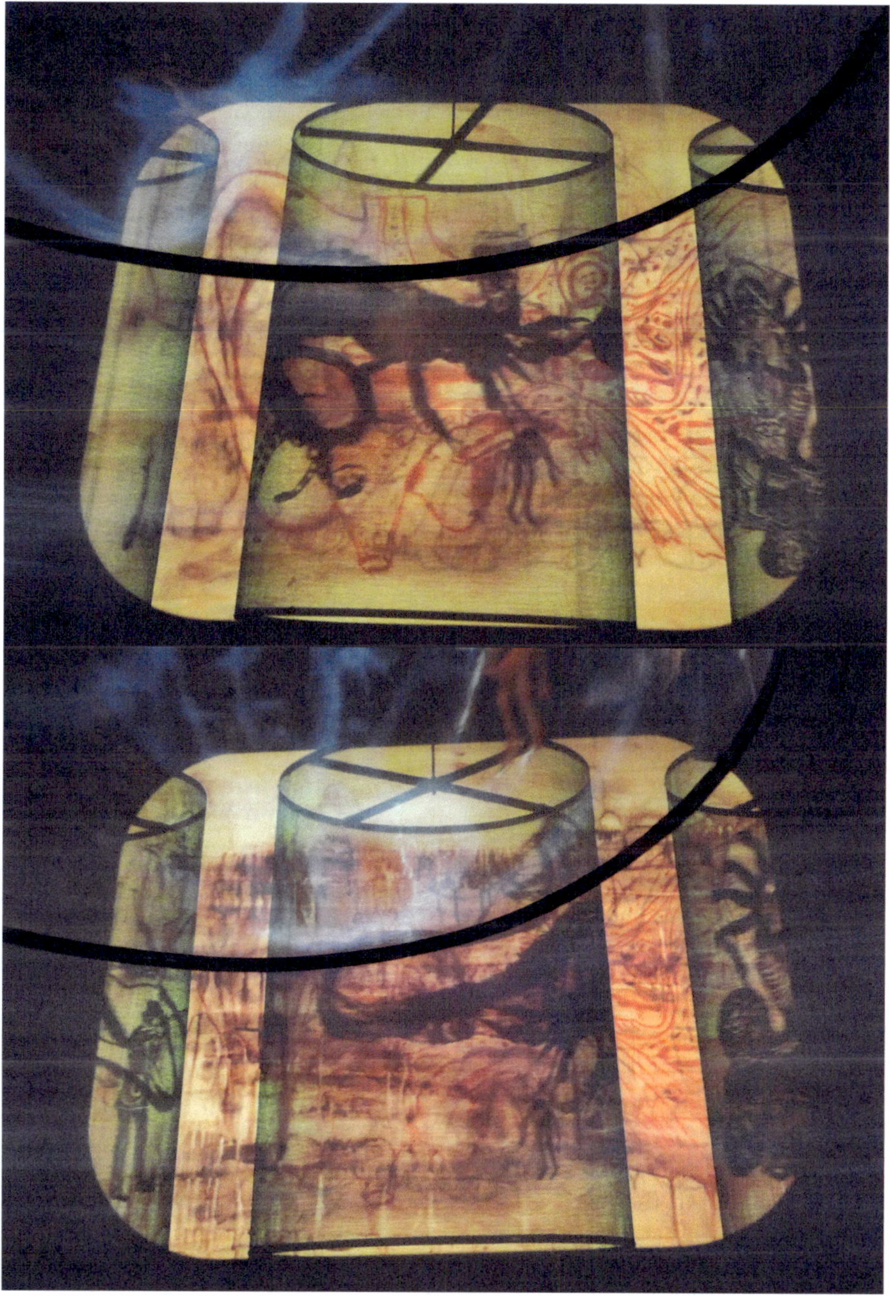

Figure 9.   Nalini Malani, *In Search of Vanished Blood* (2012). Detail.

after more than a minute. It is the artist's voice, but attributing the speech to a mythical figure. The meaning comes from the name: Cassandra invokes the woman from Greek mythology whose prediction of imminent catastrophe could not be heard. Her gift of prophesy came with the curse of being ignored. This mythical character will return later in this book. And in the well-worn spirit of blaming the victim and killing the messenger, she was killed when she refused to shut up. "In the heart of darkness," replies or continues Malani's distorted voice, again pluralized by means of asynchronicity.

This play with voice creates a sonic shadow play, as the voice is accompanied by its own shadow. The pluralization of the voice is meaningful, not only because of its eerie mechanical sound but also because it speaks a plural identity in the linguistic first person singular. The phrase "in the heart of darkness" quotes the title of Joseph Conrad's 1899 novel. This adds the spatial positioning "in" that might be seen as saying something like "Africa, including Conrad's-Kurtz's 'the horror! the horror' is here (here in India, here in this exhibition space in Germany)." The quotation is indirect, passing through Heiner Müller's 1977 play *Hamletmachine* where Ophelia speaks these words, but there saying, "This is Electra speaking." Three mythical women speak in one personal pronoun "I" and claim their voice. All three were victimized; all strong, and refusing to give up their subjectivity. What the voice says – a bit difficult to understand – becomes grimmer, and the pluralization more meaningful.

Then the abstract sound takes over again. But now the visitor has the memory – let's say, the cognitive-sensorial shadow – of those words to help her imagination make sense of the sounds. These continue to reject their function as illustrations; yet they now become narrative. For after having heard the name Cassandra we know that both the difficulty of hearing and the need to understand are crucial. And thus we make an effort to understand and engage more intensely with the sound track, preparing for our role as narratee. The words "Under the sun of torture / To the capitals of the world / In the name of the victims" don't tell a story. In this, they are different from the myth of Cassandra, activated through Christa Wolf's (1984) rewriting of it that puts it back into the present. And they differ from Conrad's book title.

Instead of telling, these words only set a story up, recall and invoke it, and together they add up. They set the stage: they position what follows in a political place, define the addressee, and specify the speaker as plural and in need of a spokesperson. That speaker is layered, for it is triple, at least. It is up to the visitors to take a place and choose their relationship to what is to come. This is how this artwork embodies the idea of "in medias res": the visitors cannot stay outside it, for then they would not be able to experience the artwork as it has been made. The visitors must do this for the story to take place – the latter phrase to be taken literally here, since this work concretely *takes place*. They are provided with the clues, the links, to connect what they see to the invisible invoked by the word "vanished" and the need for the search, with the help of their imagination. They are given all the tools to become part of the searching subject, to join the title's search and thus increase the chance that a result may be found. Art is a product of the imagination and addresses the imagination of its audiences; and this in the most literal sense.

This entails reflection on the status of art as fiction. Fiction is not the opposite of reality. It is a special inflection of reality, the latter enriched by the imagination. In this way, art is able to provide visions, including knowledge, that other forms of knowledge production have difficulty achieving. Addressing a contemporary audience and compelling them to imagine, hence see what history has done to people, this artwork seeks to enable Cassandra to be finally heard, so that the future, too, can be seen or imagined. The narrator cannily uses the device of quotation to enhance recognizability and thus make visitors part of the game. Through quotation, it also inserts the work in a kind of ephemeral community that art can forge. These works make such imagining almost irresistible.

In addition to the abstract sound and the pluralized first-person speaker, made unidentifiable through that very pluralization, quotation is another important device deployed in this work's narratorial discourse. The poetics of quotation implies an acknowledgment of the collective nature of art – the works, the experience, and what the imagination does with these. It is a form of collaboration. This is a tool to pluralize the narrator. Quotation is not repetition; it is, rather, engaging in a dialogue with others, with what came before this contemporary work. The narrator quotes motives, images, styles, and in this work a novel and poetry. Quotation is also an acknowledgment of art's need for materiality. The quoted precedents are primary material, building blocks that help the new work to provisionally stand on its own. The reason I insist on the status of the quoting agent as a narrator is not only to make it possible to analyse it, but also to avoid infringing on the status of the artist. Quotation does not contradict a measure of artistic autonomy.

If I speak of the artist, it is to present her not as the narrator but as the creator of a work of art that offers a narration and, consequently, a narrator for our consideration. For, as I said above, the historical artist is not irrelevant; not at all. The analysis of the text, the creation that the artist has given over to the public domain and put in touch with the imagination of the public enables doing justice, precisely, to the artist through avoiding conflating the artist with her work. Malani's invention of the particular genre of the video-shadow play as her medium relies on earlier technologies and aesthetics as much as on actual motives. She merges intertextuality with interdiscursivity, if I may introduce two concepts that are not specific to narrative but frequently relevant when we wonder about the narratological question of the narrator: Who speaks? The former consists of the quotation of traceable precedents such as extant texts and images. For this, we can sometimes recognize the precedent, the earlier use of a word or image. "This is Cassandra speaking" is a double and stacked quotation: from Müller's play, modified through Wolf's novel by the change of name. Both can be traced and referenced; both are cited in the bibliography of the present book.

The latter consists of borrowing earlier discourses, including technologies and the traditions of their deployment. This does not have a specific precise precedent. Conversely, the artwork can still claim a measure of autonomy. For autonomy is not isolationism, arrogance, or cultural autism; the text does not speak for itself. Autonomy is self-governing on the basis of collaboration, moral and political responsibility, and most importantly, a relatively free subject position. Free, that is, in acknowledgment of its interconnection with others. In recognition of this complex wavering between quotation and autonomy, the "I" that the narration keeps implicit is here exuberantly plural. I bring in this form of narration to suggest that the concept of the narrator is not a simple personification of a narrative function. It is, in contrast to that common prejudice, an instance that performs a function that needs to be made visible, discussable, in order to understand that and how narration is culturally and politically embedded. Within that general questioning of the responsibility, both singular and plural, both individual and collective, we can then zoom in on some particular forms in which the narrator manifests itself.

All Kinds of "I"s

I now consider the instances that the narrator shows up in the text and refers to itself as "I," while also thinking that this "I" is not by definition a character, not an actor as in these examples. This I indicate by the addition of the term "perceptible" or "non-perceptible," by which I mean perceptible (p) or non-perceptible (np) as specifically mentioned or not by the narrating agent in the text. The formula for such a sentence might then be EN(p) [EF1 [CF2 (name of character)]-name of actor spoken of(p)]. Here, EF means external focalizer, and CF a character-focalizer. Please take note of the obvious fact that these abbreviations are just for speed-noting; they have no added intersubjective meaning. Thus there is a partial correspondence of two of the three agents, while there are still three different functions or identities at play. This form occurs quite frequently in older literature, such as Dostoevsky, Tolstoy, Balzac, Dickens, and also Cervantes's *Don Quixote* (1605, 1615). It often serves to state a truth claim – the best guarantee of fictionality. It is safe to assume that a narrator-"I" who claims to be speaking the truth is thereby declaring his/its fictional status.

Cervantes uses this ploy frequently, with the claims of veracity attributed to different narratorial postures, incompatibly so. This happens especially in the chapters 1 and 9 of the first part of his long novel in two parts. These two chapters constitute the basis of an episode in a video installation I (co-)made in 2019, titled *Don Quijote: Sad Countenances*. I will draw here and there on this work and the issues of intermediality it raises. In the beginning of the novel *Don Quixote* we read, "But this does not much concern our story; enough that we do not depart by so much as an inch from the truth in the telling of it" (31). A bit later, the narrator claims to be the most truthful among his competitors by giving several versions of a fact (37). This goes so far as to turn the truth claim completely around: in chapter 5, a tale that is disqualified as coming from the kind of literature the novel consistently ridicules is thus framed by the external narrator who shows his hand or EN(p):

> a tale familiar to children, not unknown to youth, and enjoyed and even believed by old men, though for all that no truer than the miracles of Mahomet. (53)

This alleging of clichés is a way of enlisting the reader as a witness.

Such a position of the witness may be less crucial to the fabula but can be key for the reader. In this example, the combination of invoked categories of listeners-readers is clearly ironic. A non-ironic, straight-faced witness can convey suggestions of compassion, laughter, suspense, or other affective responses to the reader. They can also influence the plausibility of the narrative. Hence, neither the quantitative presence nor the participation in the fabula determines a priori the importance of a particular type of narrator. Here, that narrator declares himself only when claiming the truth. For the rest of this long novel, the main character is the one who speaks in embedded narration; he is it who sees in the story and acts in the fabula, and the narrator recedes to an anonymous background position (an EN[np]). And since he is not alone, there are also the people around him such as his squire, host, or opponent, and the narrators of inserted novellas set up as tales told by people the Knight encounters by chance, at the inn or, for him, "castle" where he stays between adventures.

Who is this man Don Quixote we all know but who never existed? He is the carrier and spokesman of many of our own preoccupations and questions. In the fourth episode of my installation, "Who Is Don Quijote?" an artist and a narrator, simultaneously, are respectively photographing and describing the portrait of Don Quijote – as a historian and as a fictive figure. This scene should account both for Don Quijote's worldwide fame, but as a book; and for the character's looks, which have become so emblematic, in spite of the fact that the well-known long horsey face and emaciated body never lived. If we can recognize a figure who is entirely fictitious, what does that say about the presence of the imagination, carried along by the heritage from past attempts to imagine unthinkable things?

This question is built into the narrator's discourse. In our video exploration of these issues, the figure is the first to be astonished by the way he looks, speaks, and thinks. Looking in a mirror (Figure 10), he seems to encounter himself for the first time. It is also a commentary on the relationship between fiction and reality, the imagination and history. In this particular photograph, he also addresses the viewer through the mirror, as if he needed our confirmation of his identity. The episode combines tiny fragments, bits and pieces from chapters 1 and 9 of the novel's first part and quotations from Borges's 1939 story "Pierre Menard, Author of the Quixote," with improvised views uttered by three discussants, intellectuals who care about historical truth. (More on Borges's story in *Narratology*, 55–7.) The mirror emblematizes the self-reflection we constantly practise, whether to see what we look like to others or to think about the point of what we do.

Through this example I broach an issue that will also return in the course of this book: the way narratological analysis can support theoretical reflection, in a variety of disciplinary fields. In the Introduction I have given a glimpse of this issue. The images of Don Quijote in the video episode intersect with those serious discussions by people engaged with history. Quotations from the past and contemporary views present inter-temporality. The discussions among the three staged thinkers who at first ignore, then begin to listen to and interact with the narrator who reads from the Borges story, evoke the polemics that were the after-effect of Hayden White's groundbreaking analysis

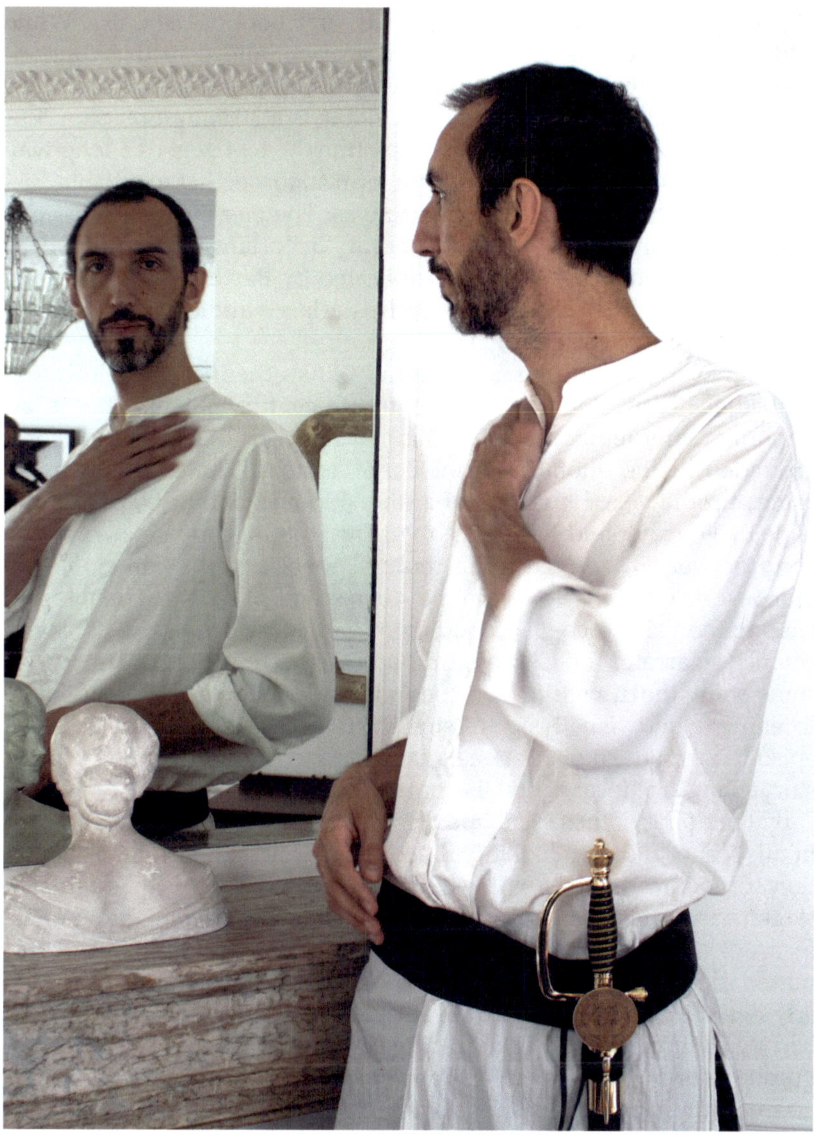

Figure 10.   Don Quijote (Mathieu Montanier) in FID-focalization. Photo: Jeannette Christensen.

of the rhetoric of history writing in his 1973 book *Metahistory*. White addresses nineteenth-century history writing, and considers rhetorical concepts rather than narratological ones. In fact, given that history writing is so predominantly narrative, this is a striking omission. But a key concept he proposed was "emplotment," which goes a long way to tie up the link with narrative. That term suggests that inevitably, historians turn their accounts into narratives. The passionate discussions that followed indicated that contemporary historians felt implicated; as strongly as literary scholars felt implicated by Barthes's "death of the author" thesis. The discussions reached a large audience, with many non-academics participating.

Hinting at these discussions actually links them to the views described in Cervantes's early seventeenth-century novel. This is an important inter-temporal bond. This anachronistic link is, in turn, foregrounded in the quotation from Borges's story. The scene thus also brings up the vexed question of authorship and authority, put on the table by Foucault and Barthes in the 1970s, but here anticipated by the bond between the seventeenth-century novel and the contemporary video work. Over the voices, in the video scene, of the three people discussing the value, need, and possibility of history, we hear that staged character-narrator, or CN, quoting and discussing Borges's story. At some point, the discussion becomes one, and the three discussants start listening to and visually addressing the CN. That is the moment in the episode when the bond between narrator and the direct content of the storytelling, the focalization, becomes visible.

By the doing of these scholars discussing the issue of historical truth in this scene, and then looking directly at the narrator, the latter's function turns into that of a witness. The idea or image of the internal / staged narrator as witness occurs in much literary, cinematic, and other forms of narrative. It allows the narrator to remain invisible yet committed to the story it tells. It is also a figure that can be used as a readerly device. Considering the narrative as told by a witness is a way of barring indifference and encouraging compassion. This, in turn, solicits questions of modesty, or a resistance to an attitude of voyeurism and appropriation: hence, questions of an ethical kind.

However, as we will see in the next part of this book, focalization need not remain with the same narrating agent. Technically it would even be almost impossible to maintain such continuity. As I have argued in *Narratology* (20), a spectacular example of a novel in which focalization rests from beginning to end with the character-focalizer, or CF, and narration with the EN(np) is Alain Robbe-Grillet's *La jalousie* (1957). It is curious that precisely the consistency with which the technique is maintained has had the effect that almost all critics have termed that anonymous agent a specific character: a jealous husband. Clearly, the technical device alone does not satisfy interpretation-eager readers.

Of course, the title has also been of influence here. Yet it is meaningful to distinguish the two levels a bit longer. I propose to take a look at a visual instance of such play with the theme of jealousy in a painting by Norwegian artist Edvard Munch, who figured the topic of jealousy quite frequently. But my example here does not address that topic. I invoke it to lay the question of the narrator's identity to rest and instead bring in another question: that of the characterization of the narrator's discourse. For this purpose, and to stage an intership, an encounter between the disciplines of literary and visual studies, I connect the narratological concept of the narrator to the one that linguistics terms "syntax." This I construe as the pictorial equivalent of a narratorial "I." In linguistics, syntax concerns the logic of the links between parts of a sentence, divided into either juxtaposition, where the parts are functionally equal, or subordination, where a logical link such as causality pertains.

Given the sequential nature of language, this logical link is also a temporal one. This can be considered on the level of narration, therefore, the agency of the narrator. In the case of visual images, the most widely used concept is iconography. I distinguish the special form of iconography I term *syntactic* from *semantic* iconography, which focuses on single motifs and their meanings. The distinction is important for the analysis of visual art, and can then be returned, so to speak, to the analysis of literary narratives. Munch's painting helps us achieve that intership.

Red Virginia Creeper (Figure 11) is a horrific image, an image of horror; a land- or cityscape gone awry. As occurs frequently in Munch's work, the tradition of linear perspective is both endorsed and questioned by making the perspective excessively steep. The perspectival excess, the path running uphill and around the corner of the fence divides the image into an illusion of three-dimensional space, and a flat image, that of the man in the foreground. In American culture, a white picket fence stands for petty bourgeois, suburban tranquillity, which can also degenerate into spooky scenes, such as in David Lynch's 1986 film *Blue Velvet*. The more tranquil it seems at first sight, the more horrific it becomes. Munch's narrator welcomes such ambiguity.

The fence is just there, on two sides of the path, separating plots of land, delimiting gardens as tokens of private property and individual happiness, misery, fear, jealousy, or other forms of existence in which people can become mired. The right-hand fence leads the path and the gaze away from the red house, around its corner, into the street of normality.

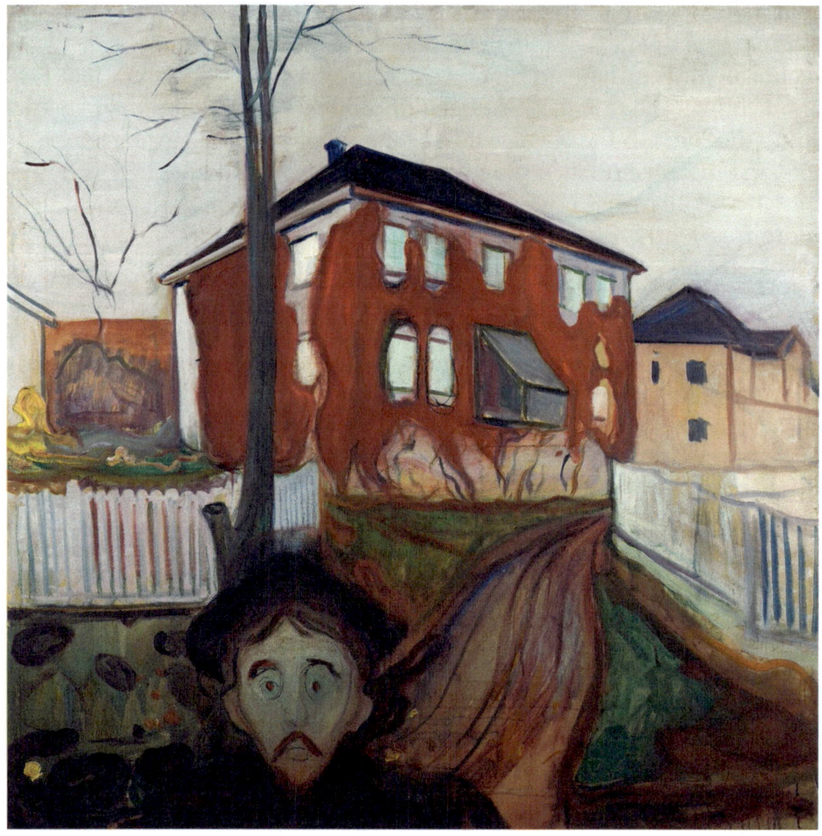

Figure 11. Edvard Munch, *Red Virginia Creeper* (1898–1900), 119.5 x 121 cm, Oslo, Munch Museum.

It is the bright white fence, on the left, that is not quite "normal." It de-limits nothing; its two ends finish into nowhere. The one ends at the edge of the painting, and only if we see it with the cinematic concept of "hors-champ" (out of frame) can we imagine that it continues outside the frame. This invokes yet another intership: the relation between painting and cinema. The other fence ends at the corner of the building. The logic of fences as lines in landscapes is disrupted. This is an effect of a syntactic kind; the fence's relation to what it is supposed to delimit is broken.

The house stands on a hill. This elevation is indicated not only by the mounting and narrowing path but also more forcefully by the way the house itself is distorted, as if filmed from too close and below – in cinema, this would be considered a "mistake." The perspective with lens-based distortion clashes with the close-up view of the horrified face in the foreground. This gives the painting two distinct points from which the picture is taken. The work's title focuses exclusively on the plant growing on the walls of the house. It normalizes the colour red a bit, although other associations refuse to disappear; and it ignores the man. Behind the white fence there is also some red, as if blood has seeped into the garden. Realistically, this indicates probably some red plants, but realism doesn't always work. Also, the path, which almost leads to the house but then deviates its course, is orange, alluding to fire but without "being" it. And due to the curve, its shape becomes like a flame blown to the right. This makes the lower side of the creeping plant look like fire, too. Along with the tall white windows behind which nothing can be seen, the house looks like an Addams Family House of Spooks. Very present in American culture, the Addams Family is a satirical inversion of the happy suburban American family. The black-and-white cartoons created by Charles Addams were initially published in *The New Yorker* between 1938 and 1988 – long after Munch.

Syntactically, the tension that we frequently encounter in painting between the production of an illusion of three-dimensional space and the foregrounding of the flat, two-dimensional image is the clearest manifestation of the pictorial narrator and the text it produces. Moments where this tension is played out can be seen, for example, in the syntactical bond between the man's face and the dead tree. In a flat interpretation of the image, the dead tree seems to come straight out of the figure's head, which is cropped just below the shoulders. This figure, so close to the picture plane, competes with the large, looming house for our attention, raising the question of depiction. Is it scale, figuration, colour or form that determines what the visual centre, the "main clause" of an image is? In connection with composition, the disruption of the unity of the image has a flattening effect. There is no unified pictorial space. We are thereby alerted to the potential performativity of the figure, as if imploring viewers to give up their passivity and become active participants. He can be seen as coming forward from the flat image into three-dimensional space towards the spectators.

Thanks to the composition as well as the mode of painting, the dis-unification comes across, leaving its cause ambiguous. This man is not looking at us. His eyes are unseeing little red blots in large round saucers of greenish white. The moustache is a red triangle over the lips, with only a little excess on the left that gives it life beyond the geometry. It rhymes with the triangle of hair above his forehead, where, again, the left side is a bit longer. The man's face is greenish in the middle, turning to yellow at the edges, with a white forehead. His mouth is pinched close. Fine lines on his left cheek accentuate the shape of his skull. The man's shoulders have been painted over, with a leftover visible on the right shoulder. Or, perhaps, this doubling of the shoulder is a small detail alluding to cinematic movement. By means of that doubling, the movement indicates that the man is raising his shoulders, perhaps out of fear, terror, shock. This allusion adds to the sense of horror-in-the-suburb: the Addams effect.

When we consider the painting as narrative, all this suggests that the man, as an embedded focalizer, has seen something horrifying, from which he is running. All the features of the image I have mentioned so far can be seen as the narratorial agent, the "I" that tells the story. And so, it seems, has the landscape itself. The trees are bare of leaves, black, as if burned. The sky is white. The house is almost tilted backwards. The incongruous single yellow dot on the left rhymes with the yellow bushes higher up on the left, growing beneath an orange wall or screen. On that square something is depicted. It is unlikely these are bushes, because the wall looks otherwise impenetrable; but they could be an allusion to bushes. Which would frustrate our attempt to understand the painting in realistic terms. This incongruity in the left background, the distortion of the house and the excessively large head of the horrified man make us ponder the syntactical logic of an image that does not obey the rules of perspectival unity, but instead creates flatness out of portions that refuse syntactic subordination. What could be the horror this figure is running away from? Is it the fire, or has something inside the house set him emotionally on fire? Whatever it is, it is not limited to what is inside the frame.

Jealousy is only one of many possible causes of the horror, but one that, through its banality, cautions us against leaping to such semantic interpretations. The face is quite like the frequently recurring one in depictions of jealousy in Munch's work. This would be an iconographic interpretation; it would fill in a single meaning for a single pictorial unit. Iconography is a tool to make associations where the picture itself reveals little. The downside can be that the method stimulates figurative reading over sensitivity to the work of art. It can also stimulate us to focus on seeing what is not visually there. But language not only has syntax; it also comprises semantics. I want to make the case for iconography as a helpful method to get at meaning, but to be used with caution and not in isolation. An eye for narrativity not as a story told as an illustration but as the narrative work of design, composition, and colour together, and a recognition of the painting as narrator, can prevent simplistic interpretations.

Based on a recognition of what we already know, semantic iconography can crush our view of the work, reducing it to banal realism when it replaces what we see with a meaning instead of the double nature of allusion remaining in sight. But in connection to visual syntax, it can help make sense of what would otherwise stay unseen because un-understood, as well as refrain from explaining too much. The horror on the face of the man must remain unexplained, simply because there is nothing other than the colour of a plant to allude to – but not really show – a possible cause of horror. But it is the content of what is being told, including the ambiguity that leaves the viewer in charge. Similarly, the consistent focalization in Robbe-Grillet's novel, in spite of the title, cannot be turned into a semantic unit. For the novel as a whole, the entire narration, contains a syntactic unity rather than a semantic one. And this can also, conversely, stimulate more complex thinking about jealousy itself; for it, too, has a syntax.

Second-Person Narrators?

After all these confusing "he" and "I" questions, one more narrator question remains: second-person narration, the "you" form. I won't go into the epistolary novel, a genre that systematically deploys second-person narration. This is quite common, and some of Western literature's masterpieces are just that: a stack of letters. Pierre Choderlos de Laclos's 1782 novel *Les Liaisons dangereuses*, which got a new actuality when in 1988 Stephen Frears made an award-winning film based on it, starring Glenn Close and John Malkovich, is a famous instance. Another example is Alice Walker's *The Color Purple* (1982), on which more later. In this genre, there is an expectation, implicit or even explicit, that "someone," a narrating agent, has collected and ordered the letters of which the novel consists. Whether or not this is a useful way of approaching the genre does not concern me here. I would like, instead, to consider the possibility, or impossibility, of writing a novel entirely written by a primary narrator in the second person. Such a form is difficult to sustain; yet is important as an idea. Michel Butor's *La modification* (1957), belonging to the French experimental narratives called *le nouveau roman* (the new novel), is one of the better-known instances. The following passage from *La modification*, for all its brevity, already fails to sustain the second-personhood that is its overt narrative mode:

> If you were afraid of missing the train to whose movement and sound
> you are now already accustomed again, it is not because you woke up
> later than you planned this morning, since, to the contrary, your first

> movement upon opening your eyes was to extend your arm to prevent the
> alarm from going off, while dawn was beginning to sculpt the disordered
> sheets of your bed, the sheets which emerged from the dark like defeated
> phantoms trampled on that soft and warm floor from which you tried to
> tear yourself away. (21)

This passage has all the appearance of a so-called interior monologue, that equally artificial mode of narration "in the first person" – with a character-bound narrator, or CN – that seeks to eliminate reference to the first-person discourse in favour of a silent, "pure" first-person focalizer.

The relapse into the first-person form that lurks throughout is a consequence of Butor's refraining from taking on board what the second person is: to be, to act out, the essence of language, in address and its mutuality. This is not to suggest that the novel is a failure – on the contrary. It is a masterpiece of staging the ambiguity, the threatening collapse, of the entire linguistic structure of pronouns, verb forms, and first, second, or third person. Butor's narrator is not addressing anyone but himself. Only when speech is addressed to a second person can language fulfil its mission to communicate, however. This is the nature of words called deixis: words that have meaning only in the context in which they are uttered, such as "I" and "you," "yesterday" and "tomorrow," "here" or "there." What matters in language is not the world about which subjects communicate but the constitution of the subjectivity required to communicate in the first place. What is lacking in *La modification* is the key feature of deixis: the reversibility, the exchange, of the first and second person; not their respective identities themselves, which are semantically empty outside of the situation of utterance. The novel becomes a soliloquy, an interior monologue richly filled with direct observations, with very concrete sense perceptions.

Instead of a formal "second-person narrator," then, I propose another excursion into the way narratology can help us think narrativity at work in other domains than literature. The question of the narrator's "you," the second person, can also be thought of in relation to the potential for interaction between, not within artworks. In his short story "The Garden of Forking Paths" (1983), Jorge Luis Borges manages to tell a gripping, suspenseful story with a beginning, a middle, and an end, that is about and that performs the absurdity of a world where time is not singular. The reflections on temporality increase in complexity during the unfolding of events. It takes a spatial structure to militate against the temporality of Aristotelian poetics. Thus, Borges experiments with what visual artworks are condemned to do: reckon with time's flow in a space of duration.

At first, the duplication of time in the story is simply a ploy to inspire courage in the face of a dangerous task: the external narrator must "imagine that he has already accomplished it, ought to impose upon himself a future as irrevocable as the past" (22). Soon, this duplication maps time on space, "one sinuous spreading labyrinth that would encompass the past and the future" (23). In the second part of this book I will return to the issue of temporality in more detail. Here, I allege it to make a case for a dialogic relationship not within but between artworks; here, even in different media and moments of making. This collapse between the two dimensions of existence will be a parable for the problematic I will broach in the following commentary on a work by Louise Bourgeois belonging to the series of those works that emblematize the spacetime, or chronotope, at stake.

Parallel, intertwined, supplementing, and opposite to Borges's forking paths, I posit Louise Bourgeois's "crystals of time," of which her *Cells* series constitutes the central figure. I call this figure a literalizing metaphor, a figurative thought-image that works through a literal embodiment of an idea that shapes a narrative through a mutuality of first-second person narrator. Borges's figuration of the problem of time in a fictional *character-plot knot* likewise allegorizes the forking quality of temporality, "literally." Toward the end of the story things have grown endlessly complicated, to become an "infinite series of times in a growing, dizzying net of divergent, convergent, and parallel times" (28). Bourgeois's *Cell* called *Spider* (1997), a work in which two of her most powerful series converge – *Cells* and *Spiders* – proposes just such a network of parallel times. In this sense it is a good counterpart of, or interlocutor for, Borges's story. The gigantic spider hovering over her nest, filled with future-holding eggs, also protects a multilayered temporality, ranging from Bourgeois's own past – the tapestry fragments literally taken from her parents' restoration workshop – to the time of weaving, and to the antiquity evoked in the figures still visible. What I am driving at, though, is not a similarity but a dialogue between these two works; the way they address each other and thus, as through deixis, they exchange "I" and "you" status.

One can imagine the horror of a story modelled entirely on Borges's spatialized temporality. Like the one by the Chinese writer Ts'ui Pên in the story projected, such a narrative would never end. In Borges's story, however, this temporality does not lead to unnecessary proliferation. The story is saved because convergence and divergence allow for both proliferation and collapse. The result is that after a mere ten pages, this story about an infinite story has a satisfying, totally logical ending, in which time and space collapse, the deed is done, the perpetrator is arrested, tried, and sentenced, and the enigma raised by the opening lines is explained. The story has retraced its steps, or, to speak in terms of Bourgeois's work, it has completed the circle of multilayered temporality.

Because entering a different macrocosm – in Borges's story, the house – is also a powerful figure in *Spider*, Borges's probing of time's complexity can be brought into dialogue with Bourgeois's more peaceful experiment with contradiction. For Borges, the figure through which time is played out is political murder. For Bourgeois, it is intimacy. Since Borges's hero must enter his victim's house to experience the victim as a person with a face, the notion of intimacy is not entirely absent from the philosophy of time that Borges develops. With Bourgeois, we can make more sense of that philosophy, see better how it affects our lives, not just as an abstraction but also as a concrete, embodied sphere of intimacy.

In Borges's story the temporal structure returns, full-circle, to the beginning, of which the ending is the future but also the past. This circularity parallels a casual visitor's walk around *Spider*, blocking out the desire to enter the work, which the half-open door evokes in the viewer. This temporal structure is satisfying, even classical, yet also a denial of the passage of time as the basic structure of narrative. Instead, it proposes infinite spatial extension. Making the story more like a spatial object, it finds *Spider* on at least one of its forking paths. For Bourgeois's *Cell* is not satisfied with such a roundabout circular vision.

Two elements of *Spider* supplement Borges's easy integration of his story into a fundamental narrative structure: the half-open door and the chair inside, on the one hand, and the fragmented state of the tapestries that are nevertheless emphatically figurative, on the other. The former ruptures the circle and offers a path to the inside without giving access to a centre or core. The latter, especially emblematized in the cut-out genitals of the woven putto, visible in Figure 12, refuses to yield to a clear-cut return to beginnings. Both propose, as an alternative to Borges's neat structure, something we can call crystals of time. Note that I am using this metaphor here not in the specific conceptual sense of Deleuze, but as a metaphor that helps construe the two artworks as in dialogue. Because it is, in turn, through Borges that we notice this. His splitting and multiplying of the first-person pronoun are his glosses on *Spider*. Through this literary experiment we understand better, in visual art, and in Bourgeois's complex literalizing metaphor for it, how the viewer's "I" is seduced into giving up the safe identity of individualism in favour of an adventure of heteropathy.

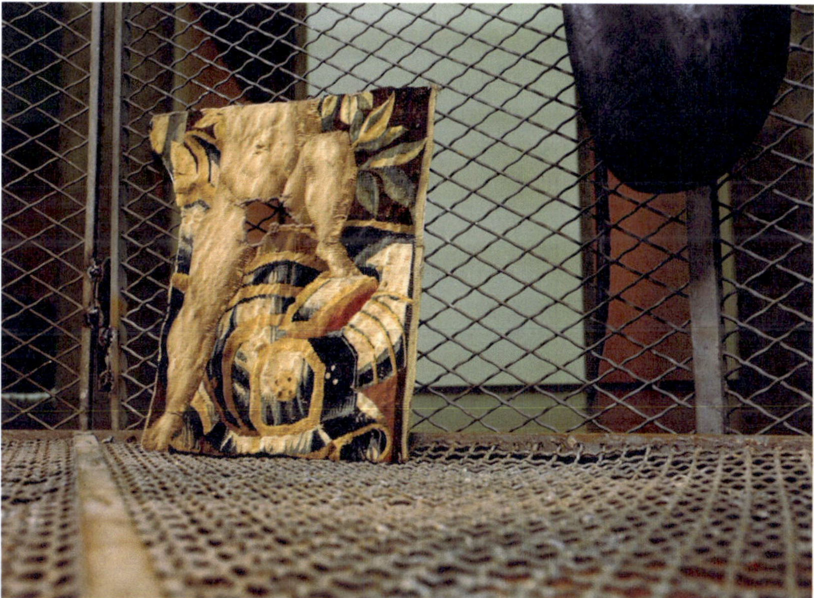

Figure 12. Louise Bourgeois, *Spider*. Detail.

The term "heteropathy" points to the sense-based, emotional, and affective move out of oneself into a subjectivity that is neither one's own
nor One. Characteristic of the kind of postmodern literature that blends
philosophical musings with narratives in which they are acted out, this
story's fanciful imagination offers an alternative for the most problematic terminology in which both literary studies and art history – as well
as philosophy and other cultural disciplines – couch their analyses and
results. That terminology arises from what I like to call the "anthropomorphic imagination," underlying so much of our analyses and understanding of cultural objects.

With a wink to the Western tradition, the Eastern tradition imagined
in Borges's story offers, by means of the spatial metaphor, the possibility of rethinking and revising some of the basic terms of the reigning
paradigms in the field of cultural analysis. The Western tradition has,
after all, grounded – and continues to ground – so much of its ontology
of humanity and its subsequent moral and cultural legacy on a story of
a Garden that is also a story of origin and diverging identities. In the
Biblical story of the Garden, there is also a problem of temporality that
undermines the certainty regarding the priorities and primacies that

Western culture derives from it. That problem concerns the chronology of the creation of the sexes, and the values attached to that chronology. That garden, too, poses problems of forking paths among which choice is impossible.

Given the status of Borges's story as a parable or allegory that duplicates the parable of the Garden of which the story speaks, I invoke it here, in turn, as an allegory of my interpretation of Bourgeois's work. In the eye of Borges's labyrinth, Bourgeois occupies the philosopher's chair. But the viewer this chair beckons can occupy it too: in desire, in movement, and in change. Bourgeois's *Spider* helps us to reflect on how we talk about art by talking *to* it. A number of different deployments of narrative predominate in this work. All are both solicited and questioned by Bourgeois's work in general and by *Spider* in particular. But the latter work does not stop at questioning the deployments. It offers a revision of each, proposing new ways to think this age-old mode of communicating through stories, so that in the end, narrative can come forward again, but in a new guise. What distinguishes the old narrative from the one *Spider* articulates and activates is temporality. By the imposition and foregrounding of the messy temporality involving the present, Bourgeois's narrativity binds sculpture to architecture. But narrative in general is no longer the cement.

The most common narrative modes can be characterized by their positioning as "anteriority stories." In the sharpest formulation, a visual work is thus considered an illustration of the narrative that precedes it and to which it is subordinated, its success being measured in terms of the degree to which it matches the story. Various practices of iconography exemplify the problems this narrative mode of anteriority poses. For example, iconographic analysis is often a search for antecedent works of art, for other images in which motifs, poses, compositional schemas, conceptualizations, or allegories were already used, whereby the later work becomes affiliated with visual predecessors. The narrative of anteriority uses the prior text, or image, as a measuring stick. This is what iconography does to Bourgeois's work: the spiders are metaphors for the artist's mother; the tapestries come from and hence are metonymies of the parents' workshop. Why, then, can we not "own" those stories, read them "off the page" so that they replace the mute objects we see?

The major thrust of such anteriority narratives is its diminishing of the studied work's originality in a justified impulse to shed Romantic notions of art. Thus, where Caravaggio or Rembrandt were once considered geniuses, they have now become craftsmen doing a job for patrons, who, it must therefore be deduced, really invented the work. Artists have cannily led the way to this much-needed revision of Romantic preconceptions of art. A work such as *Spider*, which integrates discarded perfume bottles, pieces of bone, and old fabric, a work where nothing in itself bears the artist's signature as "hand," must certainly agree with such a rejection of the idolatry of originality. It has, in fact, proposed that rejection.

However welcome this anti-Romantic attitude may have been at the time, though, it has now become a paradoxical tool to undermine the art it is alleged to serve. For it risks defeating the point of visual art, which is not to reiterate but to innovate, in the sense of offering for its viewers' experiences and insights, sights and sites in the present, that we did not as yet possess. This has nothing to do with Romantic originality. It has a lot to do with art's efficacy, rather than its "essence," with an understanding of art as process, with cultural life at the crossroads of significant events.

Thus, by specifically ignoring the visuality of a particular work, a narrative of anteriority bypasses what the work of art, as a theoretical object, has to say. To reject this, I contend, is one of *Spider*'s and Bourgeois's other artworks' theoretical propositions. They effectuate that proposition, enunciate it, through its imposition of a bodily participation by the viewer, who, caught between narrativity and sculpturality, builds a home for the old stories in the now. This, not the explicit use of "you," is what give this artwork a second-person narrator.

Yet if we want to dream about a non-reductive engagement with visual art, Borges's reason-based subjectivity must be allowed to go to sleep. In its dreams, then, it will meet its counterpart. With this metaphor of sleep, I am alluding to the contribution of psychoanalysis to this discussion of second-person narrative. As is well-known, psychoanalytical criticism is by definition committed to exploring unconscious impulses alleged to pour forth from the work. Pouring forth as address, going towards the second persons. Strictly speaking, such criticism cannot appeal to intentionalist statements at all.

The conception of the subject underlying such criticism is, or ought to be, that of a split subject, who, to use Freud's words, is not master in his or her own house. In the case of Bourgeois's *Cells*, and particularly of *Spider*, this Freudian phrase is strikingly apt. The *Cells* are, or represent, houses, in a literal sense, through the enclosed shape and shelter they suggest (Figure 13). This is their primal sense of architecture. They are both building blocks and complete houses. Body-houses. The *Cells* militate against the predominant model, in that art of building the house as a unified, idealized, symmetrical body. And they are, represent, or rather perform the house where the Freudian subject, whose own house it is, is not the master. For by deploying address, the house is unmasterable but yields to the second person the power it declines for itself.

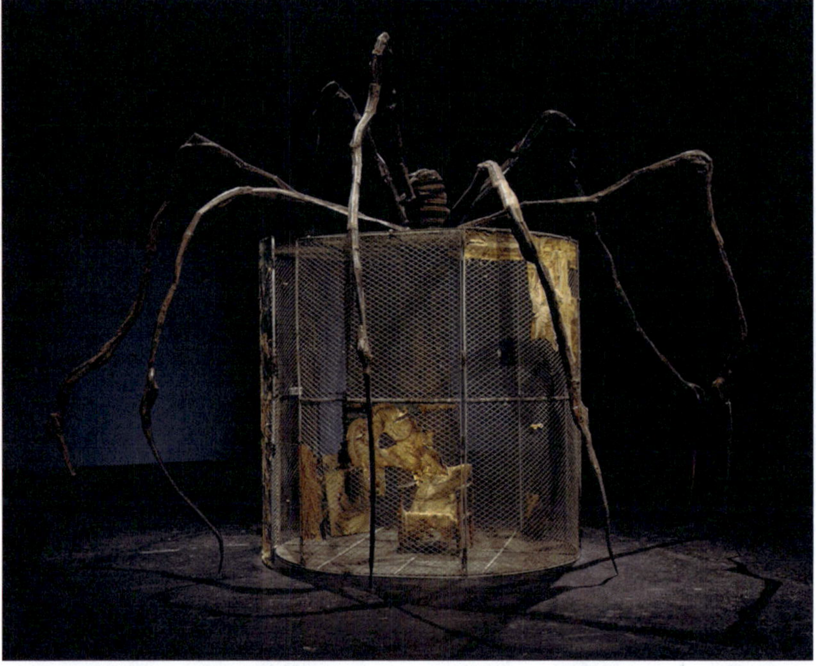

Figure 13. Louise Bourgeois, *Spider*.

According to Bourgeois's *Spider*, there are two reasons for this. First, figuratively, the *Cells* are houses of the mind, facilitating the childhood memories they obviously shelter. The huge spider brings in its wake the small child who first saw it. That anteriority, rather than the biographical one, infuses the work with an outrageous instability of scale that turns a sculpture into a building and back again. This is the level on which the narrator's utterance – not specific narrative content – serves as the cement that builds the house. Second, the particular "theory" of conceitedness, which speaks through Bourgeois's installation sculptures, requires a house, a habitat, for the subject to be, precisely, not master of. Instead, conceitedness functions on the dual level of the relationship between subject and other, in a one-to-one connection, and, simultaneously, on the level of the relationship between the subject – the one – and her surroundings, embodied by the house. In this duality, the subject cannot, by definition, be master.

The Freudian sensibility, rather than the content of the *Cells* as houses of the mind, consists, moreover, of a precise, sensitive, and very subtle resonance with the famous master/house metaphor from the creator of psychoanalysis. For masterful works of art as these are, "mastery" is not the sense they convey. Instead, "mystery" is more like it. Their strong affect and power of meaning-production suggest precisely the kind of subjectivity that would generate what psychoanalyst Christopher Bollas (1987) felicitously termed "the unthought known." This is something the subject senses and on which it acts but which it cannot articulate in a fully rational discourse – the intellectual discourse of artist's statements, for example. Yet at the same time, this "unthought known" is something the subject does know thinkingly and needs to make and mould so that it can actively – but outside intellectual discourse – participate in the cultural process that leads to knowledge.

Boldly, then, Bourgeois's work engages in a theoretical debate with Freud, pushing this master's tendency to anteriority narratives back to where, according to *The Interpretation of Dreams* (1982 [1900]), they emerge: in the visual present. The strong sense of mood, memory, and mystery that all the *Cells* emanate partakes of this realm of the unthought known. Accounting for the *Cells* through the words of the artist (alone), then, does them a profound injustice. If Bourgeois is such a strong spokeswoman for her own work, it is because thought, reason, is so very important to her art. The *Cells* are the work of Descartes's daughter, who grudgingly takes up Vitruvius's legacy in a revisionist conception of architecture that does not allow reduction to reason. If she makes works that are so replete with childhood memories – fragmented, allusive, yet powerfully present narratives – it is because she is also Freud's friend. She knows, even if many of her critics don't, that listening to her is fine but that repeating her words (only) reduces her work to just one side of a multifarious, multilayered complexity.

Process happens when the narrative of viewing rivals the narrative of memory, whose presence one senses but cannot grasp. This is also the Borgesian moment when identity flounders, its uncertainty leaking from the work into the viewer. This is art's way of performing narration with a second-person narrator. The viewer drawn into heteropathy does not emerge self-identical from the experience. The processual aspect of Bourgeois's works is a strong counter-force against chronology, against the linear unfolding in time and the anteriority narratives it generates. The evocations and associations of the viewers function like the scraps of tapestry and the pieces of bone in *Spider*. The memories there are found objects that we routinely integrate into narrative frames derived from the cultural stock available to us. By presenting memories as found objects, Bourgeois makes them appear as scraps of a past. Through the need to experience the temporality of looking, the narratives that turn this particular Cell into a house also slam the door on the viewer who is trying to read the stories, to turn them into anteriority narratives and thus cannibalize them. Her stories of the past stick to our stories of looking, but they remain opaque. What characterizes second-person narrative most profoundly, then, is not the "person," which is mutually interchangeable anyway, but the tense; the present.

3: Non-narrative Comments, Narrative Arguments

Non-narrative comments occur everywhere within narratives. Since these pass mostly unreflectively, opinions and inflections do not affect the status of the narrator as the "I" hidden behind a "he" or an "it." Together, they may begin to sketch the shape of the focalizer, whose vision the narrator tells. The reverse is also true: non-narrative texts, including scientific ones, are also replete with narrative. The following example demonstrates the relevance of the search for narrativity and the identification of the narrator even within apparently non-narrative discourse. Physicist and philosopher of science Evelyn Fox Keller (1992) has conducted studies on the connections between language and science. One of these concerned the way scientific inventions and ideas are presented to the larger public. This study focused on the word "secret" as in "the secret of life." Another study was about the language in which biology continues to build on evolutionary theory. A central concept in that work was the term "competition"; traditionally, after Darwin, related to "struggle for life" and "survival of the fittest." The price to pay for this attention to competition was a lack of attention to collaboration, an evidently indispensable element in the sexual reproduction of organisms. One doesn't need to be a biologist to see that this privileging of one term over another has potential consequences for the further development of the theory itself and the social influence of such thinking in relation to gender. Bringing narrativity to bear on both competition and collaboration facilitates a diversification of the theory itself.

In the study I am looking at here, the issue was the use of metaphors one can still maintain to be "innocent," "just language": rhetorical. It concerned the discourse the developers of DNA used to present the importance of their research to the public. That discourse was filled with words carrying a long tradition. Thus, the initial molecule was called mother-molecule, and nature was constantly referred to as a woman; the unknown that it was the project to understand was "the secret of life," which had to be found out, if necessary by means of violence. Keller interpreted this discourse as follows:

> And if we ask, whose secret life has historically been, and from whom has it been secret, the answer is clear: Life has traditionally been seen as the secret of women, a secret from men. By virtue of their ability to bear children, it is women who have been perceived as holding the secret of life. (40)

I focus on the metaphor in that word "secret," which sounds so common and ordinary. Whereas the word "secret" in combination with "life" or "nature" has indeed become quite usual, the word is here a substitute for something else, not a single term but, I argue, a narrative.

What is unknown, as the negating prefix suggests, can be known. The subject of that knowing is the researcher. What is secret can also be known. But here, the subject is not quite the researcher. The word "secret" implies an action, hence, a subject of withholding. If there is a secret, then somebody is keeping it. This differentiates the secret from the enigma, which is subjectless, a situation or state, and the noun denoting it, descriptive. Hence, the choice for "secret" is not necessary; it is an active choice, which fits into the network of gendered language in which nature and life are made feminine. And it implicitly tells a story in which secrecy is seen as an act. "Secret" as a metaphor for the unknown, when considered a mini-narration, establishes a focalizer who perceives an opposition between two subjects: the researcher who wants to know the secret and "woman" who withholds it. This opposition between acting agents is easily turned into hostility, as the well-known metaphor of seventeenth-century British philosopher Francis Bacon (1561–1626) shows, according to which the scientist wanted to put nature on the rack to torture "her" secrets out of "her."

But this gendering of the unknown comes with a second aspect of the word "secret," which is of an altogether different nature. A secret that must be found out implies a process in which that finding out takes place. If we compare this to detective fiction, the series of events involved in that process can be considered a fabula. That narrative is implicitly told by the user of the metaphor; the male scientist's spokesman is its narrator. The narration is subjective in the precise sense of emanating from a subject. The word tells the narrative in the version of – from the focalization of – the subject of not-knowing. This subject feels excluded by the lack of knowledge, and experiences it as an action by an insider, the subject of knowing and withholding. That subject, now an actor, is the narrator's opponent. This implied battle between two actors intimates that the narrator may well be an imperceptible one (an np) but is certainly not an external narrator (EN).

This interpretation of metaphor as mini-narrative yields insight, not into what the speaker means but into what a cultural community considers "normal" interpretations; so acceptable that they are not considered metaphorical at all, and certainly not narrative. It requires analysis – cultural-narratological analysis – to follow up on the question of cultural interaction involved here. This is a case of ideology in ordinary language that becomes visible through narratological analysis. It may sound paradoxical, but I contend that the argumentative, hence, in itself non-narrative nature implied by the metaphor becomes apparent as soon as we consider the metaphor to be narrative. This is one example of how narratological analysis is inherently able to facilitate political or ideological understanding – an understanding that does not even let science keep immunity from narratology-based critique. It demonstrates, therefore, that all approaches that either isolate ideology from structure or reject structural analysis because it is not considered political are missing an important point of narrative theory.

4: Description

Description can be defined as the attribution of features to fabula elements. The attribution comes with a specific colouring or look, which is what binds it to focalization. Because of this it has great impact on the ideological and aesthetic effect of the text. But it is also a particular textual form, indispensable, indeed, omnipresent in narrative. It makes the elements of the fabula concrete and visible. It does that through slanting what we get to see, as the next part of this book, with the concept of focalization, will show. The present section briefly substantiates the discussion of aspects of description. Delimitation, motivation, and the rhetorical features of description together all appear relevant in descriptions (*Narratology*, 26–31). They constitute the textual body of the description, separating it from or binding it to the text as a whole.

In film, the near equivalent of delimitation is called suture: the shift or cut from a character who looks to the spectacle they see. I briefly mentioned this in my remarks on *Schindler's List*. This is primarily an aspect of focalization, but the textual showing of what the character sees is a descriptive unit. In painting, we tend to assume that the image as a whole is the object seen, and thus, it seems, no separate descriptive passages are called for. We have seen in the painting by Munch that this wholeness assumption fails to account for the painting as image, with its own narrator. From the house, the plants outside it, and the path to the large face of the man who walks away from the scenery but also, thereby, narrativizes the image, we can derive a descriptive portion as distinct from the narrative one, while both pertain to the pictorial narrator. Literary narratives, conversely, contain descriptions that we need to notice if we are to become aware of the image as text.

The passage from Djuna Barnes's *Nightwood* (1936) cited and analysed in *Narratology* (32–8) makes the complexity of the descriptive participation in the narrative abundantly clear. There, the introductory frame represents the difficulty of keeping that frame within its own bounds. In this way framing was put on the table. The passage posits itself as ostentatiously far from naturalizing the description through character-bound focalization. Binding each element to a larger whole, which is not a woman but a domain of sense perception, a painter's studio, a painting, and an object that refuses to stay still, respectively, Barnes's modernist descriptive discourse comments on the coherence within narrative as an altogether different kind of order.

The novel *The Ten Thousand Things* (1984 [1958]) by Dutch writer Maria Dermoût consists practically of descriptions; at least, that is how the first ten pages appear. The island evoked seems to be the main character. Small narrative bits or fragments intervene occasionally later on and serve mainly to give the descriptions a sense of purpose. That purpose is memory; the memories of a Dutch colonial subject whose memorial work completely erases the violence of colonization and the horrors that came with the decolonization. Instead, the descriptions of idyllic landscapes are literally a setting; but a setting that stays behind and remains almost empty of narrative. Nostalgia and grief go hand in hand to make sense of descriptions that are eerily beautiful but so extensive that one wonders if this text can still be called a novel. In an impressive syntactical icon, like the tropical plants they portray, description here overgrows the narrative of events.

This seems very different from the way description functions in realist narratives. In the case of a person, for example, the description would move from head to foot and from the eyes to the rest of the face. Or so we expect. For landscapes, the order might be from foreground to background, vague to clear, left to right in Western images, right to left in Eastern ones. Alternatively, the description could run through the different senses involved in the perception of the object. However, the best writers of the realist tradition are the worst realists in this sense, thus offering through their practice a critique of customary assumptions concerning narrative. Realism is the most widespread and, in its common conception, flattening of these assumptions. Again, Flaubert comes to mind. Famous for his realism, his work compels us to revise such preconceptions about realism as what "imitates" or "represents" reality. Flaubert's realism is not an imitation of reality but a critique of it. In this sense, his realism is couched "in the second person," if we can consider his readers as part of the narration in the same way as I proposed to do for Bourgeois's viewers.

The "second-person" constitutes the contemporary culture Flaubert fiercely critiqued, instead of representing it. In the seventh chapter of the third part of *Madame Bovary* (1971 [1857]), a chapter that is longer than most, we see, hear, and overhear what could almost be considered a descriptive passage, although small actions are being performed and many different voices heard. But what happens, if anything, is the staging of the social setting within and through which Emma is about to meet her end. Neighbours are gossiping, the tax collector is cheerfully-selfishly working on his amateur wooden sculpture, and Emma, socially excluded, is alone. This quick characterization of the scene can be traced in more detail in the final pages of the novel's chapter. The relentlessly isolating "third-person discourse" in the quoted speeches and the insinuated focalization of the villagers predict Emma's hopeless situation: isolation, social ostracism, is what dooms her, more than anything specific of her own doing. And that social hostility is the object of description. The events don't matter; the looking and gossiping do.

In the making of our feature film *Madame B* (2012–14), with Michelle Williams Gamaker, we were keen to substitute the problematic concept of "faithfulness" in adaption of literature to film with "loyalty." The difference is enormous. Faithfulness as a criterion focuses on similarities. For us, "loyalty" was a goal of doing justice, not to facts and details but to artistic-political thrust, which in Flaubert's case is primarily focused on his cultural critique of his time. In view of this, we played with the scene briefly described above to confuse narration and description. The mediating force is *affect*, a concept we take from Gilles Deleuze's (1994, 182) conception of it as an intensity that can be communicated, between people but also between artworks, objects, and people.

The resulting combination between affect and narrativity is best seen in the opening sequence of the film. Here, we respond to, or take on, that scene that in the novel is situated towards the end. The temporal reversal is an issue of narrative sequence, but here I seek to explain something else: namely, the narrative intermediality between literature and film on the level of the text. The images of the opening credits of our film posit ruin. This is their predictive tenor. This is poignantly visible. In the wider shots of this scene, it is noticeable that the ruined, half-collapsed house in which Emma stands is positioned on an abandoned field, as alone as the character is. The equation predicts that other equation, between the ruined state of the house and that of the character's life.

This sequence can be seen as descriptive. In this photograph (Figure 14), this is foregrounded by the blurred grass at the lower edge of the image. This ruin signifies the present state; what follows, the film we are about to watch, gets us back there. This happens in a circular movement that turns out to be, narratively speaking, a vicious circle. Thus, the opening credit sequence foretells the mode of storytelling: based on circularity, repetition, and an undermining of the narrative movement forwards, it posits the multiple moments that build up the story together. This circularity proposes the power of habit. This, too, is in loyalty to the novel, where habit is constantly put forward as destructive. And description is one of its master modes. It is more predominant in the novel than, for example, dialogue. That sparsity of dialogue is also a potential equation, in that it underlined Emma's loneliness.

In addition to this, and rather than deploying narrativity for suspense, our idea for the film was to immerse viewers in affect from the beginning, with our revision of Flaubert's alleged statement, "Madame Bovary, c'est moi," into the saying "Madame B, that's us" constantly in view. In our film, we have taken up Flaubert's famous ambiguity of narration and the implication of witnessing through focalization, which he staged directly at the opening of the novel, as discussed in *Narratology* (39–40). We turned this also into a beginning image by taking up the later passage, so as to posit the "pre-posterous" temporality that makes us all peers of Emma, like Charles's classmates at the beginning of the novel. This becomes an intersubjective multiplicity that implies the social, even philosophical point of fiction.

Emma precariously hovers in the ruined house that stands for her ruined life. But this is film; not a still image, although in this book it is. This, too, needed to be accounted for in film's own capacity, so as to avoid the flat criterion of faithfulness. This was necessary in our attempt to be loyal to that which makes Flaubert's text primarily such an artistic success. He did all he could to make language, his medium, work for his project of aesthetic perfectionism, including audio – in the sound of sentences – and critique. Hence, we had to do something that would also make the most of the cinema as an artistic medium. A visual change occurs through which Deleuzian affect and Flaubertian narrativity join forces. After some thirty seconds, when the title *Madame B* slowly shifts into the top of the frame, the image becomes slightly wobbly. This small change would be barely visible in a less continuous,

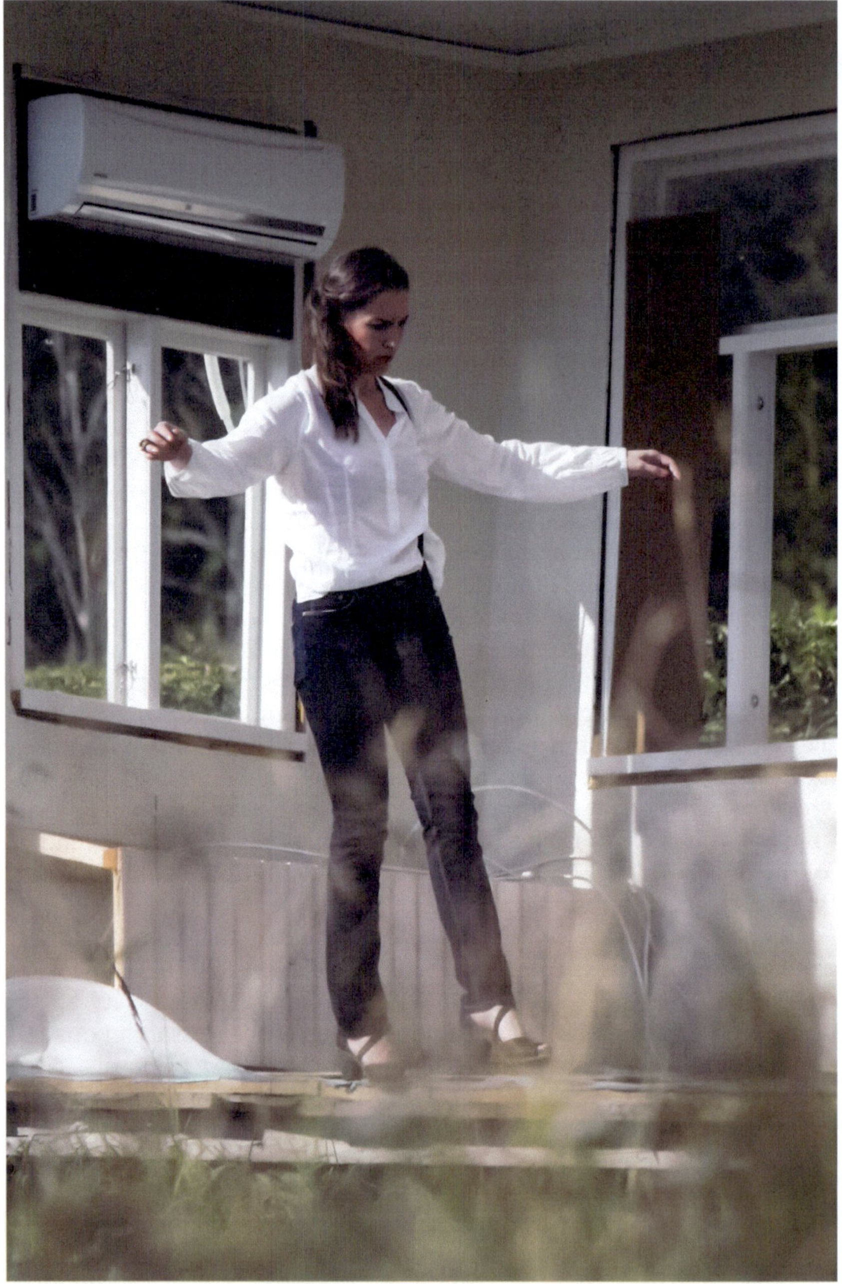

Figure 14.   *Madame B:* "Broken House" (2014). Photo: Thijs Vissia.

descriptive sequence. In cinematic language, wobbly images tend to indicate hand-held camera work. That typical cinematic feature is either a mistake, an aesthetic sloppiness, or, when meaningful, it can signify the presence of others. This was the point of our decision to edit from stable to wobbly footage halfway through the sequence, making the edit practically invisible.

These evoked others remain out of the frame; which is termed *hors-champ*. How, then, to make their presence visible, focalizable? In the novel, they are the inhabitants of the village who gossip about and despise Emma, and who, as characters, barely have a distinct identity. But these others indexically signified by the wobbliness also include the second persons: the contemporary viewers Flaubert's critique targeted, who witness, with relish, when the image hints at spying or meddling. But since the others remain out of the frame, the hand-held footage can also suggest possibly empathizing others and can shift from the past to the present tense: the tense of looking. The hand-held camera creates the "nous," the "we" of Flaubert's opening sentence, quoted in *Narratology* (39): "We were in study-hall when the headmaster entered, followed by a new boy not yet in school uniform and by the handyman carrying a large desk."

While chronologically speaking, our image of ruin occurs at the end of the fabula, and indeed, returns later in the film, we use it at the very beginning to introduce the "nous," the plural subject of witnessing, asking viewers to determine their own attitude. It is a kind of guideline for reading or, here, looking. Such a request to viewers is a second-person discourse, anchored in affect. This affect is a condition for what thinking in film can do. It helps viewers watch with a delicate balance of empathy – hence, understanding – and critical distance at the same time. For the emotional content of affect is also multiple. And since this is how ambivalence, complexity, and change of opinion are possible, it is important to propose this through artistic form. We aimed to make the destructive power of habit affectively tangible. In this, we attempted to be loyal to Flaubert's fiercely critical stance towards the culture of his time and place by offering our own culture a choice of attitude while also trying to deploy the medium's affordances to achieve this. The combination of the descriptive setting and the character who is literally falling down, results in a motivation that absorbs descriptions within the narrative.

In literature as well as in visual art, conventions of motivation have been criticized and challenged. In postmodern literature the motivation of descriptions is sometimes exaggerated to the point of collapse, in a motivational madness, or made blatantly incoherent. In film, a medium that is plagued by an excess of realistic effects, the opposite of motivation is often necessary. Descriptive takes that are not motivated by the suturing together of shot and reverse shot can be disconcerting, but also refreshingly surprising. This ambivalence towards motivation is not only the case in postmodern challenges to realism. In modernist literature, the emphasis on the subject's access to the world tends to blow up motivation to the point of completely subordinating the described element for which it was invoked.

In early cinema, the then-recent invention of the medium was still such a marvel in itself that the registration of the visible world was more important than the often tenuous fabula that was set in it. For example, the earliest specimens of the western were not at all primarily stories of suspenseful adventures but resembled, rather, a kind of travelogue, with the camera mounted on the top or the back of a train to register the landscape, as a form of visual tourism – called "phantom rides." The fabula was a rather meagre pretext to take the viewer on a trip. Even in the more or less realistic cinema that is currently predominant, many strategies have been developed that counter the unsuitable realistic effects the medium tends to entail. *Schindler's List* is again a case in point.

Let me preface the following example briefly. It is by now a common albeit also contested view that the horror of the holocaust cannot be represented; yet as time goes by, the need to make sure that it be remembered becomes more and more acute. Film is an expository medium: its narrative mode is showing; and its power to produce affect and thereby implicate viewers is based on that showing. Films on the holocaust have not been very successful in avoiding the pitfalls of representation. They either use the tragedy as a backdrop, sideways (*Sophie's Choice*, 1982, Alan J. Pakula), or sentimentalize it through individual identification (the TV series *Holocaust*, 1978, Marvin J. Chomsky). It cannot, ever, be adequately – realistically – represented, and I suggest that Spielberg didn't try. The reason for the severe criticisms of his film is, I think, that critics assumed he did. Instead, however, he "touched" it, established a relationship with it, based on contiguity. He explores ways to do so through a medium that can hardly avoid the pornographic effects of showing torture, shame, and sadism.

To at least complicate that effect, the film's narrator deploys a cinematic discourse that counters the effects of realism. For example, when showing victims, it deploys a descriptive technique that consists of quick takes, avoiding the grazing gaze of mastery and sadism. Also, the visual images struggle with emphatic musical accompaniment, which sometimes even takes over, monitoring transitions from the story. This monitoring is necessary because the film represents a fabula that interweaves the lives of a number of individuals with the history of mass events. The film text deploys excessive close-ups combined with movement that confine and make faces hard to see and thereby avoid a pleasure-giving visual experience.

The use of black and white, often misunderstood as historical pretension, can also be seen as part of this anti-realistic style that denaturalizes what we see, even as it also evokes the connotation "history." We have seen this also in the film *Ida*. By alternating "telling" and "showing" – making us sympathize with the predicaments of a few families and individuals, but alternating those moments with broad historical evocations that remind viewers of the worldwide scale of the catastrophe – the narrator keeps sentimentalizing identification at bay. The combination of emphatic symbolization and constructedness contributes to the narrator's rhetoric, which aims at representing not "it" (the horror of the holocaust) but the index that touches (it): the girl Danka's hand.

One anti-realist strategy in the film's description is a poetic of doublets; rhyming, repetition, symmetrical reversals. It allows real historical and mythical-biblical allusions to develop together, intertwined. This strategy undermines the tendency of the anecdotal to take over and impose realism as sentimentalism, the tendency of individual stories to overrule the historical tragedy. Yet it manages to individualize the Jews. Carefully, the same characters are made to appear in the mini-stories of daily life so that they are real persons, but their stories are framed by history. The strategy of doublets demonstrates the parallel development of good and evil (Schindler versus Goeth) within the evil party, as two possibilities. Goeth sometimes almost looks like Schindler; as a result, when Goeth looks at himself in the mirror he potentially doubles himself, just for a brief moment, into a good and an evil person. All these strategies are forms of motivation of description that, instead of supporting realism, counter it.

5: Levels of Narration

In most linguistic narratives, a narrator quotes speeches or thoughts of characters. Within such quotes, other characters can hear the second-level narrator or speaker, but this is not always the case, nor is it always indicated whether others do hear the quoted words. If one character has thoughts that contain devastating judgments about another but does not express these to that character while the thoughts are narrated so as to appear like quotes, a fundamental inequality results.

As mentioned in *Narratology* (39), French writer Colette has put this in-equality to strategic use, for example, in the novel *The Cat* (1977 [1933]). There, a young couple's first months of marriage are presented as an inexorable decline of their relationship. The man, it turns out, loves his cat more than his wife. But that is an oversimplified account, based on the fabula only. In the text and the story, something else is at stake.

When it comes to narrating, systematically, the thoughts of the man, who judges his wife mercilessly, are quoted as an embedded second-ary narration, often without the attributive verb that would make clear that the thoughts are not uttered out loud. The woman, in contrast, is only quoted when speaking, mostly to her husband. As a result, the criticisms the man holds against his wife are told to the reader over her head, so to speak. They are displayed in focalization. She does not have a clue that he is so dissatisfied; nor does she get access to his negative responses to what she says to him. The discrepancy between narrating and focalizing becomes the text's tool of manipulation. For the reader does get access to the man's thoughts. Taking sides becomes irresistible. We, too, tend to find the wife, Camille, cold, and her hus-band, Alain, sensitive and vulnerable. Only a technical analysis of the text levels will reveal the more hidden issue: Alain is incapable of com-municating, and Camille, as a consequence, becomes more and more lonely and miserable. She is an object of focalization, like Emma in that first sequence of *Madame B*, but rarely gets to speak. No wonder she blames the cat!

This example demonstrates that in the enquiry into the question "Who speaks?" it is as relevant to ask the question "Who does not get to speak?" Whereas linguistic narratives are structurally suitable for such manipulations of the reader, in film this is very different. There, too, levels of narration occur, but the distinction is much clearer. So far, I have only spoken about a filmic narrator as a unit. But where relevant, such a narrator can be differentiated into a visual and an audio narrator. The concept of the filmic narrator comprehends these two. This is not a distinction in narrative levels. Quoting characters is the most common ploy in film to embed the text of characters within the overall narrator's text, visual or audio as the case may be (Verstraten 2009, 7–8).

In our film *Madame B* we have experimented with this idea of a dual first level of narration as well. There is a scene based on the Flaubertian sentence in chapter 7 of part I: "La conversation de Charles était plate comme un trottoir de rue, et les idées de tout le monde y défilaient …" [Charles's conversation was flat as a sidewalk, a place of passages for the ideas of everyman …"]. This is a typical narrator's sentence, with a comparison no character would come up with, if only because they would all fall under the biting sarcasm of the comparison. More on this sentence later, concerning focalization. In the film, we could not incorporate this sentence; Claude Chabrol's decision to have a narrator say this most famous narrator's sentence of the novel leads to disastrous results in his 1991 film *Madame Bovary*. We learned from Chabrol's film to avoid making a narratorial voice appear as an EN(p).

Instead, we asked the actors to enact the sentence. This is an example of how filmic narration is inevitably, and fortunately, a collective activity. The actor playing Charles (Thomas Germaine) improvised a series of dinner conversations so flat, so full of "the ideas of everyman" that the addressee, Emma, shows in her face an exasperation that corresponds with Flaubert's devastating critique. This is the filmic narrator's equivalent of the literary narrator's sentence. The audio track is in tune with this. Not only the conversation's content, but also the voice of the actor is indeed exasperatingly boring. The household clock ticks, something our audio narrator systematically deploys to tell Emma's boredom. For example, when earlier on she sits bored in her empty house, the clock ticks loudly. When she picks up a magazine and browses through it, the clock stops; as long as she is interested in something, she doesn't hear the clock.

Because this sound motif is already in place when the flat conversations occur, the boredom is echoed not only by the visual narrator, on Emma's face, but by the sound narrator by means of the embedded voice and the clock working together to drive Emma mad with boredom.

These dual narrators on the first level each embed second-level speech. Charles's entire conversation is, so to speak, quoted. In film, this is so standard that it seems not to matter to analyse the levels of narration. That this is a quote becomes clear, however, especially when the servant brings a dish and Charles looks up and says to her, "Thank you, Milja." This small side speech, still embedded as all the rest of the conversation, has one effect: it interrupts, and thereby foregrounds, the manic monologue. The audio narrator also embeds the conversation clearly, in this case within the descriptive sounds of the house, such as the clock. This makes Charles's voice a second-level internal audio narrator.

The visual narrator deploys specific techniques to further elaborate on the embedding. During the entire dinner-table scene we don't see Charles, except once or twice very briefly. Instead, while the camera is entirely on Emma and the audio recorder on Charles, Charles's droning voice suits well with the image of his blurred shoulder. The face of his victim is filmed in an over-the-shoulder middle-close "dirty" shot. We see only this patch of dark blur that in an imagined three-dimensional view looks like a shadow hovering over Emma. It encloses her visually. Thus, Charles facing his wife can be seen as a second-level visual narrator, an internal one, to which she responds through her exasperated face.

This leads to a brief consideration of the intermediate forms where levels of narration and embedding cannot be distinguished: indirect discourse and free indirect discourse (FID). Flaubert is a master of confusing narrative variations of discourse, making it often impossible to disentangle them and distinguish between direct, indirect, and FID. The latter form also facilitates a multiplication of subjectivities. These features make the novel "immersive," a term usually reserved for exhibitions, not novels. The immersive quality of Flaubert's text consists in its tendency to move from narration to FID without warning, transition, or clear indication. To get a concrete sense of this immersive quality, I will now call on an instance of visual art where the narrativity itself is, at first sight, dubious. It only becomes visible and relevant if we focus on the interference between narrative subjects. Again, as with Bourgeois's *Spider*, I contend that narratological analysis, even in the face of abstract visual art, can help enliven the way we understand art. This is, then, another instance of the interdisciplinarity that narratology can inspire.

Finally, narration can occur even in abstract, clearly non-narrative visual artworks. An instance of this closes this part of the book. The artwork is an allegedly abstract sculpture by Belgian artist Ann Veronica Janssens titled *Corps noir*, from 1994 (Figure 15). With the help of the question "who speaks?" I will argue that, far from abstract, this work is as immersive as they come. In blandly descriptive terms, *Corps noir* is a deep black, perfectly round, shiny, hemispheric Perspex bowl, hung on a wall. It couldn't be simpler. Yet, it is not, in terms of its agency; of what it does to us and makes us do. And when there is action, there is agency; and hence, an agent or subject doing it. The action this work solicits from the viewer, its performativity, and its perceptual basis, are mirroring. And this becomes the object of complication, so that narrativity can creep in.

The shiny material mirrors the viewer; but the spherical form reverses the mirror image. Left and right as well as up and down are inverted. The viewer who looks into it is also diminished into a miniature. In view of the commonplace interpretation of mirroring as seeing oneself, it is an unsettling mirror to look into; as unsettling as the one of *Don Quijote*. There, the figure's gaze so directly addresses the viewer that it is as if the latter constitutes his mirror image. In both cases, the mirror is not simply a device for self-reflection, for which this motif has so often been deployed. More direct, in relation to bodily perception,

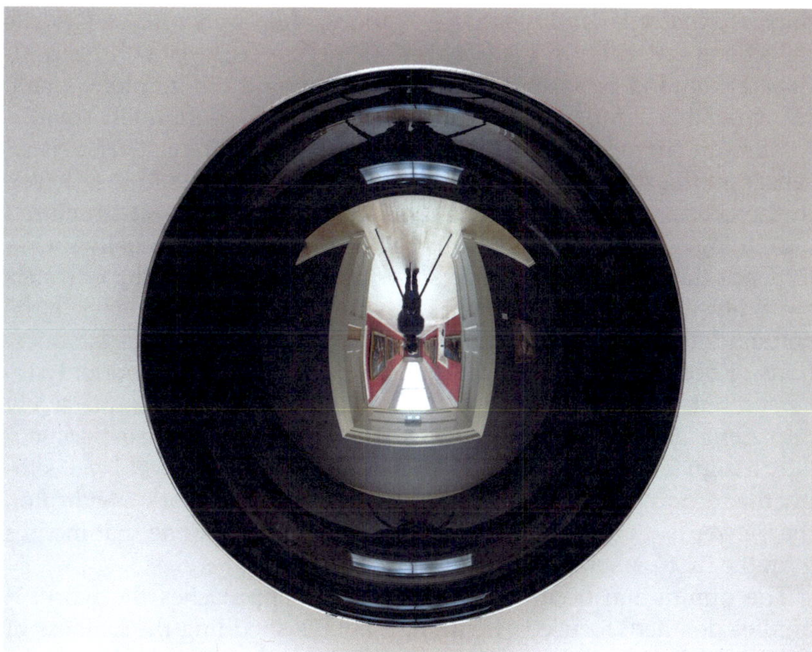

Figure 15.   Ann Veronica Janssens, *Corps noir* (1994). Black Perspex hemisphere, 50 cm diameter, 25 cm depth. Photo: Marc Dommage.

the ordinary mirror is also the flat surface that enables self-perception in space. But Janssens's mirror – and this is its primary material difference – is concave. This sculpture foregrounds the bodiliness of looking, positions the work in a non-linear history, and offers reflections on its political potential.

As an object, especially seen from some distance, it wavers between two- and three-dimensionality. *Corps noir* deploys the mythical trope of mirroring as a literal incorporation of space, and explores what combining illusionism and the round shape can do. The artwork obliquely questions the Renaissance obsession with linear perspective – a questioning we have seen Munch perform through the excessively steep path – and the difficulty of simultaneously depicting the vanishing point and the "window onto the world," as Alberti called it. Moreover, the Baroque interest in the "infinitely tiny" acquires a fascinating actuality in it, available for the viewer's experience. For the mirrored image of the viewer is rigorously miniatured. Thus the diminutive subject mirrored in *Corps noir* invokes the Baroque philosopher Blaise Pascal's reflections on scale. In his *Thoughts* (Pensées) (1910 [1660]) he positioned mankind between the infinitely large and the infinitely small. He wrote that compared to the universe, humans are infinitely small.

All in all, these are quite some actions. But who is doing it? The visual sensation this object provokes, or even creates, happens to the viewer. In the act of viewing, an event occurs. And in the subject-structured narratology I am proposing, this makes the work potentially narrative. But the question is, who is speaking here? The crossing of different art-historical and philosophical issues in a visual experience in the here-and-now also produces a crossing of agencies. It raises the questions of how and why the viewer must see her reflection not only reversed but also in miniature when looking at, or rather, immersively into, *Corps noir*. All this becomes easier to understand if we experimentally assign to the viewer the position of actor. For the viewer is not simply the second person of the narrator. Directed by the work-as-narrator, the viewer is an embedded second-level speaker, but one that merges with the first-person narrator.

The diminution occurs when the viewer approaches the work. It implies detailed, focused attention; it entails shedding the laziness of routine looking and the arrogance of overseeing, surveying modes of looking. In mirroring, the subject, always eager to see herself, can be enticed to do just that. That is why traditionally the mirror stands for vanity. This mirror does not accommodate that at all. One is compelled to come closer, and closer, until sticking one's head inside is the desired thing to do. But this doesn't accommodate vanity any better. This process has a temporal effect as well. When we realize that the viewer is compelled to approach, spend time, and produce events of viewing, the narrativity comes to the fore. The object, its concave shape, and shiny surface together, can be seen as a narrator. But that narrator does not speak alone; it can do so only in merging with the viewer. If there is narrativity, then the narrator is in interference with the viewer. In other words, this is an instance of FID.

Anticipating later discussions of temporality, the phased approach also produces an effect of timing. Due to the difficulty of seeing the tiny and upside-down self-image and in confrontation with the inherent narcissism of subjectivity, time slows down. And spatially, it enfolds the viewing subject into something outside that is larger. Janssens's shrewdly constructed impediments to vision help us unlearn what routine has inflicted on us in the form of what can be considered as a visual limitation. After that unlearning, looking provides renewed access to the microscopic world of the infinitely small. This, I submit, is the way in which this work is baroque; not belonging to this historical movement but affiliating itself with it by means of its form.

If we attempt to historicize this sculpture in the way I have historicized literary narratives in *Narratology* (39–44) with the opening passages of a realist, a modernist, and a postmodernist novel, *Corps noir* is certainly not to be reduced to its affiliation with baroque. At first sight, the work comes across as an abstract modernist "pure" object. It is austere in form and devoid of any baroque curls, folds, waves, and colouristic tricks; it seems rather minimalist, even if its rigorously round shape can be seen as baroque. To position it in relation to history, both affiliations are equally important. They qualify each other, and their apparent opposition is the bridge between present and past; a bridge that is a two-way street. Here, too, we could speak of interference. Janssens links baroque matter with meaning-making as an active semiosis, conceived as an embodied process.

This work engages the body in a way that is congenial to Janssens's famous, eminently immersive mist installations, yet different in its specific activation of bodily coordinates. In the mist installations, sight and its deceleration inflict slowness on the body's movement. In *Corps noir*, it seems that sight attempts to but does not manage to colonize touch. Inside a mist installation one almost *feels* space; one feels being inside the space that materially envelops the visitor. Here, the viewer is bound to stay outside. Slowness affects looking even if the body is not moving and is not compelled to move. Although this work is solidly black, like most of her other works it too questions as well as adopts conceptions and experiences of light. Janssens's work consistently probes, examines, and challenges the materiality of light. This happens in this work with particular force. The only light inhering in *Corps noir* comes from the outside. It is the absence of light in the object itself that precludes a firm distinction between convex and concave.

Corps noir engages us in a questioning of the semiotic practice of space and the spatial dimension of semiosis, without divorcing either from time. This experiential feature of spatial ambiguity becomes the focus of what would otherwise be an abstract sculpture. Through the performative force that compels the viewer's participation in the storytelling of the events of seeing, it takes on a very concrete shape. Up close, there seems to be a round disk of light floating between the edge and the inner "vanishing point" of the sculpture. This disk looks so solid that one is tempted to put a hand behind it to see if it is going to destroy the light disk. Again, the viewer is compelled to act. The gesture does not manage to wreak any havoc on the disk, however. It remains impeccably round; its edge remains sharp. But what matters is that the viewer is enticed to try.

As an artist of today known as abstract, Janssens does not include any representational signs and hence, does not overtly refer to painting. Instead, she makes the "pure" sculpture into a *theoretical object*, an occasion for and solicitation of reflection, not as mirroring but in the sense of thinking. This object theorizes that, visually, concavity and convexity can be very close, alternating and wavering – performatively, as between event and thing, like fire. Hence, purity – of meaning, of effect, of experience – turns into its opposite – a messy, time-bound ambiguity that cannot be disentangled. Binding time to space, its theoretical point lies in this hovering on the edge for a certain duration. This work, then, lays out the many consequences, or tentacles, of the textual confusion of FID.

Thanks to the miniaturizing of the self-reflection in the sculpture, deixis anchors semiosis in the subject, but not in narcissism. For what can subject-centredness be when the subject is by definition a wavering double I/you subject that cannot be pinned down at any single moment in any particular spatial position, as *Corps noir* intimates? This question brings the artistic search for a political relevance beyond representation to the next stage, by giving a new turn to the dialogic relation to space. In the historical moment that we begin to realize how space is threatened by our own human actions, this is profoundly political.

The anchoring of deixis in the body of the subject, together with the I/you wavering, binds the subject irremediably to her "other," in this case the artwork. The relevance becomes greater rather than lesser. Through the swerving and the experienced or felt process of it, the subjectivity of the self-assured mastery of the free individual is challenged. This simple-seeming object, then, harbours an amazing number of ideas, made concrete through a con-fusing of narratorial agencies. Enticing us to discover those ideas is what politically relevant art must do. In this sense, the work, like all Janssens's works, is *activating* rather than *activist*. This becomes visible when we let narratological questions loose on this abstract visual work. This distinction is my proposal for a further fleshing out of Mouffe's concept of the political.

Remarks and Sources

My commitment to clarity for intersubjectivity comes from my lifelong passion for teaching as a communicative endeavour. See Lutters (2018) for my view of teaching, especially in relation to vision. On the concept or approach of "cultural analysis," my alternative to both separated disciplinary fields and to the general term "cultural studies," my book *Travelling Concepts in the Humanities* (2002) gives clear arguments and details. The present book must be seen in that context. Of the many critical publications on *Schindler's List*, my favourite is the nuanced, in-depth analysis by Miriam Bratu Hansen (1996). For *Ida*, I have not found useful critical analyses in English.

The generalizing term "text" for artefacts in any medium is often wrongly taken to suggest a linguistic bias. Instead, it indicates a semiotic artefact that without being isolated from its cultural frames can function autonomously. It has a beginning and end, or a frame. See Martin Fuchs (2001). An alternative term that is not medium specific is "media product," which has been launched and further developed by the Swedish scholar of intermediality Lars Elleström (2021) and the research group he leads in two very useful recent volumes. I refrain from using that term here because it is bound to an elaborate systematic theory that I cannot lay out here.

Narrativity in visual images is not an issue of the earlier stories that constitute the content of, for example, the works called by the genre label "history painting." I have argued that – and also on what conditions, and with which transformations – narratological concepts can be brought to bear on visual art throughout my book *Reading "Rembrandt"* (2006 [1991]). On moving images and the narrativity that inheres in them, again, with transformations, see my book *Emma & Edvard* (2017).

Interdisciplinarity is the red thread in my book *Travelling Concepts* mentioned for cultural analysis. For a useful collective volume, see William H. Newell (ed.) (1998). I published an article, a "case study" in a collective volume in 2011 that Newell co-edited, in which I analyse the inter-ship between art, philosophy, linguistics, and history. The examples from the biblical book of Judges are a summing up of my book *Death and Dissymmetry* (1988). In that book I make the narratological concept of the subject more complex. I have further developed interdisciplinarity as "intership" in an article on the novel-film interaction (2017b).

On the issues of authorship put on the table by Barthes and Foucault (see bibliography for references to their key texts) I have recently published an article that takes the issue also into the visual domain (2020a). On Malani's shadow plays my book *In Medias Res* (2016) contains extensive information, and chapter 1 of that book is entirely devoted to *In Search of Vanished Blood*. More on the figure of Cassandra in the second part of the present book. The words of Malani's voice are based on Heiner Müller's play *Hamletmachine* (1977).

Currently, there is an interest in eliminating from narratology the concept of the narrator as a general starting point. This trend, called "optional narrator theory" which emerged in the wake of the founding work by Ann Banfield (1982), is also influenced by cognitive narratologists, such as David Herman (2002; 2003). I admire Banfield's work and its strong argumentation. The reason I cannot endorse her position is that it eliminates responsibility from narratological enquiry. For a collective volume that underwrites "optional narrator theory," see Patron (2020).

In this chapter, only the narrative status of the narrative agent and its relationship to what is narrated have been discussed. Narratology studies narrative texts only in so far as they are narrative; in other words, in their narrativity. In particular, the topic of this chapter, the text, is also studied elsewhere in several other aspects. Linguistically oriented disciplines such as stylistics, but also grammar, syntax, and semantics, are important for different kinds of investigations of the text. The so-called (with a misnomer) "omniscient narrator" describes the fabula as if objective, letting the actors do their thing without interfering. I entirely refrain from using that concept from classical narrative theory. I find it both fantasmatic and ideologically manipulative to even suppose such a possibility. See Culler (2004) for a definitive critique of that concept and its cognates. Wayne C. Booth (1961) introduced the concept of the implied author, which I reject (*Narratology* 17–18; and here, in Preliminary Remarks). The term "mise en abyme" – spelled with a y to recall Gide, who came up with it – has been extensively theorized by Lucien Dällenbach (1989).

Nevertheless, the connections with related disciplines have made themselves felt at several points. The distinction between direct, indirect, and free indirect discourse, discussed here because it concerns the status of the narrative agent with regard to the object of narration, is one of the classic topics of linguistics.

With the heading "In Medias Res" I want to make the point of the provisional nature of the impression of coherence that may arise, as well as allude to the most interdisciplinary narrative artwork I know: the "video-shadow plays" by Nalini Malani. I had no other choice for a title of the book I wrote about these works than "In Medias Res." Malani is an artist whose "image-thinking" and the resulting "thought-images" has been an inspiration for me ever since I encountered her art.

On Maria Dermoût and the repression of colonialism in memory, see Paul Doolan (2013). For more on memory in the context of such political issues as colonialism and the holocaust, see Rothberg (2009). On Mary Longman and her relationship to her Aboriginal (Cree) culture, see McMaster (1996). McMaster is himself of Cree origin and is a master of critically looking with nuance at the "fine line" between adopting Indigenous perspectives and cultural appropriation (2017, 70).

For *Don Quixote*, I quote from the most commonly read English translation, and in the bibliography, I cite the English, used here, as well as the Spanish edition currently in bookstores. For information about my video installation based on the novel, see my book 2019, bilingual English-Spanish 2020. The spelling of the main character's name differs widely. To keep the distinction in mind, I use the Spanish Quixote for the novel and Quijote for the installation. Hayden White's work (1973; 1978) is not narratological, but his position as a historiographer can be better understood when narratological concepts are brought to bear on it. His concept of "emplotment" in *Metahistory* alludes to the narratological affiliation.

"Character-plot knot" is a term put forward by Nanna Verhoeff in her study on the early Western (2006). It refers to the inextricable link between the plot, where time evolves, and the characters, who carry the plot. On Louise Bourgeois's *Spider*, see my 2001 book. This is a detailed case study of that single work that offers a succinct overview of the issues brought up in this intership between two anachronistically dialoguing works in different media that I have staged as talking to each other. This book contains many more images than the two included here. I recommend a recent book on Bourgeois's *Cells* by Fernanda Negrete (2020).

Both Freud (1982 [1900]) and Bollas (1987) contribute each in their own way to this whimsical dialogue. The important work of Evelyn Fox Keller is most readily understood in her books from 1986 and 1992, from the latter of which the example of "secret" is taken. The example of competition is from the earlier book. Keller is a theoretical physicist who, without using the conceptual apparatus of narratology, has a strong sense of the importance of narrativity in scientific theories. The differentiation between "secret" and "enigma," which is important here, I learned from Hernández (2020, 169), who borrowed it from Mario Perniola (1995).

On affect, which is relevant for many of the issues discussed in this book, see Ernst van Alphen (2008) for succinct lucid explanation, and his co-edited volume with Tomáš Jirsa (2019). On baroque art and thinking, see my book *Quoting Caravaggio*. In that book I develop the "preposterous" sense of mutual temporality, against the standard of chronology.

Finally, a serious recommendation. On the constellation of memory, history, and fiction, including trauma, many have written wise words. I am most impressed among recent publications by the masterly book by Griselda Pollock, who brings it all together with analytical clarity and historical precision in a book the title of which already speaks volumes: *Charlotte Salomon and the Theatre of Memory* (2018). The entire book is important. Especially the pages 386–8 are key, but every page is worth reading. The integration between visual analysis, historical understanding, and interdisciplinary theorizing makes this for me the book of the decade.

2

Transition: Between Text and Society

1: Preliminary Remarks

When there is text interference, narrator's text and actor's text are so closely related that sometimes a distinction into narrative levels can no longer be made. The relevance, then, is in the attempt and its failure. When the texts do not interfere but are clearly separate, the degree to and manner in which the embedded actor's text and the primary narrator's text are related can still be very different. The primary narrator is named primary, not to give it importance but simply to distinguish it from the narrators on other levels. In fact, the importance may be greater for the embedded narrator. The dependence of the actor's text on the narrator's text should be seen as the dependence of what is called, with equally dubious terms, a subordinate clause to a main clause. These technical terms are all bothersome, seemingly echoing social relations. Below I will foreground examples that demonstrate that structural properties of texts are important precisely because of the pernicious and oft-forgotten analogies between textual and social structures. This is emphatically not a realist, mimetic, imitative analogy; far from it.

What goes by the term "frame narratives" are the clearest examples of the structure of embedding. In *Narratology* (52) I gave the example of the primary narrator of Emily Brontë's *Wuthering Heights* (1847). This is an internal one, a CN, the snowed-in guest called Lockwood. After a strange experience during the night, he asks the servant Nelly Dean about the family, and thus she becomes the narrator, already on a second level. As a servant, she is a typical narrator-witness, and it is as a witness that Lockwood asks her to tell the tale. The mostly invisible servant, in the class hierarchy of the day, sees everything, precisely because no one takes her seriously enough to hide things from her.

Her tale is so long, elaborate, and containing things she cannot have seen that we soon forget that she is the agent-subject telling the story. Thus, we act as the other members of the household: Nelly is just as invisible to us as she is to the others. This produces a liminal affiliation between the structure of narratorial embedding and the social structure of a class society; one that the analysis in narrative levels may counter (a bit).

American historian and anthropologist Ann Laura Stoler (2002) wrote about the comparable but even more poignant situation in colonial households, where the mistresses interacted in intimacy with their servants. In Brontë's novel this power inequality is not as obvious, but precisely therefore is worth looking at with a narratological magnifying glass. This structure can also encompass many different narratives, more short stories than novels, embedded within a frame narrator. The most widely known example of such a narrative cycle is *Arabian Nights*. The less-known but better title for the same collection is *A Thousand and One Nights*. This title is closer to the Arabic *Kitāb alf laylah wa-laylah* and already suggests the enormous number of stories – one for each night – and the length of the collection, a dozen to twenty fat volumes in most editions. The stories are all embedded as second-level stories told by an internal narrator, and some are embedded on further levels. The structure is an early instance of the cliffhanger: each story ends on a moment of heightened suspense.

The primary narrative presents the story of Scheherazade, threatened with death by her husband, the king, who kills all women he marries after the first night because his first wife had been unfaithful to him. Only if she succeeds in fascinating the bad sport with her stories will she survive the night, night after night. This frame narrative, then, concerns the power of storytelling, and by extension, the life-saving capacity of cultural activity. Every night she tells a story; in that story new stories are embedded. In this case, it is possible to say that the structure of narration echoes the king's paranoid view of women. When the story is interrupted, he does not kill his wife because he wants to know: how the story ends, as much as if she will be faithful to him. The paranoia and the suspense are mutual representations of each other.

In this transitional part I will delve deeper into the theoretical issues of part I as I have proposed to practise them, with a special view – not biased, but rather partial, in the double sense of "not whole" and "engaged" – to counter those theorists who blame narratology for being blind to social and political issues. This is a rather general development, which also has an oedipal tendency to reject, or put away as "classical," narratological theories that pay close attention to formal and structural issues. Throwing away the baby with the bathwater is what they then do. It reduces literary studies to thematic-political issues. I maintain that a political analysis that does *not* do away with the literary-artistic nuances but instead makes these socially meaningful is better equipped to counter the superficiality and intellectual laziness of an approach that is rightly considered with a derogatory term: "politically correct." My alternative is not simply to maintain old positions but elaborate these in such a way that they can analyse and demonstrate how art can contribute to political debates in more nuanced and more profound ways.

2: Frame Narrative's Invisible Frame

How would such a narrative structure as a frame narrative, the clearest instance of the need for the concept of embedded levels of narration, work in film, where the primary narrator is mostly invisible, whereas the narrative text is primarily visual, or rather, audiovisual? This is not in itself an issue of "medium-specificity." One of the ways in which relations between primary and embedded narrative levels can be deployed for important effects in any medium is the mixture of genres. When we made the experimental documentary film *A Thousand and One Days* (2002–4) with the small collective Cinema Suitcase, a film devoted to the many days an Arab immigrant "sans papiers" had to spend struggling for political, legal, and social acceptance, we turned the Arabic classic into an inspiration for the intercultural connection we sought to demonstrate. For this purpose, we tried to do justice to the structure of the literary precedent of *A Thousand and One Nights* by rigorously avoiding a voice-over and instead letting all participants tell their story of what was happening, independently of the others. The figure of the king in the classical Arabic narrative would be, in this case, the French police, whom we kept at a distance. "He" held the strings of power but didn't need to speak. In other words, we kept the primary narrator in a subordinate role and opened up the world of the many second-level narrators.

This led to a fragmented film, in which a multitude of voices sound – "A Thousand and One Voices" became the title of an article I wrote about the film. In the making and in many discussions of the result, the question of narrative voice came up. The narrative was so closely situated in inseparably overlapping cultures that it seemed impossible to give it a single particular voice – to attribute, implicitly or explicitly, the narrative to a single speaker. Instead, the story asked to be multi-voiced, with the singularity of each voice being audible. Yet for potential viewers it was precisely that situatedness and the resulting intermediation that might be perceived as a lack of clarity, political or otherwise.

For, bringing along the singular into the multiple rather than the general, which preserves the traces of the singular that enriches the multitude, and transfers back to the singular the generality of the political domain, is where I place a searched-for universality that does not exist. This film with its many moments of specificity offers a good platform for such a discussion. The primary filmic narrator, who remains out of the frame, was heavily leaning on the audio narrator to edit the speeches of each participant so that the contents of the speeches became autonomous on the one hand and resonated with visual takes on the other. They resonated without systematically corresponding to them. The major intervention was to retain the idea of paranoia but not as a narrative structure. Instead, it was diminished to be a trigger of the stories, yet attributed not to the main character but to the big absent: the French police.

Even though film is predominantly a narrative genre, the one-utterance, one-narrator assumption of narratology does not readily apply to it. Yet if the common assumption holds, then film, even if it does not necessarily contain a narratorial voice as such, can also be assumed to have a single narrative agent. Therefore, I deploy film here to look at the common concept of the single narrator in order to denaturalize but not reject it. Compelled by the current world of intercultural relations as well as by the dialectic relationship between (academic) theory and (artistic) practice, I am subjecting the singular-narrator thesis to a critical re-examination. I feel compelled to do this for the sake of clarifying the inextricable bond between text and society.

The concept is at stake not in its defining properties but in the way we use concepts to think. Like people, concepts cannot be rigidly determined: instead of being universal, they travel. I will consider this travel in the confrontation of the concept of voice with cinematic narrativity, but overdetermined as it is by the individualization of narrativity. *A Thousand and One Days* tells a story of events that happen to many, shown through the intimate life of one. This would make it particular. But it is steeped in a sociopolitical situation that makes it exemplary. In principle, exemplarity turns a particular into a general, frequently confused with universal. In order to grasp the point of the narrative structure it is best to consider the film in relation to three aesthetic traditions, or genres, that meet in this film: documentary film, classical tragedy, and "oriental" tales as exemplified in *A Thousand and One Nights*.

As a collective of filmmakers, we sought to address these traditions at a moment when they were tested to their limits, in a time when they were not quite obsolete but no longer vital either. *A Thousand and One Days* is a film on migration, or rather what I prefer to call "migratory culture." Hence, thematically as well as structurally, it is situated in a space not reducible to one specific culture. Consequently, the film resists universalizing concepts from the Western tradition, such as the single narrator.

In *A Thousand and One Days* we celebrated the outcome of a long and intricate journey, of the anguish, struggle, loneliness, and financial constraints of Tarek, a young sans-papiers in Paris. The joyful three-day celebration of his wedding establishes the here-and-now of this documentary, which is organized through an Aristotelian unity of time, space, and event. But within that same event, pockets of history weigh in with darker times and tougher spaces. The people in the film descend into memories of fear and uncertainty, only to bounce back again and rejoice in the outcome. This temporal structure already precludes any particularity of a single narrator.

If I were to tell the story in my own voice, as a perceptible narrator or EN(p) – usually called "first-person" narrator – this is what it would sound like. Once upon a time, in 1999, Tarek (27) came to Paris from the small town of Remada in southern Tunisia to pursue an education. Despite the difficulties of his status as an "illegal immigrant," he made a living doing odd jobs, taking a course in computer science at university and obtaining his diploma. As he was pursuing this double life of earning a living and studying, the French authorities tried to expel him. They did not succeed. After some 1,001 days, his marriage to Ilhem (18), a young woman belonging to the second generation of Tunisian immigrants, finally established him in the ordinary life of a legal resident of Europe. At the heart of the film is the fact that the police tried to prohibit the marriage. Tarek had to go underground, appealed, and his appeal was granted. The prohibition was, thus, even for the French authorities, implicitly recognized as harassment.

But, as in so many films, this story is never really told. Tarek's complex adventure cannot be offered as a coherent narrative in the film; nor does a unifying, identifiable subject or narrator mediate the content. The function of the primary narrator is hidden, limited to the organization of the embedded stories. It remains in the shadows. The film tells a story through the voices of the people involved who, by definition, are embedded in it; they also provide closure through celebration. Like the collection of Arabic tales with which the film's title interacts, the film organizes a multiplicity of stories around a single

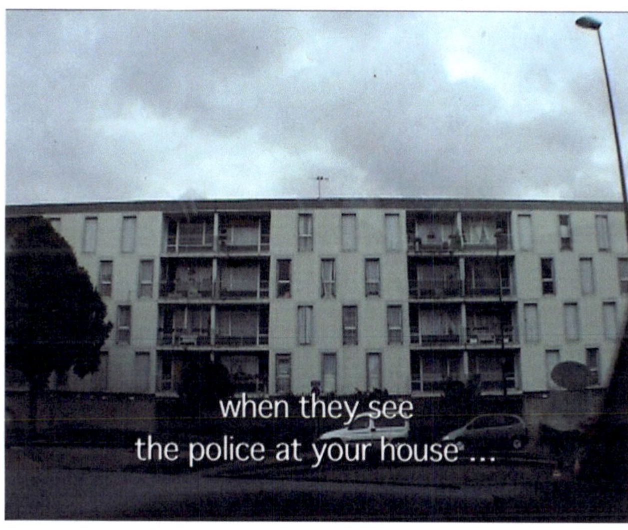

Figure 16.   *A Thousand and One Days* (2002–4): Who is speaking? Video still.

event, a wedding. Through intimacy with the men and women in front of the camera, the film invites the viewer to become acquainted with their situation – to be a guest at the wedding. This intimacy further hampers assigning an overall narrator to the film (Figure 16). Even its viewers cannot easily step out of the diegesis. The multiplication of voices extends across time as well as worlds.

With the wedding celebrations in full swing, four generations of Tunisian immigrants give shape, each in their own way, to the predicament of migration and its different opportunities and hardships. The politics of immigration thus never cease to haunt the present. However, not all generations talk about this constantly present and pressing theme. Consequently, adding up the voices does not cut it either; there is no unified or collective narrative voice that tells this story. Instead, what narratologists would call the film's voice is dispersed through a multitude of voices and images, none of which can be considered unifying. But there is a "primary-level" narrator, made visible by the embedded speakers, when sometimes, they are being addressed by the latter, as in Figure 17.

The unifying narrator's voice that is usually expected is not only lacking but even actively foreclosed; only recognized in the second person. Just one example. Against the backdrop of political machinations, the

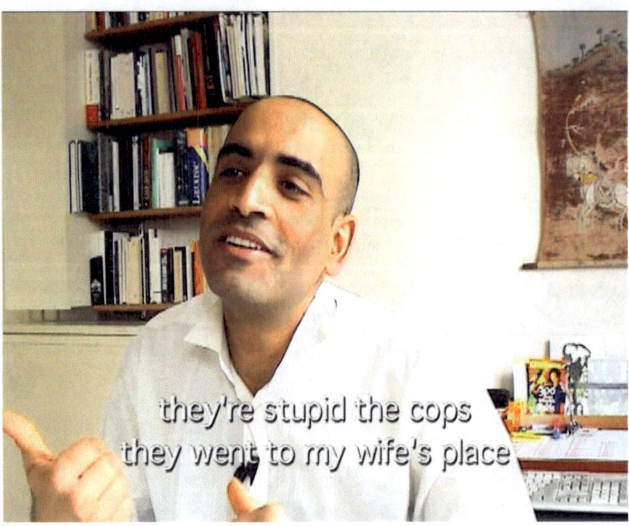

Figure 17.   *A Thousand and One Days* (2002–4): Tarek cannot believe the cops looked for him at his fiancée's house. Video still.

film offers a consideration of what is easily dismissed as an "arranged marriage." This is presented through the voices of the bride and her parents, the groom and his future brother-in-law, in a mixture of denial, endorsement, and doubt. Importantly, the issue is never named, never voiced by a primary narrator, nor by any of the embedded speakers. If anywhere, the topic suggests itself in the many concerns for the bride's future life. Western viewers, considering arranged marriages a token of cultural foreignness, might have expected an explicit discussion – and perhaps would have demanded political clarity, a position for or against. But it is the very naturalized status of arranged marriages in the culture from which the parents migrated that in fact precludes a clear narrating subject addressing this issue. Hence, using a narratorial voice would violate what is most natural to the couple and their guests.

In addition to the politics of immigration and arranged marriages, a third theme that is highly present but not narrated, not even narratable, is time (Figure 18). Cast against the shadow of his father's failure as an earlier immigrant to cope with capitalist time, Tarek seems obsessed with time's speed. Meanwhile other elements of the film appear to solicit more straightforward identificatory viewings. For example, an insight into the social fabric of immigrant life is given, as well as a tender portrait of a young woman and her friends reflecting on the

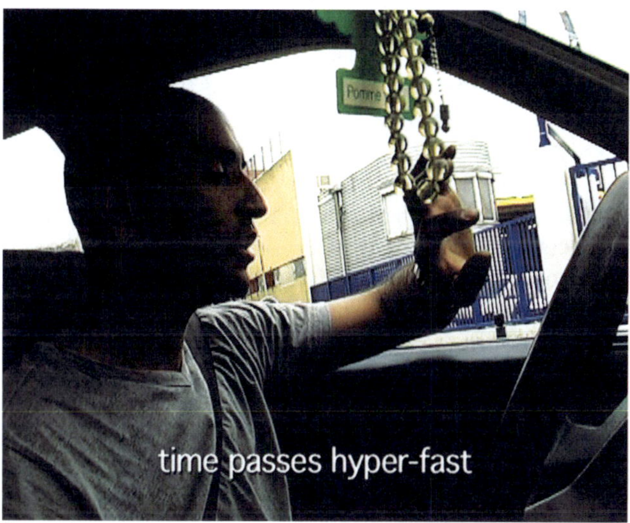

Figure 18. *A Thousand and One Days* (2002–4): Tarek always feels the hot breath of time. Video still.

transformation of one of them from schoolgirl into adult woman. The profound grief of loving parents about to see their eldest child leave home and move to the big city – a change they barely seem able to confront – alternates with the joyful anticipation of and preparations for a wedding that gives expression to their love for and pride in their daughter. All these motives facilitate affective connections, such as identification across cultural differences. I assume they speak to Western viewers as much as to the community of Arab immigrants; to a cultural plurality rather than a universal humanity.

A third doubt about the single-narrator thesis stems from the voices of a misguided official and a faux journalist. Their contrary views open up – rather than shut down in consensus and prejudice – the question of how the administration ought to deal with situations where rules and people appear to be no easy match; where politics clashes with the political. Here, the contradictory views cannot, indeed must not be resolved in a higher, universal truth. Instead, what is universal, perhaps, is the film's performativity. The contradictory nature of much of the film's speeches constitutes that performativity.

Rife with bureaucratic violence but also with the characters' vitality, determination, honesty, and intelligence in outsmarting the system, the film's content and aesthetics together constitute a plea for a world without borders. Such a world could unite in something so general as time. Yet here, time, it seems, constitutes a border. None of the people in the film are aware of this, and no connection is therefore made – through a voice – between, for example, time and borders. Yet, the unliveable nature of Western time comes to the fore with the insistence borne by repetition. I contend that it is in the false universality of time that another universal occurs: the performativity, not the nature, of experience.

As the concept of narrator travels from its theoretical anchoring to confront this object, the film *A Thousand and One Days*, it turns out that it is useful to the extent that it fails: the situation for which it fails to adequately account stakes its claim for a migratory aesthetics that honours this failure. This migratory aesthetics affects the theoretical status of the concept – its deceptive appearance of universality. Thus, migratory aesthetics partly emerge from the putting under erasure of the single-narrator thesis, while the concept of the narrator, in turn, foregrounds aspects of migratory aesthetics that might otherwise remain invisible. A travelling concept, therefore, called primary narrator, is here a concept under assault that fiercely defends itself. And indeed, the mixture of genres, between the folktale collection and the contemporary migratory situation, can thicken the effect of the storytelling, even regardless of the difference between the literary and cinematic media.

3: Con-fusing Meanings

What may seem, at first sight, confusing, can be something else. A friend suggested to term con-fusing with a hyphen; merging in togetherness. The result of con-fusing is not a lack of clarity but the emergence of a new clarity. In this way, the hyphen becomes a concept. In this chapter, the transition from lack of clarity to new insight developed through merging together will come more sharply in view. I begin with a simple example: a novel. Dutch author Carl Friedman's novel *Tralievader* (*Nightfather*) (1994) is written with a child as the primary narrator. The novel concerns the aftermath of the holocaust. It literally mixes the discourse of fairy tales and other fantasy domains with that about what is called in the novel "camp." The father of three young children feels compelled to tell the details of his ordeal and cannot stop talking about it. Although the father talks almost all the time, his narration is embedded in that of the child, who barely understands it. Any daily event or situation in post-holocaust life evokes in him the urge to go back to the past and narrate it to his children and his wife. The father relates his holocaust stories all the time. But the stories are not about the father and his concentration-camp experiences. The question that the choice for a child as primary narrator raises is, What kind of relationship with his children does the father's obsessive telling establish? Or to put it differently: What kind of problem does the father's obsessive telling cause for his children? This is how the novel foregrounds the child's focalization as the direct content of the child–primary narrator's story-telling instead of that of the adult survivor.

Although the age of the three children is never specified, it is clear that they are all very young and still have to learn the exact meaning of words, the ontological status of stories, fairy tales, and reality, and the difference between words and reality. Not yet knowing all these things is part of the child's focalization. Strikingly, at their age, having to listen to their father's holocaust experiences creates, above all, a semantic problem – a confusion of the meanings of words. Not that the knowledge of history, of the world, and of humanity assumed by the father's stories is too enormous for them to grasp. Instead, they do not understand where these stories stop and their own world begins. This confusion, again in a sense a confusion of genres, is where the fairy tale meets Auschwitz. This is emblematically present in the father's use of the word "camp."

The father, as it is sometimes phrased in the novel, "has camp." The phrase sounds like an illness and makes the place, the camp, into an illness in the present. This is a clear instance of trauma. The hyphen is needed so that confusion can become con-fusion. This use of the word "camp" by the children is both strange and adds serious meaning to the idea of the camp. The first of the forty short chapters is all about the way the father uses the word camp and how his children struggle with its meaning. It is one great explosion of unbinding meanings. The father never mentions the camp by name. He talks as if there had been just one. He is outraged when he watches a film about "the camp" that shows inmates frying eggs for breakfast. "An egg!" he says shrilly. "In the camp!" His daughter deducts the following conclusion from his outburst:

> So camp is somewhere where no one fries eggs.
> Camp is not so much a place as a condition. "I've had camp," he says. That makes him different from us. We've had chicken pox and German measles. And after Simon fell out of a tree, he got a concussion and had to stay in bed for weeks.
> But we've never had camp. (1–2)

The comparison to chicken pox and German (!) measles adds to the sick quality, the idea of contagion, which sheds light on the contamination in the aftermath. The narrator perfectly understands the distinction between place and condition. Nor does the fact that she and her two brothers "have never had camp" imply that this condition uniquely applies to their father. When the siblings visit the zoo, she starts to cry when looking at the wolf. Her older brother, Max, comes to her:

> "Well?" he said in a bored voice when we were standing in front of the wolf's cage. "What's the matter with him?"
> "He has camp!" I sobbed. Max glanced through the bars.
> "Impossible," he said. "Wolves don't get camp." (2)

At the moment the scope of the word "camp" seems to become limited to the past and the condition of her father as an illness, which is fore-grounded by the verb "get." Her vision of the world is con-fused again when Nellie, her school friend, uses the expression in an unfamiliar con-text. Nellie goes to the Girl Scouts, the "Brownies," every Wednesday af-ternoon. The narrator asks her parents if she might also join the Brownies. That, however, is out of the question because before and during the war, the Dutch scouts maintained very good relations with the *Hitler-Jugend*. The next day, the narrator informs Nellie that she is not allowed to join:

> "Too bad," she says. "Then you're going to miss a whole lot of things, movies, tracking, things like that. And camp."
> "Camp?" I repeat, wide-eyed. (40)

She must again reconsider the tentacles of the term. Wolves cannot have camp, but nor is camp restricted to the past and the condition of her father. She is touched by the unexpected proximity of camp. The family's experi-ence of the word "camp" differs from Nellie's. This becomes a fluctuation of the word, an extension of its affordances, rather than a confusion.

> In this respect, the term differs from others, which she never encounters outside her father's stories:
> "What a funny father you have," Nellie says, giggling. She looks at me expectantly but I avoid her eyes. What can I say? She knows nothing about hunger or about the SS. Words like barracks, latrine, or crematorium mean nothing to her. She speaks a different language.
> Nellie's father doesn't have camp, he has a bicycle that he rides to the factory, with a lunch box strapped to the carrier. (21)

Here, the verb "to have," like "get" above, is up for con-fusion. Posses-sion and being contaminated become synonymous, and so do a state and a thing. If the past and the condition of her father are fundamentally different from her own world and other people's condition, then his stories can be compared to fairy tales and, hence, also function like them. Indeed, the father sometimes talks as if he were telling a fairy tale. When the children hear a camp story in which the father's pants suddenly begin to talk to him, this solution is seriously considered:

> "What did they [the pants] say?" I ask.
>
> "They spoke in German," says my father. "I don't feel like translating all of it right now, but one of the things they told me was that they answered to the name of Heinrich and that they had once belonged to Adolf Hitler. They'd been looking up Adolf's asshole for years and had learned the most confidential state secrets that way. Then, one day, they were arrested and sent to the camp because they knew too much."
>
> "Talking underpants? But that can't be true!" says Simon. My father raises his hands helplessly. (87)

When the three siblings go to bed, they evaluate this story:

> Simon still finds it hard to believe.
>
> "Clothes can't talk," he says while we're getting undressed. Max, who doesn't have to go to bed for a long time, leans against the closet.
>
> "Why not?" he says. "Crazier things happened in the camp, people were gassed there." Simon shrugs his shoulders.
>
> "Of course people were gassed there," he says. "That's what a camp is for, isn't it?" (88)

All three siblings come to different conclusions. The adult survivor feels the need to relate his experience through fantasy, while Simon, the youngest, feels he is too old for fairy tales, in contrast to his older siblings. They are untrue, they contradict his frame of reference for reality and normality. The camp, however, is part of his frame of reference. He has heard so many stories about it. So camps are places where people are gassed as a matter of normality; this is known.

All these children's experiences are so meaningful, and for adults so completely understandable that it becomes attractive to step in and adopt the children's logic. The children are con-fused, but they each seem able to pick up the allusions. The German-speaking underpants, enabled to look into Hitler's asshole, alluding to the idea that the man who wore them as a whole was an asshole, is both the strongest fairy tale–like statement and comes closest to historical reality. The fact that the three children are so different in the way they each process what the father says turns them into emphatically plural focalizers embedded in the storytelling of the primary narrator, each bringing their own childhood memories and the focalization that fits these. Talking underpants are no weirder than talking cats. Even without understanding what happened to their father, they live in the con-fusing realm where reality is as strange as it would be in a fairy tale. The constant allusions in both domains to the other one makes it possible to see what the child's focalization picks up from an adult's obsessive talking that is not itself a clear and effective communication.

4: Between Narrative and Theatre

But not all embedded texts are narrative. More common is the narrative situation where the direct discourse of characters is quoted by the primary narrator. For dramatic embedded texts, the theory of drama and a general semiotic theory are indispensable sources. To give an idea of the way narratology here spills over into semiotics, here is one example. Imagine overhearing the following dialogue in a hospital's consultation room:

"Ever had scarlet fever as a child?" "No, doctor." "German measles?" "No, doctor." "Ra … Rickets?" "Eh … no, doctor. "Do you know what rickets is?" "Well, no, doctor." "Why do you say 'no' then?" "I was afraid that you would ask further questions if I said 'yes.'" "But you can also say 'I don't know,' can't you?" "Is that allowed, doctor?" "How many times have you been pregnant before?" "I don't know, doctor." "You don't know?!!" "Yes I do, doctor. Eight times." "Eight?" "No no, doctor, eleven." "Are you absolutely sure?" "To tell you the truth, no … eh … doctor." "But you must be able to tell me how many children you have exactly?" "Oh dear, professor, you look so intimidating." "I am not a professor. I am a training resident." "Really … my friend was also delivered by a training resident. She had some very good laughs with him." "No wonder. I bet your friend knew exactly how often she had been pregnant." "Or, that resident was not as intimidating and less precise. Good, now you are laughing. What a relief. You were just glaring at that paper from behind those glasses. To be exact, I have seven children, and I've had two miscarriages and one was still-born. Is that clear enough for you to do the counting?" "And, eh … your last period, could you guess, approximately, no need to be precise, about which month, which week it was perhaps? Before the vacation or after?" "The 28th of June." "The 28th of June?!!" "Absolutely, the 28th of June. A woman does know those things, you know."

In the beginning, the exchange of signs between the two people pursuing the same goal, adequate medical treatment, is very unsuccessful. The resident uses normal English (originally, Dutch) words, and if the patient is reasonably educated and English-speaking, there should be no problem. Yet, there is. The accompanying signs preclude communication at the expense of both parties. And this is not because the patient comes from a different language. This all happens within the same linguistic community.

The doctor gives signs of various kinds which the woman interprets as intimidating: his impatience when she hesitates, the rebuff when she gives an inadequate answer, and his looking at the papers instead of at his interlocutor; his firing off question after question, leaving no room for hesitation; the whole setting in his office, and the social context of power that pertains to it. These signs, subliminal in various degrees, are not intended by the speaker but are nevertheless decisive. As such, they are part of the primary narrator's rhetoric, even if not a single word uttered by this primary narrator occurs in the text. This speaker does not want to produce the sign-events that have this negative effect. But he or she could not help their occurrence.

The theory of speech acts is relevant here, too. What is meant as a question, an open request for information, becomes, in the eyes of the intimidated woman, an order. This confuses her and prevents her from responding adequately. The result is the total linguistic incapacitation of the woman: she can no longer answer any question. To see this woman as stupid, uneducated, unable to cope, or shy is one way of interpreting her behaviour. But that would be a pretty rude, unsophisticated response, unworthy of the competent sign-user.

To think with the doctor that it is utterly stupid not to know how many times you have been pregnant is missing the various possibilities in the question. Did he mean the number of medically acknowledged pregnancies including miscarriages, the number of deliveries, or the number of actual living children? For a woman for whom each of these possible questions yields a different answer, the question is hard enough, and some time to think should be granted her; but the situation of intimidation does not let her. This exchange in fact shows that in some ways, the doctor, who does not realize this, is no more competent at communication than the woman; I'd say, much less so. His question is unwittingly ambiguous.

The kinds of signs the doctor intends to send out – questions clear enough to yield clear answers – do not match the interpretations the addressee makes of them. She sees them either as orders or as unanswerable. This situation could go on forever, and the interview would turn out to be useless. The woman manages to reverse the situation, however, by breaking through the false relation of authority, and restores communication. Exchange of information becomes possible. Now that the sign (question) is no more interfered with by the subliminal sign (order) and by the other contextual signs, it can be answered. No trace remains of the impression of incompetence.

The dialogue was, in fact, a short story by Hanna Verweg, entitled "Anamnesis" and published in 1984 in a Dutch newspaper. The title is the only utterance of the primary narrator. It is highly relevant: it is a word that not all readers know; I, for one, did not. It is certainly not a word expected in a small newspaper column. As a consequence, the word is intimidating. It makes the reader insecure. As the sole stuff of the primary narration, it is a mirror image or mise-en-abyme of what is going to be the story's point. The fellow patient overhearing that dialogue may respond by identifying with the patient – if she is next – or by proudly taking her distance and looking down on her – if she has been more successful. Unlike such reactions, the reader intimidated by a difficult word is likely to sympathize with the woman immediately, warmed up as such a reader is by the story's title at the doctor's expense. There is, then, a continuity between the first embedded narrator, who is also the first speaker of the story, the woman-speaker who speaks secondly in the embedded story, and the reader at the other end.

This example also lets me raise the issue of the narratee: the addressee or receiver of the narrated text. In this case it is particularly important to realize that the interpretation of signs is dependent on the subjects who use them. The narrator of the piece could tell the story in this way because he or she had, for whatever reasons, sympathy for the intimidated woman. The narrator's reticence, which turns the narrative into a virtually dramatic text, is part of that sympathy: the narrator turns the narration over to the embedded speakers, presumably to empower the woman to get to make her victorious point herself. The addressee of the text – the narratee – is strongly suggested to invest sympathy in the same figure, but training residents who read the story before setting off to their first practice may very well put their sympathy elsewhere.

The narratee, as much as the narrator, is an abstract function rather than a person. Actual readers will have different responses. Women readers are likely to better understand the final exchange, and probably be more strongly gratified by the role reversal at the end than most men readers will, but this division according to gender lines does not hold for every single person. Each person brings to the signs her or his own baggage. This theoretical point is part of the metanarrative thrust of the text. For, the story itself shows that roles are not fixed. It displays how the initial incapacity to get the message is changed into adequate semiotic behaviour that includes, aside from the information requested, a surplus to it, a subtle and humorous message, a view on gender boundaries, and a sign of restored self-confidence. In the original Dutch text, the resident is clearly male; in English, the language does not show he is male, but the traditionally male role she or he takes on suggests as much. And just to prevent gender essentialism from taking hold, let me add that the author, signing the narrative with a woman's name, turned out to be a man.

The clash in "Anamnesis" between the (man) resident and the (woman) patient dramatized the misunderstanding, the non-communication, that occurs when two people seem to speak different languages, like the embedded father and the child as primary narrator in *Nightfather*. Both this novel and the very short text "Anamnesis" have that dialogic quality that brings narrative very close to theatre. It is through the dialogues, the most theatrical aspect, that the differences and discrepancies between the characters' sense of language and meaning come to the fore. According to the theory of the Soviet philosopher of language Mikhail Bakhtin (1981 [1934]), who wrote – probably under different names – in the 1930s, this is a general feature of language. He developed the notion that language use – or rather, discourse – is always an intertwining of different discourses coming from a variety of backgrounds. This principle is known as the dialogic principle. What Bakhtinians call dialogue, however, is better understood as a metaphor that underscores the heterogeneity of discourse. In fact, "heteroglossia," also called "multilingualism," is another key term in Bakhtin's work.

The most widespread term Bakhtin's work offered is "intertextuality." This term refers to the quotation, in a text, of another text. Such quotations are not always marked as such; in fact, according to the philosophy of language Bakhtin proposed, any discourse is always already a patchwork of quotations. No narrative text makes this more dramatically clear than Cervantes's *Don Quixote*, with a hero – or anti-hero – who allegedly goes mad from his reading and can speak only in quotations. These quotations are cleverly dramatized, reversed, and ridiculed passages from sources one can actually trace. I like to reserve the term "intertextuality" for such traceable cases.

On the other hand, since discourse is for Bakhtin always a mix of different discourses, there are many instances where tracing actual sources makes no sense whatsoever. In "Anamnesis," for example, the resident and the woman speak in different discourses in the sense that they each have their own points of departure, assumptions, manners of speaking, and also things they do not say because they seem self-evident. In this text the discrepancy is clearly marked by the different speakers who each speak in their own discourse. But if a single narrative voice speaks a mix of different discourses, the more suitable term is "interdiscursivity." American experimental novelist Kathy Acker's novels are good examples of an ironic use of interdiscursivity. They consist of collages of a variety of textual modes such as dramatic dialogue, prose narrative as well as poetry; narrative modes, including character-bound narrators as well as external narrators; genres such as autobiography, art and political criticism, travel literature, pornographic literature; media, mostly words and images, and typographic styles.

But in spite of current interest in and extensive use of interdiscursivity, the phenomenon is by no means limited to contemporary culture. Again, *Don Quixote* remains a paradigmatic if not founding case. And in her "loa" (a kind of dramatized preface) to her play *El Narciso Divino*, the Mexican baroque author Sor Juana Ines de la Cruz has an allegorical representative of the native population called "America" not only speak in what was perceived as the language of the "other" but also in the discourse of Native religion. This was a smart political gesture: under the pretext of showing how Native people ended up converting to Christianity, this play, meant to be performed at the Spanish court, confronted the Spaniards with the existence of a religious discourse different from their own but which was in many ways congenial to Christianity.

Nor is interdiscursivity always so self-consciously deployed. Let me briefly return to one of the oldest texts of the Western tradition, the biblical book of Judges. There, I have seen cases of interdiscursivity that could point to the seams where the text as patchwork, or mosaic, is patched together. The daughter of Jephthah, in Judges 11, uses a discourse that could be remnants of a different tradition, oriented to a women's culture. In my study of this text I call such remnants "wandering rocks," in reference to the ice age while also alluding to the travelling of cultural bits and pieces. Bakhtin's legacy has a strong liberating potential. The very notion that language is not unified provides access to bits of culturally different environments within a single text. This makes readers aware of the limited importance of the individual author and the impossibility of completely repressing ideological and social others.

To realize that any text is a patchwork of different strata, bearing traces of different communities and of the contestations between them, is a fundamental insight. The analysis of "Anamnesis" demonstrates this clearly. The idea of a discursive plurality also makes it easier to envision a narratological analysis of a mixed-media work such as film, or even of entirely visual works. In "Anamnesis" the heterogeneity of the discourses spoken by the two embedded speakers produces the clash between them. So far, the theory presented here is compatible with Bakhtin's; in fact, a Bakhtinian view suffices to notice this. But for two reasons I did not incorporate this view in *Narratology*. First, although Bakhtin did put forward claims about the specifically heteroglossic nature of the novel, he did not refer to narrative as a discursive mode but to the novel as a historical genre. Second and more important, on the basis of "Anamnesis" I would like to maintain that a Bakhtinian perspective does not fully account for the narratological particularity of this story.

The technical distinction in narrative levels is necessary to account for the great impact of the minimally speaking primary narrator. And it is basically this organizing voice that makes the clash work to promote one position over the other – the woman over the resident – even though readers will respond according to their own cultural-political position. By setting the stage for the reader's own sense of being left out, intimidated, the two speakers, who are technically equal, are assigned different opportunities to gain the reader's sympathy. Whereas a Bakhtinian view is very useful to keep in mind, I prefer to complement it with a more technical narratological view for this reason.

The examples analysed so far not only demonstrate that an analysis of the text as such helps to gain access to a complex narrative text. They also help to historicize narratological analysis, as we saw particularly clearly in the beginnings of three novels by Flaubert, Proust, and Coetzee in *Narratology* (39–44). The metanarrative and ironic commentaries implied by the relation between embedded and overall text underscore the idea that postmodernism has a special preference for the use of mirror-text. Thus, another preconception can be eliminated: that structural analysis is ahistorical. In this section I have foregrounded how second-level texts make the distinction between theatre and narrative almost moot. However, by keeping in view the primary narrator and the structure of embedding nevertheless, the manipulative power of that narrator, sometimes the greater as the function is invisible, cannot be ignored. The usefulness of the small story "Anamnesis" for, in this case, the trainees in the medical profession goes without saying. But for all those who administer, teach, or guide others, it is just as useful.

5: Con-fusing Media

For scholars in the humanities, interdisciplinarity is a pre-eminent instance of productive con-fusion. The final small case study I present here as a transition is a work that belongs to the medium of visual art, specifically painting. This boxing-in is simply an effect of the self-identification of the artist and of the commercial framing of the work as put up for sale in an art gallery. It is titled *I'm Six Years Old and Hiding behind My Hands*, a title that might resonate with the case of the children with the camp father. Many of the issues raised in this part and the parallel one in *Narratology* come together in this work of visual art through which I now go through these, in order to demonstrate the relevance of a narratological analysis of the text layer, in a non-linguistic artwork. At the same time, the analysis below already glimpses at some of the concepts discussed in the next part.

On a gallery tour in New York many years ago I saw a gigantic 1996 work by American artist Ken Aptekar. It measures 120" x 120" and consists of sixteen panels of oil on wood, with sandblasted glass bolted an inch before the paint. It confused me, for although it struck me as both highly original an acutely contemporary – even, in a certain sense, postmodern – it was "simply" a copy of François Boucher's *Allegory of Painting* (1765) at the National Gallery of Art in Washington, DC – a copy as literal as Borges's Menard's quotation from Cervantes. Boucher's is a late-baroque work, art historians would say, and not a very narrative one. Draperies and flesh, clouds, and layers and layers of folds, encase the figures.

An exuberant gilded frame casts strange shadows on the portion of the painting that, although also blue, exceeds Boucher's masterpiece, thus making me aware that the copy of Boucher's painting is not the whole thing. Moreover, the glass plates cover the luxuriously visual work with words: a text so emphatically autobiographical that I almost felt voyeuristic reading it. And yet I read the text, even though my reading was constantly interrupted by the painting that was looking back at me, nagging that I ought to look at it first (Figure 19).

The narrator (CN) tells the story of himself in the voice of a six-year-old boy: the homey, familial situation, the loving mother who taught her children to make decorations and yet worried when the boy caught on too eagerly and too well. The hand of the allegorical figure in the embedded painting, also quite motherly, also teaching art to the putti / children she is portraying, casts a shadow, just as Boucher's painting casts a shadow on Aptekar's painting, and the letters of the glass plate cast theirs, the shadow of the autobiography that talks about another painter's hands, behind which the boy is hiding.

Aptekar calls himself a "re-painter," a title that avoids the passivity associated with the term "copy." And there is that hyphen again, the connectivity. His lifelong activity of re-painting old- and also modern-master paintings and mounting text sandblasted on glass over these re-paintings is a mode of making media speak to one another. Almost always the texts – sometimes very short, sometimes, as in this case, longer – have a narrativity in them, poetic as they also are. That narrative inflection this brings to the older "model" is a creative way of practising preposterous history. While it is quite emphatically also a gesture of intermediality, the inflection he brings to the older paintings not only enlivens these, updating them, but more importantly brings them in touch with social-political issues.

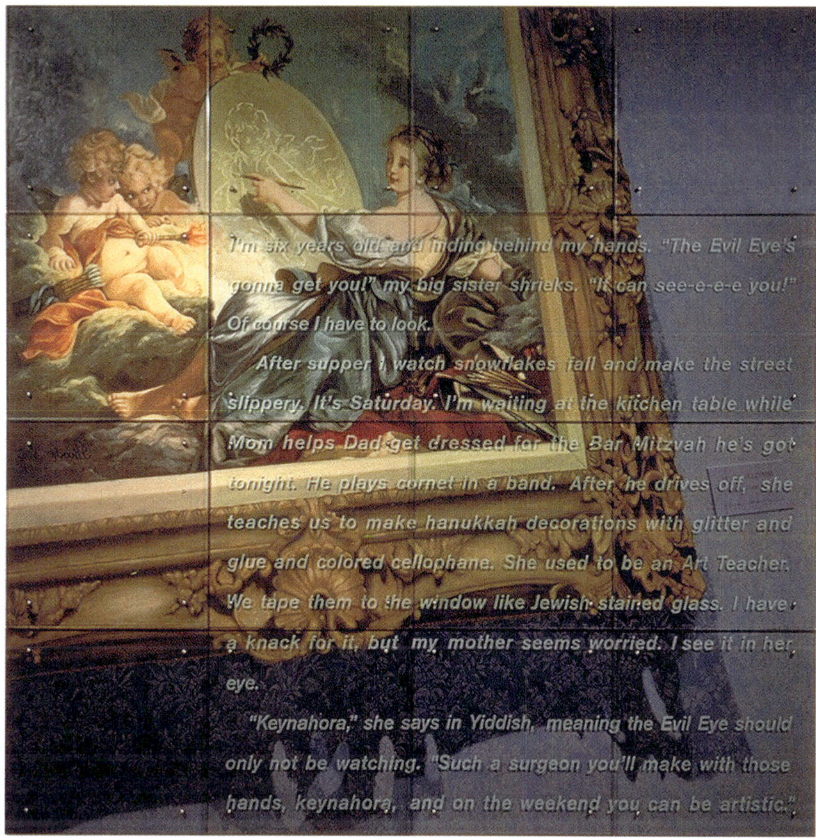

Figure 19.   Ken Aptekar, *I'm Six Years Old and Hiding behind My Hands* (1996).

In this painting, the masterpiece from the past is quoted and thus appropriated in a work that affirms its place in the present; the image is over-layered by words; and the words enhance a story of subjectivity, the torment of a subject in relation to the objects he saw and craved to make. This work emblematizes the importance of narrative structure in many ways: it posits a child narrator in the linguistic text, an allegorical figure as a CN in the quoted Boucher copy, an embedded narrator who appears as a postmodern adult narrator who knows his Boucher but who stands outside it, in the painted work that quotes the Boucher; and a mixed-media external narrator in the embedding text of the work as a whole. The question of embedding is complicated by the obvious heterogeneity of the discourses employed, including the different media.

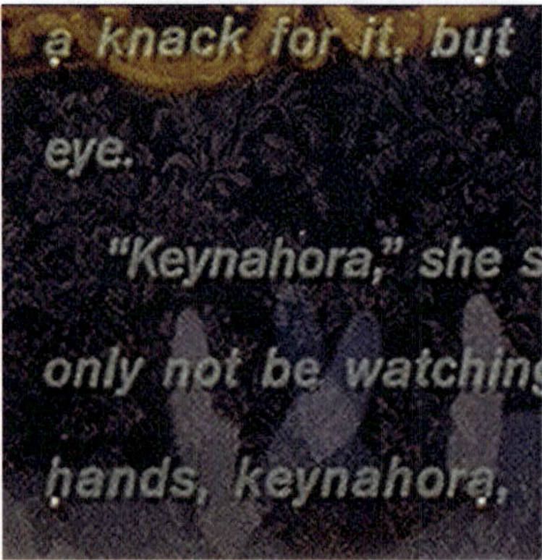

Figure 20.   Ken Aptekar, *I'm Six Years Old and Hiding behind My Hands* (1996). Detail: shadows.

The question of the relation between levels of narration can help us understand this painting. Is there a degree of mirroring going on between the linguistic and the painted narrative, and between the overall work and the quoted Boucher?

The text sandblasted on the glass plates reads as follows (Figure 19):

I'm six years old and hiding behind my hands. "The Evil Eye's gonna get you!" my big sister shrieks. "It can see-e-e-e you!" Of course I have to look.

After supper I watch snowflakes fall and make the street slippery. It's Saturday. I'm waiting at the kitchen table while Mom helps Dad get dressed for a Bar Mitzvah he's got tonight. He plays cornet in a band. After he drives off, she teaches us to make Hanukkah decorations with glitter and glue and colored cellophane. She used to be an Art Teacher. We tape them to the window like Jewish stained glass. I have a knack for it, but my mother seems worried. I see it in her eye.

"Keynahora," she says in Yiddish, meaning the Evil Eye should only not be watching. "Such a surgeon you'll make with those hands, keynahora, and on the weekend you can be artistic."

This story is a short study in hands, and a text about seeing and not seeing, and seeing differently and historically. "About" suggests a fabula, while all the acts of seeing foreground the story. Written in the present tense, the text vividly pictures the little boy who still believes one can hide behind one's hands. The homey scene is depicted with the scarcity of words that characterizes a poet. The words remain close to the vocabulary and style of the child protagonist who believes in the power of the Evil Eye, so that the narrator can be identified with this boy. Yet the unease when he sees (in the past, told in the present tense) worry in his mother's eye, is clearly interpreted (also) in the present of the adult man who became a professional painter in opposition to his mother.

"I see" is an indicator of focalization, a concept that will be elaborated more in the next part. It is an act of vision that here is not predicated on distance and mastery but on contact and mutuality. In the present tense, the phrase evokes an act of seeing (fabula) situated in the past and burdened with a past. The child has removed his hands from before his eyes; he hides no more. But his hands remain a bone of contention. The shadow cast by the allegorical painter in the Boucher is reflected in the child's mother, whose ambitions for her son do not match his desire. Here, the embedded painting begins to show its hand as a mirror-text. An embedded text that presents a story that resembles the primary fabula may be taken as a sign of the primary fabula. This phenomenon is comparable to the infinite regress generally called mise-en-abyme. I find the simpler term mirror-text easier to use.

Nor is this visual confrontation simply autobiographical, an anecdote from the domain of pure subjectivity, in that case perhaps irrelevant for the larger public. The primary narrator has made sure his readers can share part of his ideological space and know others. The absent father whose departure – to go and earn the family's bread – made possible the idyllic togetherness of mother and children in which the son's gift stands out: most of the readers of this work know that situation, its seductions and drawbacks, by experience or lack of it, in the past or in the present. The ironic capitalizing of "she used to be an Art Teacher," which implies the reflection of the adult writer, fills the mother's worried eye with a double past. The confrontation that is so subtly building up is not just one between dominating parent and powerless child, but is also one that feeds on the mother's own sacrifice of a career similar to and continuous with what she rejects for her child. And that career is precisely mirrored in the quoted Boucher. Again, this exceeds the pure subjectivity of individual experience and memory.

The reference to Yiddish in the embedded text spoken by the mother, as an index of European Jewry, is more culturally specific than the predicaments of the nuclear family. This turns this autobiography into an "autohistory" that explains and justifies, while making it the more painful: the mother's wish that her son pursue a career that will leave him less vulnerable in the world. The hand, so central in this very short story, the hand that hides and points, becomes a sign for what the son can do, won't do, and desires to do. It points to the future already prefigured by the other version of the mother, the Art Teacher in the Boucher, who points to the child she is depicting. Thus, the child, in spite of his mother's worried resistance, is an artist-to-be and, as such, his mother's creation. Both the story and the painting pay homage to that continuity-against-odds.

Although Boucher's painting is usually not considered as narrative, I would like to make the case that, by Aptekar's intervention, it gains narrative momentum; an instance of preposterous history, what many would call an anachronistic interpretation. This analysis is not a literary appropriation of visual art but a truly pictorial narratology, which does full justice to the visual aspects of the work. Starting from the back, it is noticeable that the visual narrator has enhanced, just like Borges in "Pierre Menard" (*Narratology* 55–6), the fact that even totally faithful copies must differ from their original. The painting's multilayered structure begins with nuances. The panels covered by the copy of Boucher's *Allegory*, including its elaborate frame, each have a slightly different hue.

This variation in tone is not continued on the parts beyond the frame. It suggests, then, that the meticulous copy of the older painting, done in an illusionistically faithful mode, nevertheless is a fiction. This self-reflexive disillusioning – a visual metanarrative comment from the primary narrator – in the layer that supports the painting is also present in the reversal of the model. The Boucher has been copied in mirroring symmetry. This not only exposes the copy as "just" a copy but also suggests a reading of the embedded narrative as a mirror-text. By these two gestures of self-exposure, the narrator can be said to appropriate the older work, in the mode of many postmodernist artists, but to do so with self-irony and subtle emphasis on that gesture. This alone sketches him in as much older than the boy narrator of the text panel.

There is yet another indication that this text is best read as a mirror-text. The predominant colour of the painting is blue: the blue of Boucher's clouds, and the different tones of blue of the historicizing wallpaper on which, supposedly in a realistic illusion, the Boucher is hung. The constructedness of the narrative is also emphasized by the fact that only a portion of the Boucher is copied. The slight cropping of the upper-left edges – due to the perspectival adaptations of the reversal – just like the reversal and the variation in background tone, all point to the same problematic.

But then, the blue wallpaper with whitish flowers on it presents an artificial version of the "natural" clouds in the Boucher. It is as if the primary narrator, the later artist who can only reflect – mirror – the older art, is at least not fooling himself about the natural quality of his clouds. Doubly historicizing, by the style of the wallpaper and the reference to art-historical clouds, the postmodern anti-illusionism of the painting is self-conscious and, in its self-awareness, also emulating the Boucher, of which it is a wilful misreading.

There is also a lot of blue in the baroque draperies, like clouds made of fabric, in particular the woman figure's dress. Blue, then, is the link between the signs that can only be separated through time, history, geography, and space. The woman who, in art history's past of Boucher, allegorized the Art of Painting, alias the – past – Art Teacher, is pointing, and thus narratively incorporated. Her hand points to the child yearning to learn to paint – or is it the brush, that sixth finger? But then, the finger points at the re-presentation of the child in the painting. Definitely, pointing itself is the crucial object being mirrored. And this pointing had cast a shadow – on the re-presented child.

The frame, itself a narrativizing sign that both signifies and under-mines the boundary it is supposed to be, due to its historicizing ex-uberance drips off the wallpaper up to and beyond the edge of the entire painting. There is no escape from that shadow. The shadow takes strange, uncanny shapes: of bats, hanging upside down, as bats are wont to do, and scaring little children; spooky shapes, and then lighter spots looking like footsteps – another pointer.

There is yet another pointing, narrativizing thing in this work. Inside the Boucher but in the lower-left corner – right in the copy, left in the original – where painting and writing overlap most densely, behind the Art Teacher's back, rests a bunch of paint brushes. These brushes point outward, into the wallpaper where the painter-narrator stands alone, without Boucher, framed by his bourgeois upbringing. On that blue wallpaper is painted one little object that seems out of place, different, as if it alone can escape the past as the delightful burden it appears to be. This object, painted in the same colour as the rest of the wallpaper, looks like either a museum caption or an envelope with an address on it (Figure 21).

On that thing we see writing. Painted, not sandblasted. This writing is not in English but in Hebrew. Or is it? In fact, it is gibberish, illegible, but yes, it looks like, and thus as a sign it means, unmistakably, "He-brew." Is this little detail, which is what the paintbrushes behind the Teacher's back point to, the signature of an artist whose difference as a Jew almost made him a surgeon instead of what he most wanted to be? In other words, is this the one moment where the primary narrator refers to himself? But then, is that small but nagging political message addressed to him (by whom?) or to us, viewers who crave to read it but cannot? The one thing this caption / envelope's illegible "Hebrew"

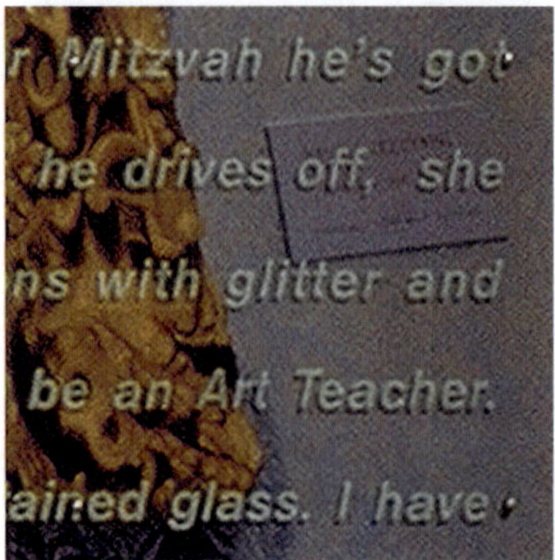

Figure 21. Ken Aptekar, *I'm Six Years Old and Hiding behind My Hands* (1996). Detail: envelope.

does is the most important narrativizing and mirroring act. Hebrew reads from right to left, English from left to right. Between the historical, gentile Boucher's representation and the image of Hebrew writing, two cultures are brought to bear on each other. They are con-fused. But it is up to the reader where to start the pointing: with the signature of the 1996 work pointing back to Boucher or the other way around. History goes in two directions, not one.

This examination not only demonstrates that an analysis of narrative levels helps to gain access to a complex, multimedia narrative text. It also helps to historicize narrative analysis. The metanarrative and ironic commentaries implied by the relations between embedded Boucher and overall text underscore the idea that postmodernism has a special preference for the use of mirror-text. In the next part of this book, the focus is on the level of the story. The main concepts concern the content of the narrator's storytelling and the way the inflection of the fabula is guided by the agents on that intermediate level that shapes that content. In standard narrative theory these are the least visible agents. I will demonstrate that this is a major omission in most narratological approaches. Instead, the subtleties and complexities of stories are greatly dependent on the agents that do the inflecting.

This work of visual art, narrativizing the older painting in a playful manner, also brings up such social-political issues as the nuclear family's divisions of tasks, interculturality and, in this case, the need to remember and rethink the way we remember the situation that brought the painter's family to the United States – in other words, the holocaust – and the question of history, the dubious consequences of linear chronology as the only way to think of history.

3

Story: Aspects

1: Preliminary Remarks

When we were making the film *Madame B*, I was frequently reflecting on the need to make the film different from the novel. This seemed necessary to me, not only in the obvious sense in which the different media necessarily require different ways of manipulating the allegedly raw data of the fabula. Nor was it needed just in that the historical difference between the 1850s and the 2010s demand a rethinking of where in historical time we wanted to set the images and events. It was, rather, in bouncing about ideas for actual casting, acting, and setting decisions that I realized how strongly the intermediate level of the novel's narrative, the story, determined the effects and affects of the text. Taken separately, the fabula is, after all, rather banal. And the text, famously so polished that Flaubert needed five years writing it, could best penetrate into our film in the form of quotations – apart from the examples already given of how we translated or, rather, "intermediated" the novel.

Some of the aspects of the story are the consequence of a kind of "story logic" (Herman 2002). Depending on how classical, realist, modernist, postmodernist, or otherwise experimental a narrative is, readers expect certain consistencies in time, place, focalization, and can be either enchanted or annoyed when unexplained jumps occur. Other aspects seem random, but may have a profound causality, only discovered when the reader or viewer accepts that randomness is relative. I will give examples of such expectation-dependent forms of operation. That this is not an issue of writing or otherwise making but of reading can be argued through a rather silly-seeming example of our film experience.

For Emma's death scene we had found a white dress that looked perfect. But it was a bit too narrow for the actress. Since we did not have the means to get another dress, we subsequently developed with a little more emphasis a strand in the fabula – Emma's eating disorders – into a thick motif in the story. Does it matter that, on re-reading the novel yet again, we saw that the motif of overeating is actually quite emphatically present in Flaubert? It does and it doesn't. Yes, it demonstrates that we had been unreflectively "contaminated" by the novel, perhaps in our attempt at adequacy or loyalty. But then, also no, because the practical solution to a practical problem is inevitably a different, later, act in an artistic work that privileges narrative. Thus the dress, which visibly stayed open at the waist, was a poignant reminder in the end scene of the many moments during her life that we had multiplied to foreground the motif when Emma had attempted to quell her mounting frustration by excessive eating.

This had the added advantage that the story got an update to our time. From a nineteenth-century pre-Freudian neurotic, she became a contemporary depressed woman. In the entire project, our challenge was to leave the fabula intact as much as possible and update the novel by means of the story. The text was divided. The visual narrator we decided was to negotiate between images from different moments between the 1850s and today in the contemporary settings. The primary and embedded audio narrators uttered discourse that mainly consists of quotations, selected to jar minimally with the contemporary while also being loyal to, foregrounding, and thereby honouring Flaubert's beautiful prose. Time, as in history, anachronism as a productive way to renew the affective impact of the novel, and in rhythm, was a key aspect in our project. Therefore, beginning this part with the issues of time makes all the sense in the world.

2: Temporality

Heterochrony between Objective and Subjective

Time, as I argue in *Narratology*, is thick and complex, not at all linear and single stranded. To realize this thickness of time, just imagine the life of an undocumented immigrant. The moment of border crossing occurs after a long journey. The heightened danger intensifies that moment, even if it can take days to actually cross. Once on the other side, inside the new country, the immigrant's inner clock starts ticking loudly. The justification for the departure, and the loss of the affective base of family and friends, is to make money to help out at home. But as long as documents such as residency and work permits are not forthcoming, much of his or her time is spent waiting. This produces a kind of temporal and also social schizophrenia, which makes the migrant in this situation always hasty and always stagnating at the same time; and always locked in a different experience of time from the residents of the host country. Then, if and when the long-awaited documents finally arrive, the hoped-for relief is slow in coming. The time lost is also a loss of the opportunity to learn the new language, acquire work skills, and make new friends. People in such situations are condemned to live in the present; a time that stretches out endlessly. As a consequence, the memories of their past that should sustain them are in fact put on ice. This living in an enforced presentism is a symptom of disenfranchisement.

Once we realize this, the thickness of time becomes impressively complex. Looking at temporality in *Arabian Nights* is rewarding, as we have seen in *Narratology* (67). And in terms of today's culture, migration is the experience of time as multiple, heterogeneous. The time of haste and waiting, the time of movement and stagnation; the time of memory and of an unsettling present not sustained by a foreseeable future. This temporality is itself complex. Moreover, it seems overruled by the predominance of measurable, linear time in the organization of social life. Heterochrony is something one can be afflicted by, suffer from: a condition. You can "have" heterochrony as you can have the flu; or, as we saw in Friedman's novel, you can have camp. When multi-temporality becomes a problem, an inhibition, and paralyzing contradiction, you "have" heterochrony. But it may also lead to a pleasurable sense of fulfilment when the multiple temporal strands in a day make that day particularly intense or meaningful.

The super-positions, tensions, and incongruous encounters of different temporalities alert us to the simple but oft-forgotten fact that time is not an objective phenomenon. Although our lives are regulated by a relentless clock and the fixed schedules it prescribes, obviously someone who is bored experiences time differently from the hard worker who never quite manages to do what needs doing. Some people are always in haste; others not. People in situations of migrancy are often torn between haste and standstill. This simple experiential discrepancy is compounded by political and economic temporal multiplicities in the so-called "post"-colonial era. It proves that the preposition "post-" is misplaced. Although temporal discrepancies and disturbed rhythms occur in all human lives, it is easy to realize that multi-temporality is specifically tangible in the life of someone who is permanently, as the saying goes, on the move.

Heterochrony, however, is more than subjective experience. It contributes to the temporal texture of our cultural world and, thus, our understanding and experiencing it is a political necessity. This texture is multi-temporal. Narratological analysis can help us understand and appreciate this texture and its relevance for the social world. It comprehends at the very least the time of telling, the time of the events, and the suspension of time wherein these two do not match up. One area where this plays out in sophisticated forms is video art. Heterochrony is a point of intersection between videographic and the migratory mobility. The super-positions, tensions, and incongruous encounters of different temporalities in video narratives – such as South African artist William Kentridge's fabulous animation *Felix in Exile* (1994) – alert us to the phenomenon of heterochrony in both objective ways, in this case, visible, and in subjective, focalized ways. This substantiates my claim for the necessity of narratological analysis of the middle layer, the story, where nuances are created that make narrative the powerful cultural manifestation it is. Precisely because time is multiple, heterogeneous, and objective as well as subjective, it is impossible to make an analysis based on fixating categories, but it is necessary nevertheless to examine the aspects of time that help us understand and experience the time of others.

Sequential Ordering, and Messing It Up

This section concerns the relations between the order of events in the story and their chronological sequence in the fabula. The analysis of this aspect is not always possible or relevant: Why reconstruct the chronological sequence? This becomes informative, however, when transformations of chronology begin to characterize a narrative in meaningful ways. In many experimental modern novels and films, we find, for instance, that these matters are deliberately confused, the chronological relations deliberately concealed. In such cases the chronological chaos we note is often quite meaningful.

Reconstructing the order of the events according to fabula logic and stopping at the result, satisfied that one has done the job, would in fact conceal or even destroy the point of the text's temporality. Films by Alejandro González Itárritu, for example – *Amores Perros* (2001), *21 Grams* (2003), and *Babel* (2006) – tend to carefully confuse in order to con-fuse the chronology so as to build an impossible simultaneity. Thus, in *Babel*, for example, he creates a truly global world, but foregrounds through temporality that this world is not unified. Such a chaotic temporality can even be concealed behind apparent chronologies, as in Gabriel Garcia Márquez's *One Hundred Years of Solitude* (1967) and Marguerite Duras's *L'après-midi de Monsieur Andesmas* (1962). (On these two novels, more in *Narratology* [70].)

Sequential ordering works differently according to media, and some literary narratives play with this medial difference. To give an example of the emulation of literary narrative with the still image: in Toni Morrison's *Beloved*, the main character, Denver, often dwells on memories of events she cannot in any realistic sense have witnessed, including her own birth, about which she has been told so many stories. These not only provide her with memories she needs to build up her sense of self but also paint for her a picture: "easily she stepped into the told story that lay before her eyes on the path she followed away from the window" (29). The play with sequence, although too complex to trace, calls attention to itself, because it contributes to the important wavering in the novel between supernatural and "real" existence. This is a wavering that, among other things, is a metaphor for the bond between history and present, group and individuals. Nor is there a direct relation between chronological play and intellectual complexity. In *Narratology*, I gave some examples of three aspects of chronological deviation: direction, distance, and range. Here, I will limit myself to demonstrate further the fundamental messiness of chronology, alleging that the failure of the attempt to analyse it is just as informative as its success would be in other cases.

A clear example is the short story "Invisible Cities," a chapter in Italo Calvino's novel with the same title (1972). A classic instance of postmodern narration, the novel consists of stories told by the traveller Marco Polo to Kublai Khan at the latter's request. Kublai Khan is the emperor of an empire that knows no limits, since all the cities Polo tells him about waver between reality and fiction. Here I invoke this text because this wavering also affects its chronology. Time jumps back and forth between past, present, and future. I won't go into the detail of this temporal anti-structure. The key declaration about chronology is this short sentence: "Desires are already memories." (8) The connection between desires, which we take to be futural, since the desiring subject strives to achieve something not yet there, and memories, which we assume to address our sense of pastness, whether or not they are based on true facts or more or less imagined: that connection takes place in the present. I have called this "acts of memory."

The complication of chronology in Calvino's novel has inspired the contemporary artist Fiona Tan in the making of a groundbreaking video work, *Facing Forward* (1999). She began her Calvino-ish reflection on temporality already in a video from the year before, *Linnaeus' Flower Clock*, where she writes on a black screen, "I try to imagine what I will remember in 30 years." This statement walks the fine line between reality and fiction as well as that between the three temporalities. Yet it is a possibility. But shortly thereafter, she writes, "I try to remember what

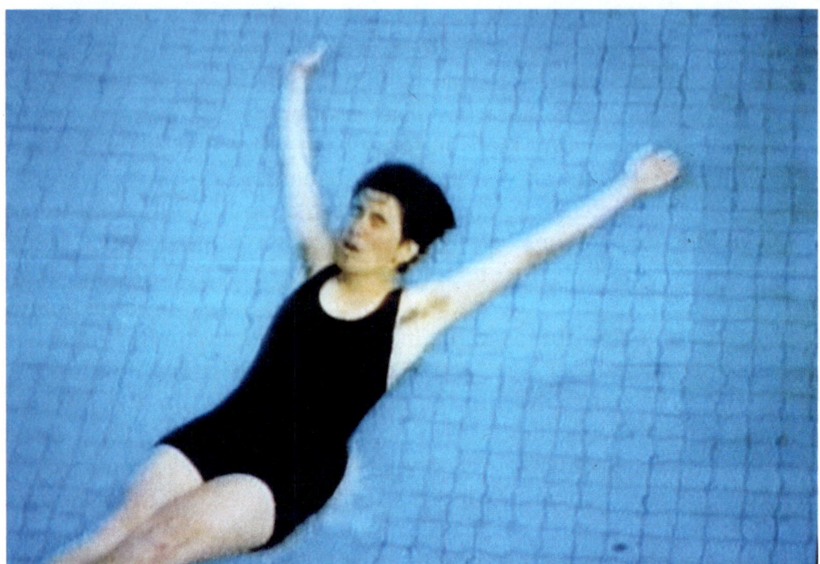

Figure 22. Fiona Tan, *Linnaeus Flower Clock* (1998). Video.

I will imagine in 30 years," which is quite puzzling. This work reflects
on the way we need images to build and experience our reality. In *Linnaeus' Flower Clock* the video consists of a combination of old and new
footage, whereas in *Facing Forward*, it consists entirely of old film fragments. In some segments of the former work, the difference between
the old and the new images is marked by the direction of the faces.

Where in a recurring segment of the old footage, men are diving,
facing forwards, these images are interrupted by newer ones where the
artist herself is diving, but facing backwards (Figure 22). This can be
read as an exploration for or inflection of the topic of her 1999 project.
For in addition to the mixture of old and new, the relation to the past
that is part of the project is complicated further.

In *Facing Forward* (Figure 23), this wavering of chronological slices
becomes visually personified through a mixture of old, archival footage
from different cinematic genres: colonial, touristic as well as footage
of a cameraman at work, seen up close. The latter wears some feath-
ers on the back of his head, as if "playing Indian." Here, the historical
reflection integrates the imaginary one through the different groups
involved in the colonial endeavour: white men sitting, relaxed; native
men standing in compulsive poses for the ethnographic camera; arbitrary city dwellers captured in their everyday-life occupations by the

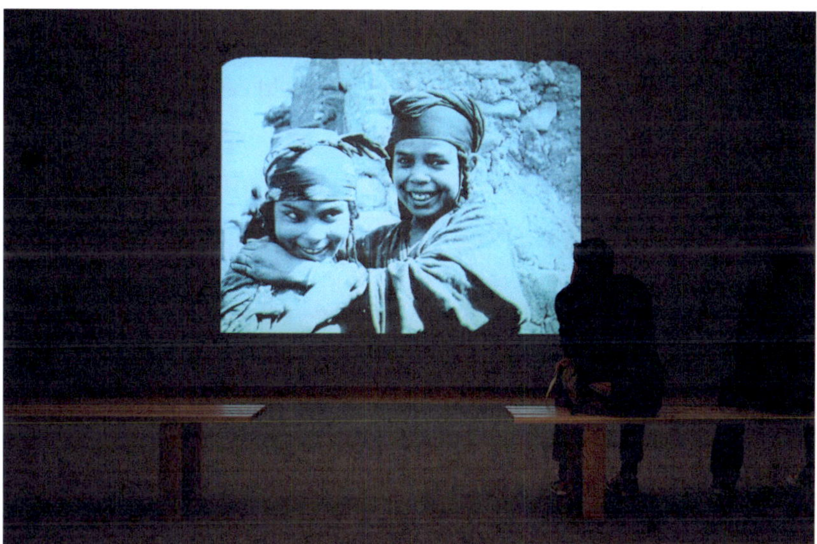

Figure 23. Fiona Tan, *Facing Forward* (1999). Video installation.

camera of a tourist, and that cameraman, concentrated on and working with what he sees. What Tan made is an archival assemblage, the fragments of which do not form a narrative. I am tempted to call this, too, a mosaic. But the work as a whole makes us *imagine*, to use a word that is crucial in Tan's work, what that colonial situation may produce as narratives – perhaps future, imagined memories of a colonialism that one day may lead to a situation that could deserve the preposition "post-."

I now want to consider a contemporary novel that complicates temporality to the point of the impossibility to retrieve chronology while entertaining the desire to do so. This is *El dolor de los demás* (The Pain of Others) (2018), by Spanish writer Miguel Ángel Hernández. The title recycles that of a short book by Susan Sontag, *Regarding the Pain of Others* (2003). Sontag's book reflects on the dilemma of ignorance and voyeurism in relation to the suffering of other people. The verb form "regarding" is meaningfully ambiguous, since it not only means "concerning" but also, visually, looking. It seems meaningful to choose that reference for a novel's title, even if we cannot assume the novel subscribes wholesale to the essay. But clearly it borrows or recalls the topic at stake in the latter. It has to do with pain, grief, or trauma, and places those emotions in other people. But as Sontag argues and Hernández narrates, this placing is precisely the problem. It is impossible without putting the self on the line.

Hernández's novel experiments with many of the narratological concepts and issues at stake in this part of my book. Here, I focus on temporality, and the problem as well as the yield of considering it. The narrative begins as follows:

> They went into Rosario's house, says your father from the next room, they killed Rosi and they abducted Nicolás.
>
> This is the first you hear. The voice that wakes you. The sentence that you will never be able to forget.
>
> For a moment you prefer to think that it is part of a dream and you stay immobile under the sheets. It is five in the morning and you have barely been able to sleep. You didn't feel well on Christmas Eve, and you have been tossing and turning for several hours.
>
> They have killed Rosi and abducted Nicolás, you hear your father say with utter clarity.
>
> When you open your eyes and, while still not hearing anything, you jump out of bed, you dress with the first thing you see, and run out into the living room.

> [Han entrado en la casa de la Rosario, dice tu padre desde la habitación de al lado, han matado a la Rosi y se han llevado al Nicolás.
>
> Es lo primero que oyes. La voz que te despierta. La frase que ya nunca podrás olvidar.
>
> Por un momento, prefieres pensar que forma parte de un sueño y permaneces inmóvil bajo las sábanas. Son las cinco de la madrugada y apenas has conseguido dormir. Le cena de Nochebuena no te sentó bien y llevas varias horas dando vueltas en la cama.
>
> Han matado a la Rosi y se han llevado al Nicolás, escuchas ahora a tu padre decir con total claridad.
>
> Es entonces cuando abres los ojos y, sin entender todavía nada, saltas de la cama, te vistes con lo primero que encuentras y sales corriendo hacia la sala de estar.]

This beginning announces the complex narrativity: second-person narration and the statement that the "you" will never be able to forget the sentence. This pertains to narrative temporality: it implies that time cannot be neatly ordered into past, present and future. The future of possible forgetting is already in the past of telling. It will turn out, in the future, to have been impossible in the past. Yet the discourse is in the present tense. Is this a classic case of what is called a "historical present" – the use of the present tense in a framework of pastness to enliven the narration? Given the unclassical mode of narration in the entire novel, this seems unlikely.

In addition, also in view of the title, we must consider the potential plurality of that "you." This is the more intriguing as Spanish, unlike English, does differentiate between aspects in two distinctions: the familiar and the polite form, more or less as in French; and the singular and the plural, in Spanish both in distinct pronouns and verb forms. These distinctions are very important to further understand who the "you" is/are, and who the "demás" are, the others of the novel's title. Not only is the novel set in a small, suburban neighbourhood, the inhabitants of which all suffered from the shattering event, but also the wider circle of others; the plural "you" also enlists the readers. This complication of tense and person already makes it impossible to put down a clear structural set-up. A novel, I called the book – but is it? That remains to be seen. A double crime in the first sentence, a sentence repeated every now and then; quite frequently, in fact. After every chapter in the first person – in other words, told by the CN(p) – there is a short chapter of about one page in the form just quoted. This turns the potential thriller into a possible poem in which a refrain is formally repeated, although the words are different. And when everything keeps shifting, no genre label fits anymore. Or they all do.

With a back-and-forth movement between time and tenses, characters and grammatical persons, literal and metaphorical uses of the same words, allusions to other novels, investigations that morph into attempts to establish contact with others, it is hard to know which genre label would apply. And yet, from the first sentence on, we know this is indeed a narrative, with events, a narrator, and all that ensues. The narrator is internal, a CN. But since the writing in this fragment is in the second person, the intimacy between narrator and character remains subject to doubt. As a turning point that undermines the genre of the thriller, later a shift in attention from the perpetrator to the victim occurs; from man to woman; from the author's own grief to that of the woman who had been the best friend of the victim, and more.

Nothing matches our expectations. The most likely genres are left behind as well: although utterly personal, this novel does not quite belong to the genre of autobiography nor of autofiction, although it has affiliations with both. It is also a chronicle, but of the research, hence, not of the central event. It can also be seen as a reversed Bildungsroman, the report on the protagonist's attempt to learn who he is and how the others (los demás) are part of that identity. It creates a new genre: one that touches life. It does this by means of passing through all attempts to tell it, on the way engaging many theoretical problems. This touch uses words we all know but as if cured from habit, in a "word hospital." With this phrase I allude to Azriel Bibliowicz's novel *Migas de pan*, discussed in the companion volume (*Narratology*, 81, 87, 128, 147, 148). A word hospital only releases the words / patients when they have retrieved their shining health of crystalline language. Not yet. Perhaps never.

The beginning I quoted is reiterated many times in an almost formulaic way within the short refrain-like passages between chapters. It is as if the "you" and the "I," who will soon manifest themselves as the same individual, must remain split. The combination of formulaic repetition and self-reflection blurs the temporality, especially the chronology. The alternation between narrative chapters in which the CN self-identifies as an "I" and where past and present alternate, and the invocation of that moment in the past told in the second person and present tense, seems inevitably full of repetitions. The repetitive nature of those fragments points to an issue that forbids the development of memory over time. I am alluding, of course, to trauma.

There is no chronology to speak of; the entire narration is an act of memory; or rather, a desperate attempt to achieve such an act, which is doomed to fail. But it is impossible to place that memory in the past. At some point, in what seems to me a crucial passage, the CN in his "I" identity is explicit about his attempt to remember the past and his incapacity to do so:

> I had gone there like a kind of *flâneur* of time, a stroller of memory, drawing the past into the present, silently, the camera in slow-down. The past did not appear as a still image without sound, however, but as a murmur in movement.

> [Había ido allí como una especie de *flâneur* del tiempo, un paseante de la memoria, a traer el pasado al presente, en silencio, a cámara lente. Pero el pasado no se apareció como una imagen fija, sin sonido, sino como un murmullo en movimiento.] (62)

Movement, but no progress. This evocative passage implies a theory of narrative time, against the odds of trauma, literally seen as odds; obstacles. It also "theorizes" time in relation to memory and to different media, such as the cinematic, in turn invoking but not quite reaching the still image. And the evocation of the visuality of memory is also remarkable. For those who know, the allusion in the word *flâneur* to Walter Benjamin's unfinished *The Arcades Project* (1999 [1927–40]), written in interaction with Baudelaire, will add to the philosophical depth of the novel, but such allusions are carefully integrated to avoid jargoned imposition and the resulting intimidation.

The narrator's search for what happened that ominous day of the beginning, presents his way to get back his sanity; to get over what we can indeed only call trauma. The traumatic state betrays itself in the temporal messiness and repetitiveness. The CN's remedy is research. He sets out, twenty years after the facts, on the research endeavour to know the events, the motivations, the people involved, including himself. This research project carries along the fiction-fact tension that subtends the entire novel. The temporal tension, in this novel, is presented as the ongoing con-fusion of past and present, with only incidental moments of clarity. For example, the narrator repetitively mentions that twenty years have gone by since the horrible event that the refrain-passage keeps mentioning. But that time frame keeps alternating between "they have" and "my best friend has."

For after an unspecified while, it turns out that the "true fact" is that his best friend was not abducted by anonymous murderers; he had killed his sister and then threw himself into an abyss. But the phrase "it turns out" wrongly suggest a punctual moment, an insight emerging as an event. This never happens; there is never a precise moment that the version of the beginning – that the friend had been abducted and the murder committed by outside thugs – transforms into the later one. That moment, which the entire novel is devoted to discovering, must stay out of time. It is also significant that the beginning is a direct discourse uttered by the "you"'s father, not by that second person himself. The narrator turns to the "I" ("yo") form after each short second-person intermission. We see that the "I" may be identified as the primary narrator, but there remains a haze of unclarity, such as in the sixth chapter. For even then, the embedded speeches by his brother and the brother of the victim(s?) are not attributed with quotation marks nor attributive verbs, so the "you" there remains ambiguous (57.) I will return to this impressive novel, which in its intense engagement of socially important issues and narrative complexity reads, indeed, like a "narratology in practice."

From Linearity to Constellation

In *Narratology* (71–9) I analysed two examples of play with chronology: one from an ancient classic, and one from a modern narrative. As it happens, recently I encountered again a classic in relation to a modern narrative, this time a modern "versioning" (a term coined by Peeren [2007]) of an old classic. This had such a poignant actuality that it enticed me to continue, or divert, the changes made by the recent author into another versioning. This was a media transfer, from literature to film. I mean the story of Cassandra, the prophetess who was seduced by Apollo by the gift of prophecy, but when she rejected his sexual advances, he cursed her: she would know, see the future, but no one would believe her. The story is briefly mentioned in books 7 and 24 of Homer's *Illiad* and more extensively in Aeschylus's tragedy *Agamemnon*, one play of the trilogy *Oresteia* (5th c. BCE). Although she is also murdered by Clytemnestra, who kills Agamemnon in revenge for having sacrificed their daughter Iphigeneia, little attention is paid to Cassandra's pre-story.

But renewed interest in this figure was sparked in the 1980s when East-German writer Christa Wolf published a novel, titled *Cassandra* (1984 [1983]), which was immediately translated into English. This novel appeared in the heydays of the second feminist wave. It struck a sensitive chord by giving the victim the almost exclusive narratorial power. A very short first paragraph by an apparently primary narrator positions the figure: "It was here. This is where she stood" and ending just a few lines later on "Into the slaughterhouse. And alone." From there, and without any indication of a shift in level, the story is told by Cassandra, a CN(p). She begins with these words, a single sentence that constitutes a paragraph: "Keeping step with the story, I make my way into death." Note, again, the present tense. What follows is all told by Cassandra. Using second-level narration, she does quote direct speeches of other characters, embedded in her account. But at no point can there be any doubt that she is the CN, narrator of the last day of her own life. The narrative gives, thus, a personal account of a woman who knows that destruction is imminent, including her own death.

But in spite of this consistent structure, the narration is also imbued with philosophically and narratologically relevant questions of media, of what thought is, and how the world is, or is not, the bearer of thoughts. And it is all embedded in a harrowing chronology that, as in Hernández's novel, puts the present under scrutiny. "What I grasp between now and evening will perish with me. Will it perish? Once a thought comes into the world, does it live on in someone else?" Although at moments she expresses fear and anxiety, and also anger, she is continuously raising questions about language and images, hearing and seeing, and the difficulties of communicating with others. For a narratological analysis of sequence leading to the establishment of a chronology, this is a challenging novel. Such an analysis is practically impossible. But as I have said before, the technical failure of an analysis is also a valuable result. Moreover, the direction of the deviances from linear chronology are all rooted in that rigorously straight line: towards evening, which equals towards death.

Needless to say, a lot of the fabula of which the figure tells the story concerns memories. This already makes the temporality as well as the distinction between the three layers and their agents both problematic and, or thereby, revealing. In terms of direction, we can distinguish the predictive statements, such as the reiterated announcements of her imminent death, from the memorial ones, where she looks back to earlier events. The fact that these are hardly ever specifically positioned in time makes it even less appealing to undertake a meticulously detailed analysis. Nevertheless, once we attempt to do so, it becomes clear that much of the storytelling is set in the present tense. From that moment on, reflections and narrations go into the direction of the past and the future, sometimes without warning of the change of direction.

And then she complicates this even more; for example, when we read,

> Affable, modest, unassuming – that was the image I had of myself, which survived every catastrophe virtually intact. Not only that: Whenever it survived, the catastrophe lay behind me.

This self-focalization is set in the past tense ("the image I had") but then it is made iterative ("every catastrophe"), and since the catastrophes lie behind her, the imminent catastrophe that is the temporal setting of the entire novel and which lies in the (near-) future is, and is not, part of the series. On the whole, this novel's temporality systematically refuses chronology as much as the idea that one thing comes before or after another.

This is the primary reason I chose this novel, with its impossible chronology, as the starting point for a cinematic experiment. When I was invited by the Łódź Film School to come to Poland and make an "essay film," the difficulty of defining that genre – if it is one – brought Wolf's novel back to my mind. I remember the term "essay" from school, where it meant simply "not narrative." This never sounded right to me; narrative can well be, indeed, inevitably is, an integral part of an essay – just think of the deployment of stories as examples or the reiterated beginning of Hernández's novel. I also find it remarkable that Adorno's extensive writings on literature (two volumes in English) begin with an essay on the essay, thus giving it pride of place within literature. But not as a genre. Rather, unexpectedly, according to the title of Adorno's text, as "form" (1991 [1954–8]). But what form is that, if none can be fixated? This is one of the reasons why I decided to give the present book the formless form of short fragments of analyses, with the theoretical concepts that are more extensively explained in the companion book as the tenuous skeleton.

The difficulty and, yes, relevance of taking a closer look at the temporal structure of a narrative, and especially in view of an intermediality experiment (on which more later) is best understood through two passages from scholars whose work has been tremendously important to me. The first is psychanalyst Christopher Bollas, who demonstrated the larger realm in which the mutuality of past and future, and hence, the difficulty of pinpointing chronology, is highly relevant. This is something where the failing analysis of narrative chronology helps our understanding. In his important book *The Shadow of the Object: Psychoanalysis of the Unthought Known* (1987) – the title of which already speaks volumes – he wrote,

> I often find that although I am working on an idea without knowing exactly what it is I think, I am engaged in thinking an idea struggling to have me think it. (10)

Not only does this phrasing express the modesty towards one's object of analysis, an attitude that I value greatly, since the author acknowledges that he doesn't know exactly what he is busy thinking about or figuring out. But also, it qualifies the intensity ("engaged") and the liveness of the thought-in-becoming. Becoming, then, positions the act in the present, even if there is a past – the beginning of the "working on" – and a future, the moment that the idea has won its struggle. With the adverb "often" the issue of frequency, that other opponent of chronology, is included. Most importantly, the idea that Bollas is trying to think is itself collaborating with him. The author and his object, the idea he is working on, do it together, *now*. The idea wishes to be thought; it even struggles to achieve the status of idea. This struggle happens in the present and points to an imminent future. There is no better demonstration of heterochrony as I have described it above.

This view has important implications for narrative between media. In a strikingly comparable formulation, Kaja Silverman presented her theory of the image of, or as memory, in the following way:

> If, in trying to make sense of this strange account of unconscious memories, I am unable to avoid attributing to them the status of a subject, that is because subjectivity itself is in its most profound sense nothing other than a constellation of visual memories which is *struggling* to achieve a perceptual form. (*World Spectators* 2000, 89; emphasis added).

Both *El dolor* and *Cassandra* are clear demonstrations of the truth and relevance of this view of the conflation or collaboration, of memory and image. Cassandra's memories are among those that flesh out her subjectivity in this struggling way, in need of perceptual form. This was the challenge in the making of the film where she is the main character, and time her primary antagonist.

That struggle is not only bi-lateral; given that both Bollas the author and the idea-in-becoming are connected to many other beings, issues, and things, it is multiple. Silverman's word "constellation" intimates that same multiplicity. And this can answer the question of the identity of the "you" in *El dolor*. The *demás* of the title could have told us. He, the "you" who wakes up to the ominous words of his father, is going to spend his lifetime searching for "what happened" in order to relieve the pain of himself and of the others, the multiplicity of the "you." Between the singular "you" who narrates it all and the "I" who performs the novel-long search-without-outcome and the multiple others who suffer (also), a constellation takes shape that the narrative constitutes and forms.

Yet even in situations where chronology is impossible and time heterochronic, the relentless ongoing-ness of time during the processing of the cultural objects that narratives are makes the constellation a moving one, whether or not the object is a still or a moving image, linguistic or visual. So this is the fundamental paradox of narrative temporality, one we owe to Silverman's memory-image struggle: in a narrative, even one with a more-or-less traceable chronology, the moments that in our reading experience constitute a certain timeline, nevertheless remain in our reader's (largely unconscious) memory as a constellation. That constellation, which I have inflected as mosaic to keep in view the small pieces that constitute it and the visuality involved, can achieve what Silverman calls so aptly, because simply, "a perceptual form." This is why narrative is culturally productive, and the analysis of chronology, including its inevitable failures, an important step towards the experience, appreciation, and understanding of time. And time is what connects reading and cinematic viewing.

In the novel *Migas de pan* (*Bread Crumbs*) (2013), already mentioned, Colombian writer of Polish Jewish origin Azriel Bibliowicz stages a situation that, like Hernández's search, never gets a narratively satisfying ending. Briefly: guerrillas in Colombia have captured Josué, the father of the main character and a holocaust survivor. The entire novel is structured around the horrible repetition of the violent capturing, decades apart. Since Josué is clearly profoundly traumatized by his camp experience, his son Samuel and his other relatives, while constantly waiting to hear from the captors, imagine what must be going through Josué's head. This can be seen as an embedded hetero-focalization. But this is a two-way street: their own waiting also becomes the experience of powerlessness their father had gone through decades earlier. For more on this novel and its fabulously imaginative "imaging" of the experience of heterotemporality, see *Narratology* (81–2, 87, 128).

This repetitiveness of capture – a tragedy without crisis – becomes the primary story line. This is an exceptionally adequate narrative of the timelessness of trauma that captivity produces.

I invoke this novel here once more because of the comparability with Hernández's novel *El dolor de los demás*. There, too, the repetition of the account, in the present tense and in the second person, of the primary moment when ordinary life transformed into tragedy, is the core of the novel's temporality. In *El dolor* the primary moment transforms a self-evident friendship of the narrator's entire childhood into a recognition of an alienating monstrosity. But full of doubt. The brief period of hardly a day when the question of whether his friend Nicolás either was himself abducted or that he did kill his sister and then committed suicide was still unresolved, hence, the transformation from friend and victim into murderous monster is often evoked, but the moment of that change itself is never specified. That moment, the primary event of the novel, remains, as the narrator qualifies his knowledge later, in the second chapter, a sea of mist ("El mar de niebla"). Uncertainty, unclarity, is ultimately the content of this novel. Mist: a noun we can also bring to bear on the narrative itself, and the temporality that, with timeline and constellation and all, must remain misty. A good case of con-fusion.

Above I mentioned that our *Madame B* (2012–14) film's beginning, during the opening credits, shows Emma in a ruined house, predicting the end. This ending placed before the beginning forecasts her demise by emotional capitalism. It was our way of stipulating that the narrative was not going to be linear. In the famous scene at the Vaubyessard Castle, which we have updated by turning it into a reception of a fictional French Association of the Pharmaceutical Industry, Emma is ostracized and, as a result, seeks comfort in eating from the desert, richly sprinkling it with powder sugar. Visually looking like the arsenic with which she will later kill herself, this image is one of the moments in which presenting her eating disorder becomes a tool to implement anti-linearity.

This hint goes hand in hand with another kind of hint at Flaubert's anti-linear poetic. One could consider this a process of pro-retrospective affiliation, in which the temporality of our search is reversed to find associations with works by other, later artists, but who, for our film made for today, become earlier and predictive. This resonates with the dialogue I established earlier between Borges and Bourgeois. Here, some visual quotations in our film in relation to experimental filmmaker Maya Deren's *Ritual in Transfigured Time* (1946) and *At Land* (1944) help understand how this works in reverse. Deren's films often depict space by showing the threshold between societal borders, intercutting wild or natural space with the realm of high society or the bourgeoisie.

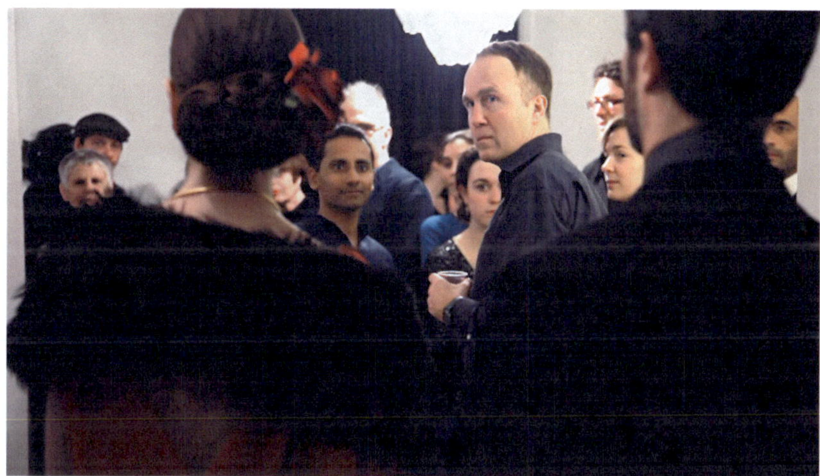

Figure 24. *Madame B*: Social cruelty, quoted from Maya Deren. Video still.

In *Ritual*, a woman enters a room in which a party is in full swing. Deren traps her in the throng by using freeze-frames to fix her position among the crowd. What plays out is an increasingly violent choreography in which the crowd's initial engagement with the woman is abandoned to the societal buzz in which they no longer see but only brush past her. In our film, as Emma and Charles enter the reception in a Paris apartment, their naïve eagerness is quickly crushed by the frosty reception that greets them (Figure 24). The guests freeze as these two outsiders enter their world, an inherently cruel act of social severance.

Another example from Deren comes from *At Land*, in which she climbs up a tower of driftwood to arrive at a dinner table lined with guests. Deren, who acts in her own films, subsequently crawls along the table, intercutting her journey along it with images of her crawling among dense foliage. Deren's "inappropriate" behaviour is mirrored in Emma's own strange behaviour at the table. Later, in the same reception scene, we have Emma appear as a ghost (Figure 25), unseen by the others, including Charles, another nod to Deren as well as an aggrandizement of Flaubert's futural hint. These visual quotations can be seen as a *politics of allusion*. Allusion is an indispensable tool for narratological analysis. It brings in other texts, in intertextuality, but it also ruins the attempt to follow the timeline of the fabula. To see these allusions to the ending we must be willing to give up on narrative streamlining (a.k.a. chronology) and consider the image as double by definition. An

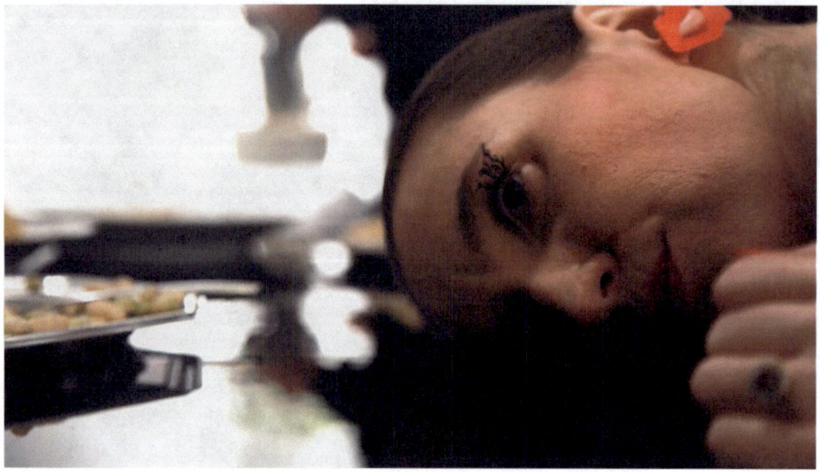

Figure 25. *Madame B*: Emma gives up, quoted from Maya Deren. Video still.

allusion is not a metaphor; instead of replacing one thing with another, an allusion enfolds the alluded into what we see. Allusions operate not on an "either/or" structure but on a "both … and" or an "as well as" inclusive model. They are not anachronies but *achronies*.

Seeking to determine direction, distance and span of anachronies, for which I have given examples in the theoretical volume, is useful as long as the narrative we are studying makes its points by means of such devices. Sometimes, however, the very search for such specific phenomena can also blind us to an aspect of the narrative that resists temporal clarity. This procures a paradox: if narratives are defined by the sequence of events of the fabula, then some temporality is inevitably part of their structure. The play of hide-and-seek the narrative stages between its events and their temporality can signify a foregrounding of another aspect that becomes predominant once we probe temporality in its inherent heterochrony: the rhythm that mediates between the timeline and the constellation, as one of those shards that shape the mosaic.

Rhythm Extraordinaire: Slowness and Hecticity

But what is it that we can call narrative rhythm? Should we take as a standard of measurement the time it takes to read the narrative? This varies from reader to reader, and according to circumstances in which the reading takes place, including its interruptions. Suppose that a rough average reading time per novel could be calculated. This reading time would then, in principle, be comparable to the time covered by the performance of a play or piece of music, even though this performance-time does not vary with each receiver (listener or spectator) but with each performance. The end product of these calculations remains dubious; and then relevance still has to be argued, to say nothing of the problems involved in working them out. In films, however, rhythm is a prominent feature. It is one of the most important tools to keep the viewers riveted as well as to make them plunge into the fictional world.

As I have explained in *Narratology*, the tools of narrative to vary its overall rhythm are the figures of ellipsis, the elision of events we expect; of summary, the quick enumeration of events that take a much longer time, and its opposite, the scene that spins out a single event over a relatively long stretch of text; and the slowdown that stretches time beyond simultaneity. The paradox of narrative, in this respect, is the use of scenes as building blocks in the face of chronology, the linearity that suggests a complete rendering of the sequence of events while such completeness would make the narrative unbearably slow. Reading cultural objects with heterochronic rhythms is a socially useful training as well as an artistically gratifying experience. It makes narratives, in whatever medium, alive and sensuously impacting.

As mentioned above, heterochrony contributes to the temporal texture of our cultural world and thus, our understanding and experiencing it is a political necessity. This texture is multi-temporal. Video is technically able to make multi-temporality visible and the experience of heterochrony tangible. This trains the viewer to be sensitive to this aspect of temporal disjunction in the lives of people among whom we live. Thus, it is now obvious that analyses of narrative in all its forms, with its capability to manipulate time in the ways described above, can contribute to both an understanding and the development of a greater sensitivity to the multiple ways cultural experience engages time.

As a short enquiry into rhythm I propose to consider two rhythms we all know: hecticity and slowness, or haste and stagnation. Both have a somewhat negative connotation: the latter easily seen as boring, the former as nerve-wracking. Both judgments fail to reckon with aesthetic achievements. They can be deployed to enhance our awareness of what art can perform; they are self-reflective, precisely for breaking routine. Both rhythms are intermedial bridges: they become more prominent when we consider the differences and similarities between narratives in literature and film, video and painting.

I look first at slowness: the time of video slowed down to the extreme, to the point that the difference between still and moving images becomes moot. This turns rhythm itself into a "theoretical object" that reconsiders the distinction between still and moving images as media specific, as in the distinction between photography and cinema. Interruption is the motor of what can then be achieved in the domain of the social. The reflection below briefly examines a few different frames within which interruption occurs and becomes an event, an act, a performance, a wound, an encounter. The issue of slow rhythm, the advantage it offers, the goal it pursues, can be slowing down for better looking. Looking at the image, that is; not at the world it allegedly represents. Slow reading, as poetry presupposes, is the literary equivalent. But narratives can also do it. Two examples from video art and photography follow.

Dutch video artist Roos Theuws shows us something about the connection between looking and slowness that diverts attention from the illusion of realism to the image as such. Technology allows the creation of perfect visual illusions. Knowing full well that what we see in a video image is a two-dimensional plane that doesn't move, from the beginning of the moving image the endeavour of the art form has been to solicit the "willing suspension of disbelief." The quality of current moving images, be they cinematic or videographic, makes it only too easy to dream away in the illusion that what we see is something "out there" – a piece of the world. While many moving-image makers exploit that willingness to be deceived, especially art video and film can also counter it. In self-reflexivity, the medium is deployed to question what it is, can do, and does. Many practitioners of lens-based art question the assumption of the world made visible and probe the properties of the technology that facilitates it. Theuws is among the most radical, profound, and creative of these. In her work she offers two very different ways of decomposing, dissecting, exploding the moving image. She takes the medium to its limits, with astounding beauty as a result.

On three large LED screens disposed asymmetrically, in her work *Kitab Al Manazir* (2013–14) we see black-and-white images of the same room of a museum of optical instruments (the Boerhaave Museum in Leiden). Yet they refuse to become a unity. The question, What do you see? remains hard to answer. Two of the screens present a very slow panning shot that moves until a reflecting sphere, visible in all three images (Figure 26), coming from the left in one and from the right in the other,

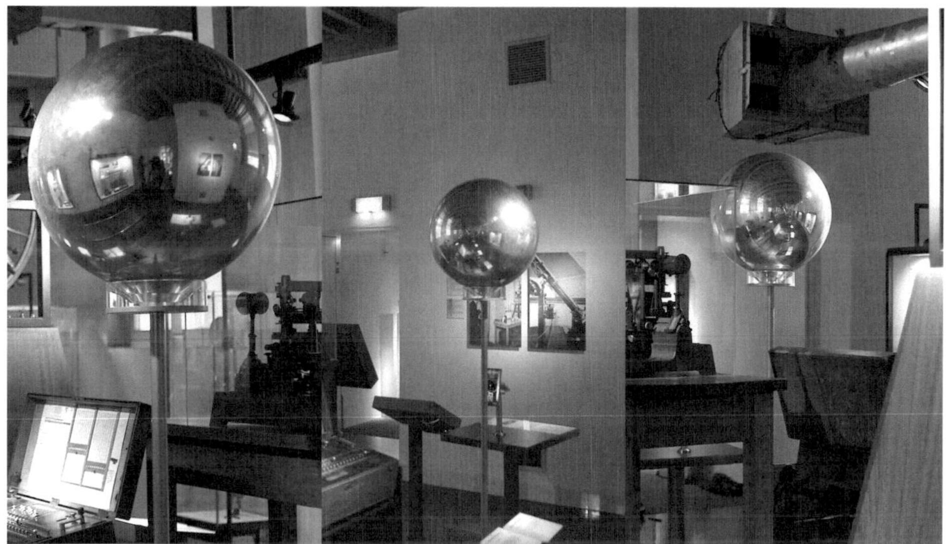

Figure 26. Roos Theuws, *Kitab al Manazir* (2013–14). Three-channel video installation.

after some fifteen minutes appears in the centre, because the sphere reflects the lens that moves in search of a focus. Of our happy stabilizing habit of looking with linear perspective, nothing remains. The images do not show anything but themselves. Meanwhile, a tenth-century treatise on optics by the Persian scholar after whom the work is titled is read in Arabic, the language of the origin of much optical science.

In the two screens – one large projection, one monitor – of another work, titled *Fences & Pools* (2012), we see again a slow panning shot. This is of a fence on a peninsula of Salt Lake, behind which at a distance is the mountain landscape of Yellowstone Park (Figure 27). The images couldn't be more different from those of *Kitab Al Manazir*: this work is in colour, blurry; and the movement, slowed down 6,000 times, is so slow that it is invisible. The only way to become aware of the moving quality of the image is by looking for quite some time at one of the screens, then going back to the other. You don't see it change; you see that it has changed. Slowness turns the present into something only visible as past. Change happens while you are present, yet becomes change only in the past tense, as was the case in the transformation from friend to murderer in Hernández's novel, which thereby manifests its affiliation with visuality. (No wonder: that novel's author is

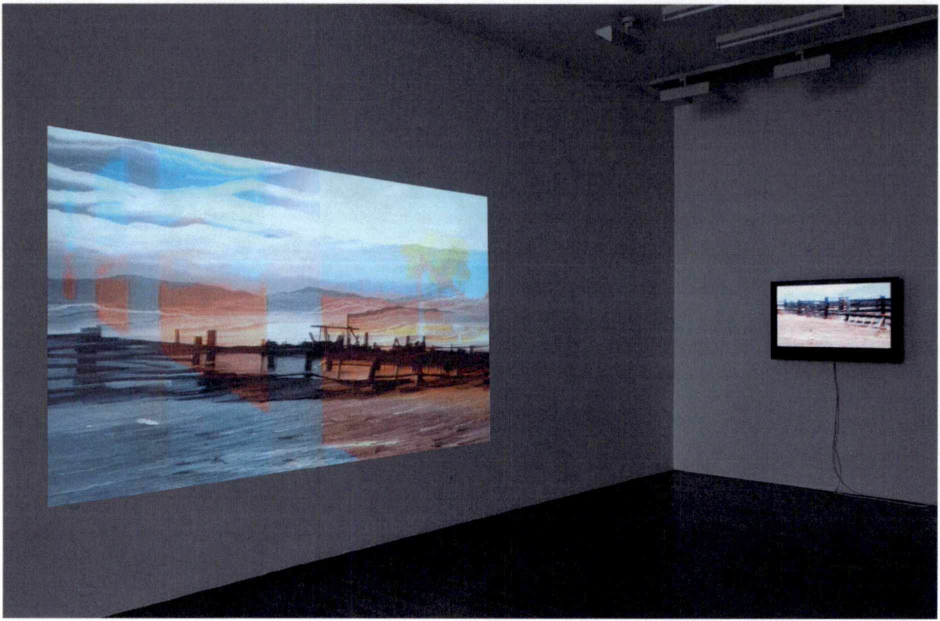

Figure 27. Roos Theuws, *Fences & Pools* (2012). Channel video installation.

a professor of art history.) This also connects Theuws's work with that of Norwegian artist Jeannette Christensen (discussed later).

In *Fences & Pools*, a voice in English reads from three texts that evoke this landscape: one from the biblical Book of Revelations, one from a Navajo creation myth, and one from the diary of a nineteenth-century scientist. The same voice, three cultures, different in time, space, and discipline, all three relevant for the space of the image. These three voices constitute a plural narrator. The voices are audible from different speakers, so that the viewer who moves from one to the other can hear only fragments. Sitting in the middle, you seem to have three ears, in a bodily exercise in sculptural hearing. When on the left of the right-hand screen a tree we have seen disappear on the large screen begins to enter the frame, an old oil-drilling installation on the right begins to leave the frame. When the tree is completed, the drill is gone; as if nature pushed economy away. The visual image decomposes in lines and planes of colour; the texts decompose the mixed society of the space. In these works, the medium dissects itself, undoing representation and revising the standard conception of perception. What do you see? Not a piece of world "out there"; only the image blown up in time, disrupted, laid bare.

Something that is also bound to slow rhythm happens with Norwegian artist Jeannette Christensen's serial work *Woman Interrupted*, from 1994 to the present. This is based on Vermeer's oil painting *Woman Interrupted at her Music* from 1632. This too is self-reflective; a work of art on art. Time, hence, also its interruption, has many tentacles, touching on the most crucial aspects of social-cultural life, narrativized in a threadbare temporality. Materially, this work started out as a series of polaroid photographs – the medium of the instant. Through temporal work, through its sheer recasting of the painting, it is already an image that interrupts the enduring silence, the timelessness of Johannes Vermeer's masterpiece. Consequently, it becomes a narrative. We consider Vermeer's paintings silent, indeed. This is part of why and how images are still. But making a snapshot of such a work is probing the question of what that means – still?

Vermeer's art can even be seen as the embodiment of stillness – harbouring the silence of images we call "still" in the double sense of (auditory) silent and (physically) unmoving. This double meaning contains a double paradox. For, firstly, still images do move, in the emotional sense, and more so due to their stillness. This is the autonomy side of art. And secondly, the interruption of the music-making silences the depicted woman, thereby drawing attention to her earlier and later sound-making in the narrative depicted. This makes interruption a motor of narrativity: because of the implied suddenness of the interruption, the times of before and after accede to the stage. The interruption is the key, the one and only event. It also foregrounds the artwork's sociality; it shows that it intervenes in the silenced movement of life. Christensen's series of polaroids shocks us into thought about time, silence, and stillness by their live models. But still, these snapshots are still – differently (Figures 28a and 28b).

But then, the artist interrupts herself, her medium, and begins to make video images, mostly with the same models. These she slows down to the extreme, like Theuws did. Christensen's video installation takes as its starting point the situation depicted. There, the artificial stillness of the pose, on which the artwork's stillness rests, is interrupted. The figure looks at the viewer, breaking the spell of the absorption of the fictional character and turning attention to this interruption of the fictional world and its timelessness. The interruption performs a subtle twist between two times, already foregrounded by Vermeer's notoriously still painting. Looking up, the woman figure breaks open the confinement of the fictional world. Her look disrupts the theatre's fourth wall and engages viewers, however much time has passed between the absorption and the theatricality. The interruption disrupts

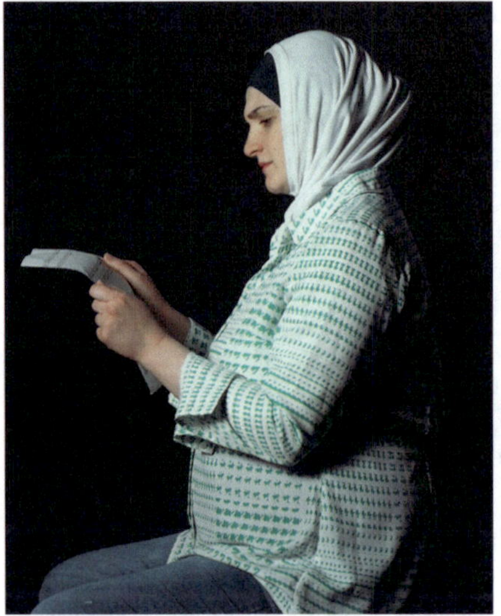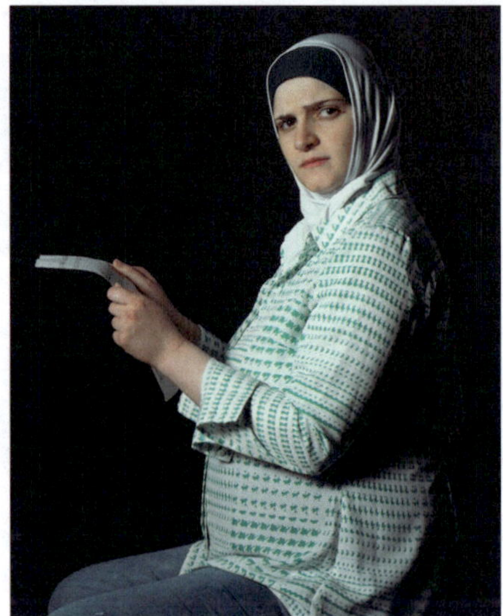

Figure 28. Jeannette Christensen, *Woman Interrupted* (2018–20). Video installation (detail: Razan).

the complacency with which we assume routine is all there is, and the flow of time is simply there – *all the time.*

We see that the figure's body and attention are divided. Even though the face and the eye are facing the viewer, the body and much of the attention are facing the sheet of notes, or perhaps the letter that, on a fabula level, already interrupted the music upon being delivered. This dividedness raises the question of the relationship between the body and attention. The woman is partly in her own time and also in a time that she shares with ours. In-between, the time of modernism has passed, of which Jonathan Crary (1999) has illuminated the interruptive quality. And as Ernst van Alphen (2017) has recently reminded us, the current time of near-permanent interruption, to invoke another paradox, remains connected to this. In a sense, we can even claim that among other artists Vermeer, through his aesthetic that so powerfully interrupts our routine of perceiving stillness in the still image, may well have intuitively called for the invention of cinema, which occurred so much later. I have made this claim for Flaubert, and also for Frans Hals. Both artists, in very different ways, experimented with cinematic devices, such as movement (Hals) and variations of close-up and long shots (Flaubert). My point is not, of course, that these artists really "invented" the cinema, but that their art was so experimental in terms of temporality and movement that the search for the technology of cinema, which occurred later, became almost its "natural" consequence. The narrativity is anchored in the temporality.

Christensen's act of re-photographing the same models in the same poses decades later, after letting the sitters age and the polaroids lose their colours and sharpness, and even mould, thus making process – hence, time – part of the artwork, is an artistic statement concerning the inevitable narrativity that time brings, even in the stillest of images. And then, filming the still scene while making the moving image rival the stillness instead of the other way around, she uses a different medium to make it respond to the photographic one. Then, she adds the medium of installation, back-projecting the resulting images in a face-to-face of a woman and a man on suspended ("floating") screens, with the viewer being invited to stand in between and choose with whom to look at whom. All this is an act of creating a multiply complicating art of interruption, with Vermeer, for our time.

For the opposite rhythm, which I call "hecticity," I revert to *Don Quixote* (1950 [1605; 1615]) and *Don Quijote* (2019) – the novel and the video installation. I argue that the interrupted slowness and the hecticity are not simply opposed but also similar. The poetics of Cervantes's novel consists of sprinkling events in which times are collapsed; in which, for more temporal confusion, the past is the present – formerly is today. In loyalty to the novel, the video project includes a conception of time that does not obey chronology with its linearity and its assumed evolutionism, which suggests that things get better while clearly they get worse.

El Ingenioso Hidalgo Don Quixote de la Mancha stands out in its intense and creative expression of prolonged and reiterated hopelessness. Formerly, in deep history, things happened that still happen, or happen again, today. Like spectres, they cast their shadow over the present – that time frame that is ours when we perceive images. The main character demonstrates, for the benefit of us all and through yet another paradox, that time is both constantly halted and hectically continuing; disempowering the subject who, deprived of the routine of life, is unable to keep a grip on living-in-time. For, Cervantes, as so many millions today, has been captured and enslaved, and I surmise, traumatized. To forecast the final part of this book, everything that happens, interrupting, makes an event.

The first screen of the installation shows the main character reading. This is an allusion to, but also a critique of, the frequent alleging of the statement by the narrator that it was reading that made the hero mad, something made dubious by the pluralization of different narrators. Although reading is not usually seen as an action, especially not compared to the anti-hero's hectic adventures to come, here it is the primary scene consisting of (tiny) actions, as interruptions. Through tiny shock effects, he changes during reading, his facial expressions and body language displaying how he transforms from sane to mad. Without uttering a word, he enacts horror, relief, loneliness, and the desire to be heard; announcing the situations of the other pieces. The scene is not suggesting to limit this transformation to reading alone – the suggestion is, instead, that there is an impossibility to remain the same when one is surrounded by the snippets of cultural and political "noise." This offers a counterpart as well as companion piece to Christensen's single and barely noticeable interruption. For, there, too it is unclear whether the woman is deprived of her concentration or offered an opportunity for contact, freeing her from the loneliness of domesticity.

To call interruption a quality of an aesthetic is assuming that the moment, act, or effect of interruption is sense based, senses affecting, and affecting the subject through the senses. The closest we can come to an understanding of aesthetic, again, not as something but as an event, act, or performance, is to consider that predominantly, the senses are engaged in aesthetic experience. This experience can most easily take place in public space, where people encounter one another in their relationship with art works or other objects that act. Hence the importance of museums and other spaces where art is put in a position to act and people to inter-act. Those are public spaces, and at the same time, they interrupt all those routines mentioned above, suspending them for a stretch of time, chosen by the visitor.

This constantly occurring interruption of routine – hastily passing through public space on our way to work or home – is necessary if the social world is to be able to continue to be "in becoming," as a Deleuzian (counter-)ontology would have it, instead of stultifying and reifying it in an oppressive yet illusory feeling of familiarity as monocultural and mono-temporal – in stillness. We must assess this in view of the non-linearity of time that the aesthetic of interruption entails, in complicity with pre-posterous history. For the *Don Quijote* project, the interruptions are primarily bound up with trauma. This entails a state not of heterochrony but of a-chrony; the incapacity to live (in) time. Such thematic accents both provide insight into the cultural meanings of the flow of time, punctuated, punctured, by interruptions. In other contexts, the hetero-temporality that results from interruption – the disruption of smooth, invisible time – has consequences for our understanding of the subtleties of the migratory culture we live in.

Attention to temporality in narrative seems too obvious for words. It is what characterizes narrative most clearly. Yet we have seen that the aesthetic value of temporality resides more often than not in the impossibility to come up with clear answers to the questions narratology poses. This makes it more rather than less worthwhile to probe temporality in narratives. And the intermediality that is one of the focal issues in this volume – as it has been in my own work of the past two decades – is the best place where temporality awareness can function as the bridge, not only between media but also between technical and social analysis.

3: Characters

The habitual kind of response that judges characters like real, modern, psychologically complex people has had nefarious effects on scholarship. It has produced the myth of primitivism in studies of ancient and folk literature, as well as on literatures from geographically and culturally remote areas. It has also produced a large body of critical literature that, while seemingly reiterating the misogyny of the texts studied, in fact projects sexism on texts whose function is not moral at all or whose standards of representation have nothing to do with what realist literature has taught us to expect. This is a major ideological trap, as well as a literary- and art-historical pitfall, for it obscures the characteristics of modes of storytelling so different from a modern and Western sensibility. It is crucial to take enough distance from this anthropomorphism, for instance, to understand that Proust's (1981 [1922–33]) Albertine, the "I" narrator's fictional beloved, is a paper person in more than one sense.

The notion that fictional characters are "just paper people" is made literal, concrete, when the Proustian "I" narrator reduces her, in a gesture of intermedial irony, to a series of photographs. Looking more closely at this character makes us aware of the extent to which the modernist masterpiece has strong features of what later comes to be called postmodernism. An anti-realistic, ironic, mocking focalization of media is one of them. Thus, such a close look helps not only to understand Proust's novel beyond realist projections, but also to relativize the periodization that forms the backbone of literary history. Albertine is an object of the narrator-protagonist's obsession, and when he no longer needs her to make his point about the relation between jealousy, love, and knowledge, she dies in an unlikely accident. I have analysed this construction of the character in some detail in *Narratology* (120–4).

Once we accept that Albertine has no psychological depth of her own, we can not only grasp the specifically Proustian construction of character, but also the aesthetic and epistemological thrust of the narrative. In contrast, a realistic reading of this character as a "real girl" will only frustrate us, make her irritating and unsympathetic, and the

CN(p) a selfish monster – this has actually been alleged against Proust in all seriousness. Needless to say that the critic who did so had fallen deep into the pit of the realistic illusion that Proust so forcefully undermines. What the character as analogue to humans loses in appeal, seen as a literary creation it gains in understanding of the art the author is experimenting with. Proust's masterpiece is much more fascinating when allowed to play with its paper people than when its characters are subjected to realist, moralist norms.

Proust's truly postmodern, and when it comes to his metaphor of photography in the series of snapshots, intermedial experiments with the paper status of characters, can be seen as a counterpoint to another narrative rhetoric of character-building. Characters can sometimes be understood through recognition of culturally current models. Here, not the experimental novelty but the predictability of characters and their features is the playground for the narrator. A Santa Claus who sets out to murder people is blatantly a fiction, or as the case may be, a fake. This possibility is used in Francis Ford Coppola's film *The Godfather* (1972), based on Mario Puzo's 1969 novel. The film begins with a peaceful Santa Claus scene in a shopping area, shattered by a murder. This scene sets the tone for numerous imitations so as to form a network of intertextual relations, if not an altogether new discourse. It is taken up in the television series *Picket Fences* (1992–6), for example, which borrows this fiction, and can serve as an acknowledgment of the way *The Godfather* made it a popular tradition.

This effect was brought about yet again, in a case of heterogeneous discourses à la Bakhtin. The action film *Turbulence* (1997) by Robert Butler makes this discursive mix the continuous line of the story. In this film at least three discourses are mixed: Christmas, with its ideology of peace and gift-giving; sophisticated, modern air transportation, including the fear of flying; and the terror stories of serial killers. Throughout this extremely terrifying film, Christmas decorations remind the viewer of this interdiscursive clash. The differences among these are not glossed over, but on the contrary, foregrounded in character presentation. When the killer confronts Carl, an African-American flight attendant wearing a Santa Claus hat (Gordy Owens), the clash enhances the artificiality of both. "Christmas" becomes a shifter where strings of meaning change gear.

In general, returning to the ancient texts about the mythical characters that have fed our culture's clichés and prejudices is exciting and valuable. It helps us both to understand how thick the historical layer is on which the present rests but in which it also penetrates; and to assess our dependence and reliance on patterns established in a culture quite different from our own. But the most adequate reading of narrative characters is to weight the experimental and the recognizable features against each other. This is necessary to gauge the text in its novelty while also understanding the common ground on which all semiosis stands. Without recognition, we wouldn't be able to understand what we read; without novelty, we wouldn't bother to read at all. And the mix is also an indication, again, that the technical and the social inevitably merge when we are confronted with narrative, fiction, and art. Character processing hovers between filling in and fleshing out.

Characters take concrete shape, so much so that we tend to experience them as living human beings, through the narratological means of repetition, accumulation, relations to other characters, and transformations. The tendency to structure the field of characters in binary opposition conforms to a widespread structure of thought; the very same one that underlies sexism, homophobia, racism, anti-Semitism, and anti-Islamism, and other ideological conceptions that constantly damage the fabric of social life. It is important to see how this is done in a story, because literature, visual art, and film are not above such ideological manipulations. But it is at least as important to keep a keen eye on how that structure functions to discredit or credit, blame, or praise, and thus create predictable categories of characters, so that we develop a readerly resistance to it. Manipulation of readers by means of character typecasting is one of the pernicious effects narrative can emanate.

The logic of opposition has it that negativity is by definition vague. It cannot be defined, hence, not articulated, and as a result it remains unmanageable; indeed, as "wild" as historiographer Hayden White (1978) has exposed it to be. He did this very effectively when he developed through this logic an analysis of the early modern fantasy of the "wild man." This concept indicates the inhabitants of wild nature outside of the control of the city. More specifically, he called the logic of negativity underlying this fantasy, using a term from logic, "ostentatious self-definition by negation." This may sound a bit like logic's jargon, but the words each speak for themselves. Ostentatious as in showing, with an edge of boasting: here, by pointing at one's "other," or opposite. White writes:

> They [the concepts] are treated neither as provisional designators, that is, hypotheses for directing further inquiry into specific areas of human experience, nor as fictions with limited heuristic utility for generating possible ways of conceiving the human world. They are, rather, complexes of symbols, the referents of which shift and change in response to the changing patterns of human behavior which they are meant to sustain. (154)

White's critical formulation of how concepts based on binary opposition are not treated, then, provides a good piece of advice regarding the scepticism necessary to work with this model without endorsing its drawbacks. And if we read between the lines, White's critique is in fact based on a concept of focalization. The negative view of the generic "wild man" constitutes the figures or people that are given that label as characters so strongly determined by the focalization of their "other" that the image bounces back onto the self.

Instead of demonstrating the structural method explained in the theory volume, I will here present a glimpse of novelistic fleshing out in the briefest of fragments. Once more I call on Flaubert's *Madame Bovary* – like Proust's *Recherche*, an unlimited source of examples of how literary texts probe and practise narratological categories. The moment is when Charles, called to repair the broken leg of the farmer Rouault, sees Emma, Rouault's daughter, for the first time; a view that will change the lives of both Charles and Emma. Please be mindful of categories discussed earlier – such as the tension between narration and description, for example.

> … while the maidservant tore sheets for bandages and Mademoiselle Emma tried to sew some pads. She was a long time finding her workbox, and her father showed his impatience. She made no reply; but as she sewed she kept pricking her fingers and raising them to her mouth to suck.
>
> Charles was surprised by the whiteness of her fingernails. They were almond-shaped, tapering, as polished and shining as Dieppe ivories. … Yet her hand was not beautiful, perhaps not white enough, and a little hard at the knuckles; besides, it was too long, with no soft inflections in the outlines. The finest thing about her were her eyes. They were brown, but seemed black under the long eyelashes; and she had an open gaze that met yours with fearless candour. (I, 2)

> [… mais, tout en cousant, elle se piquait les doigts, qu'elle portait ensuite à sa bouche pour le sucer.
>
> Charles fut surpris de la blancheur de ses ongles. Ils étaient brillants, fins du bout, plus nettoyés que les ivoires de Dieppe, et taillés en amande. Sa main pourtant n'était pas belle, point assez pâle, peut-être, et un peu sèche aux phalanges; elle était trop longue aussi et sans molles inflexions de lignes sur les contours. Ce qu'elle avait de beau, c'étaient les yeux: quoiqu'ils fussent bruns, ils semblaient noirs à cause des cils, et son regard arrivait franchement à vous avec une hardiesse.]

This description narrates how Emma, still Mlle Rouault and watched by the mesmerized country doctor Charles, is literally detailed and judged by the focalizer. The heterogeneity, here, is double: narration and description mingle and motivate each other, and the charmed would-be lover's vision – which I will further explain in the next section as focalization – is undercut by the ruthless "objectivity" of the faceless admirer. Objectivity is, of course, the last thing in his gaze. But objectification, the reduction of the woman seen to an object, is quite appropriate as a characterization of this act of focalization. Charles's surprise is an event; the whiteness of the nails is a state. White, offset against red blood; the black hair that completes the portrait of Snow White that inserts the perversion of fairy tales, is understood by implication. Emma's sucking her finger and later inserting her tongue into the small glass to finish the last drop of liqueur point to the extent of Charles's erotic oral fantasy. Brilliant, cut in almond shape, ivory: we see idealization a mile away.

But whose view is put forward in the "however" of "sa main, pourtant, n'était pas belle" (yet her hand was not beautiful)? Are we supposed to think that this man, in love and endowed with mediocre intelligence and little subtlety, is detailing and weighing what is and is not pretty about Emma? But then, in retrospect, would he be sophisticated enough to characterize the kind of ivory of the metaphoric network put in place around the nail? Suddenly, and typical of Flaubertian description, it all falls apart. Not only is Emma detailed to death by incoherence; so is the discourse that describes her. It is that very heterogeneity that fleshes the characters out – not only Emma, object of fascination, but also Charles riveted in the spectacle of her – a partial focalizer, fleshed out as such, more than as a character only. The focalization is double: Charles sees Emma, and the external narrator-focalizer details the focalization by the character in such a way that the incongruence of it becomes apparent.

Whoever says heterogeneity thinks of Bakhtin. For Bakhtin, the point is that the novel mixes discourses originating from all social strata. For Flaubert, once discourses show their messiness, there is no stopping the heterogeneity machine against which characters don't stand a chance. Emma can only die in the end, and even then, there is the blind beggar's song that destroys the moment of sublime suffering through the importation of an alien discourse. For the present enquiry into the way characters are fleshed out in the novel, it matters that this heterogeneity comprises both the story – in the always-present parody that denaturalizes the fabula – and discursive modes. Description is not only a narrative motor – as, for example, in the novels of Émile Zola – but also a narrativity machine run wild. Only narrative motivation can offer a semblance of containment, and it does so through the deployment of a multilayered form of deixis.

Let's look again at this relatively simple quotation. Charles *fut surpris*, had a surprise, hence, the poor man is bound hand and foot to the spectacle that follows, even if he cannot control it. The verb tense of the *passé simple* indicates a moment, brief as it may be, but that moment harbours an event. The primary framing suggests at first sight that the narrative embeds the description, which is part of the narrator's utterance: Charles watches, as a focalizer; Emma sucks, as an actor in the fabula, the description of her nails follows, where all three levels, embedded into one another, come together. The detail of the nail asks for the larger detail of the hand, presented in the generic singular that frame-freezes it.

But once both Charles and the external seeing reader have been sucked into the fabula by way of this stitching together of the two discourses, the master-minder of the perverse negativity – *pourtant* (however) – shows its hand and points out that the spectacle is staged for the deception of the male as a victim of fate. It is not pale enough; but by what standard? Too dry, too large. The devastating judgment "sans molles inflexions de lignes sur les contours" (without soft inflections of the lines over the contours) braids into the lover's gaze a discourse from beauty parlours, variété, and ladies' magazines, and their devastating normativity, against which Emma's mediocrity is offset. But once this devastation is achieved, we are confused yet again when the idealization reclaims the power to look. The beauty she did have – the description contradicts the critique – was in the eyes only, hence, the focalization. There is no comfort even in heterogeneity.

The enumeration of elements to form, shape, contrive a whole object, shipwrecks halfway and leaves the object in pieces. Instead of its wholeness, we have the fragile totality of Charles's paltry infatuation and a novelistic situation no more whole than poor Emma's body. This is not the mechanism through which anchoring is possible so that the object described exists within the narrative world and the description is a recapitulation or a reformulation of an element assumed to have prior existence. Instead, we have elements tied to other elements made to exist on different ontological planes. Flaubert's postmodernism avant-la-lettre will inspire Proust's, and Calvino will do his best to be at that level.

Through the triple contributions of aspectualization, modalization, and subjectivation, three modes of binding description and narrative make the former fundamentally deictic. As a result, even if we weep for Emma when she completes her gradual self-destruction, we are left with no figure except the one whose universe fails to sustain her. What we end up with is a mixture of style, world/self, and desire. Deixis versus reference: the fragment on Emma's hands displays, like a user's guide, the functions of description in relation to the act of reading the novel. It is no coincidence, then, that the master novelist is also a master ironist. Flaubert offers irony as a semantic-pragmatic theory of the novel. As a result, that emblem of readability that description appears to be solicits a decoding of latent meaning but also leads to an awareness of an inability to read. One of description's functions in reading as a cultural activity is the creation of the *character-effect*. Another one is temporalization, the slowdown discussed earlier. Here it is that rhythm is created, woven into the narrative. Deceleration, but not stopping, makes acceleration possible. Without description, no character and, more importantly, no way to read narrative; and vice versa. Characters are fleshed out on the cusp of the dialectic of description and narration.

4: Space

Space situates the characters and forms the backdrop or stage of the events. It can even inflect the events in such a way that they are unthinkable without the space as their stage. This becomes an issue in Proust's search for Albertine as the unknowable character. Later, when he is already firmly ensconced in his paranoid relationship with Albertine, the narrator describes in minute detail, how, at the beginning of the summer season, his searching eye seeks out the young girls who had so enraptured him before. The relationship is paranoid, because the descriptive exploration has demonstrated the impossibility of knowledge, hence, of the assurance as to her sexual preference he seeks. Now he does not need to distinguish the girl with whom he had so significantly but poignantly said to have decided to "have my novel." Yet distinction is still the object of the search. This time, space comes to the fore as an issue of similar magnitude. In the following fragment, the gaze, distant at the beginning of the sentence, moves closer towards the end:

> But I could not arrive at any certainty, for the face of these girls did not fill a constant space, did not present a constant form upon the beach, contracted, dilated, transformed as it was by my own expectancy, by the anxiousness of my desire, or by a sense of self-sufficient well-being, the different clothes they wore, the rapidity of their walk or their stillness. (II 867)

The issue of focalization this passage broaches will return shortly. The seeing subject transforms the incorrect grammatical form of a singular noun (face) accompanied by a plural predicate (these girls) into a zoom effect. In rhetoric this would be called metonymic. And it is a spatial trick. The combination is maintained right to the end of the sentence. It is partially neutralized by the increasingly rapid succession of nouns: clothes – in the plural – rapidity, stillness.

The search here is primarily photographic, recalling the characterization of Albertine as a series of snapshots. I contend that photography is selected as the mode of this search because it is ambiguously situated between producing and recording a slice of space, a space that fills a vision. Hence, it poses the problem of, precisely, distinction. Distinction is not only a spatial issue. It is also a temporal one. If only the model would pose for him, he would be able to fix the lens at the right distance – that is, at the distance necessary to hold the image still – and keep the focus sharp. Then he would be able to take a "photograph." This is then, implicitly, a self-reflective moment, specifically on intermediality in his writing, where depiction becomes a story, thanks to temporality.

Through photography, Proust challenges the humanistic assumptions inherent in realist literature. Indeed, photography confronts any simple idea of description as distinct from narration. With its glossy, shiny, flat surface, it is neither "profound" – it has no depth – nor stable; it resists any attempt to subordinate description to the service of the humanistic ideal of "dense" characters and "real" space. More strikingly perhaps, in a revisionist appreciation of description, Proust challenges the notion that a connection between appearance and person is possible at all, both in terms of visual bonding and of the flatness and fragmentation that vision also entails. It seems, then, that space in this fragment only serves as a framing device.

Nevertheless, space is indispensable to position the fabula "somewhere." So, other tricks can help to integrate space as an aspect of the story. In *Narratology* (126) I suggested that frequently, the rape of women is allegorically related to invasion and destruction of space. The more allegorical the fable, the more political becomes its moral. Here is an example or, rather, an abduction of the allegorical trope for a de-colonial feminist novel. Buchi Emecheta's *The Rape of Shavi* (1985 [1983]) tells of a future rape victim, the prospective queen of Shavi, who is sweeping the entrance of the guest/rapist's cabin as a sign of respect. In a typical misunderstanding of intercultural relations that remain unacknowledged by the perpetrator, this sign is mistaken for a sign of humble status, and taking the girl for a maid, the man feels free to take out his anger at his wife, who had left him, and rape this other woman, showing how inextricably intertwined are racism, classism, and sexual violence.

If Emecheta's fable ends unhappily, it is because misunderstanding –
that of the man towards the woman and that of the albino (the novel's
name for the white people the Shavians saw for the first time) towards
the African culture – is the basis of behaviour. This force of misunderstanding is possible as long as people – such as, here, the rapist – take
their preconceptions for the truth and decline to reconsider them. That
this is about space, both the natural space of the forest and cultural
space, where the meaning of the threshold is crucial, does not occur to
the raping man. The young woman sweeps the doorstep – the boundary between the man's space and the outside world – as an homage and
a welcome, but,

> Ronje fell on her and, in less than ten minutes, took from the future queen
> of Shavi what the whole of Shavi stood for. To him, the Shavians were
> savages and Ayoko was just a serving girl. Though she fought, cried and
> begged, her pleading was gibberish to him, her resistance enhanced the
> vengeance he was taking on Shona. (94)

The whites rape the space of Shavi, protected from the outside world
by the forest that is in turn a frame, just as Ronje rapes the princess.
The characters evolving within this frame and who inhabit this space are
both strange, clearly allegorical, and very much like real people. Noticing
both is essential for an interpretation that does justice to the literary and
political qualities of this novel, which, importantly, cannot be separated.

Regarding the function of objects in the representation of space, the
reader of the theoretical volume will remember the descriptive passage
from *Nightwood* (1936) in *Narratology* (32–6). It begun with – or better,
was framed by – the man looking into the room where a woman was
asleep – an eminently voyeuristic situation based on spatial divisions
between private and public space:

> On the second landing of the hotel … a door was standing open, exposing
> a red carpeted floor, and at the further end two narrow windows over-
> looked the square. (56)

The framing is primarily spatial. It is here that the man discovers the
woman he will marry. This frame overdetermines the connections between text – descriptive – story – where seeing, here, is the sole form
of focalization – and fabula – the imminent meeting of the two actors.
In the world that the narrative conjures up, a world of make-believe,
things can happen because that world is spatial. It gives space to events,
so that events can, as the phrase goes, take place.

The discovery of the woman and the special orientalist quality of his vision is overdetermined by objects:

> On a bed, surrounded by a confusion of potted plants, exotic palms and cut flowers, faintly oversung by the notes of unseen birds, … half flung off the support of the cushions from which, in a moment of threatened consciousness she had turned her head, lay the young woman, heavy and dishevelled. (56)

The objects – potted plants, exotic palms, and cut flowers – figure an embedded frame within the room with its red carpet that already framed the vision, and the bed is a third frame. Triply framed, this woman stands little chance of being seen as an autonomous subject. The space is her prison.

Sometimes, developments in new media help understand what is at stake in narrative structure. Spatial perception and the narratological issue of sequential ordering meet, for example, in the media practice called "Augmented Reality." Applications in this area use the mobile screens of smartphones and tablets to explore and experiment with the possibilities of location-aware technologies. They aim to develop new and specific ways to present archival material on site and in time. As media scholar Nanna Verhoeff (2016) formulates it, "This intersection of time and space in the use of locative media for archival dissemination is the subject of my inquiry here. These applications are called 'projects,' 'tours' or 'virtual museums.'"

In a commentary on the 2013 app The Cronovizor, developed by Romanian artist collective and media lab Colorbitor, Verhoeff writes:

> Strictly speaking, it is an application – a "layer" for one, even – but the somewhat archaic-futuristic sounding name suggests it is a viewing machine for looking into the past, for looking (-vizor) into, or even at, time (crono-). A view master for time-travel that allows the user to open up "time windows." The concept here is itself as relevant as the practicalities of the technology. Moreover, the metaphor of time windows is combined with the notion of the museum "gallery," as well as the tourist trope of visitors who walk around town. When we watch the video demo, these lively, but clearly old, on-screen images of archival footage inserted in – or stitched onto – the present-day street scenes surrounding the user of the "vizor," a viewfinder of sorts, indeed suggest a historical co-presence. (2016, 360)

And as she writes a bit later, "The Cronovizor plays with spatial continuity and temporal discontinuity" (361). The app allows us to be in the

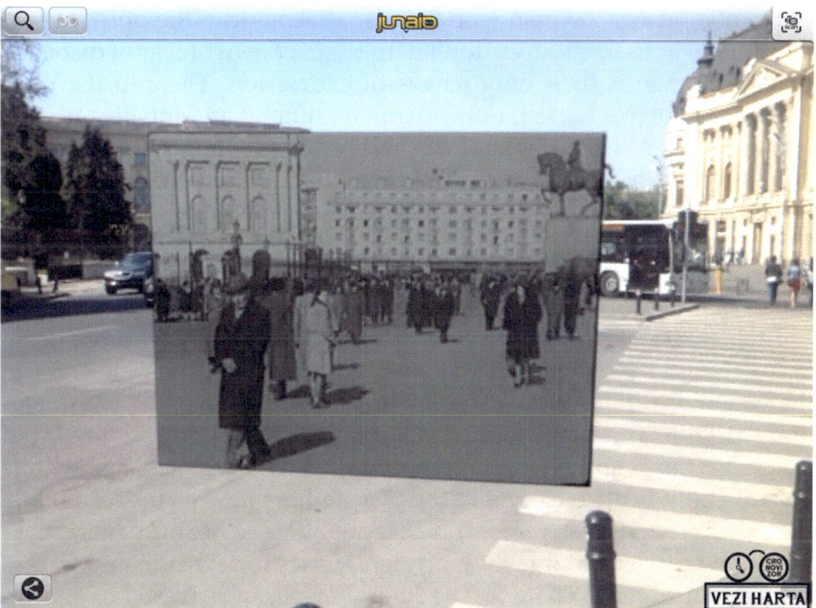

Figure 29. Cronovizor (augmented reality).

space – for example, on the main square of Bucharest – and see both the space today and, on the mobile phone, the same space as it was eighty years ago, including people who wander around in it (Figure 29).

This experience can be a model for the experience of reading a novel or watching a film that presents the paradox of being-in-space of a story in a different time. Once we get the hang of the use of such apps it becomes more understandable, even logical that space frames the events in a particular way, regardless of the moment in time when it takes place. Perception, then, this app suggests, can travel through time.

Two final examples of space and how it connects to other elements. The first one is the beginning of an award-winning documentary film by Thom Verheul, *Denial* (1992), about a young woman called Brigitte, thirty years old. Most of the beginning sequence has no spoken words, so I must describe it. In the first image you see a young girl from behind. She is walking on a deserted beach. She is looking down and is paddling a bit with her foot in the wet sand. Her back alone shows depression. She is presented by the filmic narrator as totally self-enclosed, out of reach, beyond help. A male voice-over begins to explain what is the matter with her. As the beach girl fades out, we see the authoritative but gentle face of the man who knows: an American therapist. He explains how abused children don't dare to speak, out of fear of disbelief. Body language is their only means of expression. Then, in the third image, the subject herself, now a woman, quietly and intelligently explains her case: "I was about fifteen and I wanted so much to die." Then you see her run on the beach. And then, in a different voice, she reads from a letter: "Yes, it is true that I have been raped. So what?" Signed: The Lady.

It is a documentary that shows the phenomenon of what is clinically called *multiple personality syndrome*: different personalities split off out of self-defence. The Lady is one such "alter": a tough yet well-brought-up lady, who is close to Brigitte's mother and tries to create some order in the chaos of Brigitte's life. The intelligent, impressive, beautiful, and brave Brigitte appears before us in her many diverse appearances, and each alter has a space. There is the compulsive house cleaner, who is bossed about by The Lady and must clean her apartment every single day; with a wet towel, please, no cheating. We see her only in the confining, overly neat bourgeois apartment. Space locks her in and frames her as subordinate. There is The Lady herself, who was conjured up when Brigitte was twelve, "to keep things a bit together." The Lady hates chaos, and Brigitte's life was in constant danger of becoming chaotic. The Lady sits on the stone wall in the cloister of Utrecht Cathedral. There is The Little One, who moves back and forth on a swing, her hands hidden in her sleeves "because I don't like hands; hands are dangerous," as she is in a good position to know; and she plays in the yard. The Silent Beach Girl walks the empty beach between sand and water because she doesn't like people.

The Tough One, boyish, in a leather jacket, who is like a coach for the group of alters, encourages the others to sustain the incredible effort to keep going. The Tough One appears in noisy bars, pool halls, and train stations; it's the only one who may travel. A whole team of specialists, all indispensable for that leaden burden: suffering sexual violence, and the timeless trauma that results. Each "alter" inhabits her own space. These spaces never connect. The stable relationship between space and alter is all this girl can boast as stability, but only for each of her. Ignoring that relationship would be a denial of how this film could be made into a narrative that we can process. Yet this processing is the viewer's task, bound to Brigitte's own processing that will ultimately cure her syndrome. This narrative form that binds space to character thus exposes to the viewer the social usefulness of narrativization.

Finally, an example from the most common genre of literary narrative: a realistic novel. When separate segments of narrative are devoted to the presentation of information about space alone, we have descriptions. The space is then not simply indicated in passing but is an explicit object of presentation. This is a structural tool to position and frame the characters and the events, and connect them all to constitute a story. The following passage from Charles Dickens' novel *Great Expectations* (2003 [1860]) helps us understand how this connecting works:

> I crossed the staircase landing, and entered the room she indicated. From that room, too, the daylight was completely excluded, and it had an airless smell that was oppressive. A fire had been lately kindled in the damp old-fashioned grate, and it was more disposed to go out than to burn up, and the reluctant smoke which hung in the room seemed colder than the clearer air – like our own marsh mist. Certain wintry branches of candles on the high chimney-piece faintly lighted the chamber; or, it would be more expressive to say, faintly troubled its darkness. It was spacious, and I dare say had once been handsome, but every discernible thing in it was covered with dust and mould, and dropping to pieces. The most prominent object was a long table with a tablecloth spread on it, as if a feast had been in preparation when the house and the clocks all stopped together. An epergne or centre-piece of some kind was in the middle of this cloth; it was so heavily overhung with cobwebs that its form was quite undistinguishable; and, as I looked along the yellow expanse out of which I remember its seeming to grow like a black fungus, I saw speckled-legged spiders with blotchy bodies running home to it, and running out from it, as if some circumstance of the greatest public importance had just transpired in the spider community. (103–4)

This description is linked to the perception of the character: its elaborateness is motivated by the fact that the character is entering this space for the first time. Consequently, the boy is curious and takes in every detail. At the same time, he evaluates what he sees; he judges, which is announced in the second sentence in words like "excluded" and "oppressive." These aspects of the description – the point of perception, the motivation, and the relation between perception and opinion – will become more relevant later in the novel.

By way of transition to the next section, I draw attention to verbs such as "I looked" and "I remember" and "I saw," as indication of character-focalization. The eerie atmosphere the piece emanates is entirely bound up with this feature, and what the boy will take away from this event of experiencing a space will stay with him throughout the novel. For the moment, the point to note is that in such a fragment, space is presented explicitly, as an almost independent element, indicated by the anthropomorphic-metaphoric ending of the fragment, introduced by "home." In addition to the strong subjective aspect of this description, I also note that it would not be easy to turn this fragment into a cinematic versioning. This is emphatically a medium-bound instance of the interaction between space and character.

In some realistic novels, descriptions of space are executed with great precision. In such cases, it is evidently considered important that the realistic aspects in such descriptions be clearly visible: the space must resemble, or at least be understandable and imaginable in terms of the actual world, so that the events situated within it also become plausible. Yet plausible is not the same as real, for literature is never entirely similar to the actual world. The elements that turn the spiders into anthropomorphic creatures, such as the final sentence, mediate, precisely, between fiction and our tendency to project reality onto it.

5: Focalization

The theory of narration, as it has been developed in the course of this century, offers various labels for the concept referred to here. In using the term focalization, I wish to dissociate myself from a number of current terms in this area. The most current one is point of view or (narrative) perspective. Terms such as narrative situation, narrative viewpoint, narrative manner are also employed. More or less elaborate typologies of narrative points of view have been developed. All these typologies are, however, unclear on one point. They do not make a distinction between, on the one hand, the vision through which the elements are presented and, on the other, the identity of the voice that is verbalizing that vision. To put it more simply: they do not make a distinction between those who see and those who speak. Yet this distinction is crucial for our understanding and appreciation of narrative.

True, intuitively we believe that the voices uttering the narrative sentences know what they are saying, according to their vision. Nevertheless, it is possible, both in fiction and in reality, for one person to express the vision of another. This is a key feature of language and it happens all the time.

When no distinction is made between these two different agents, it is difficult to describe adequately the technique of a text in which something is seen, and that vision is narrated. The imprecisions of such typologies can sometimes lead to absurd formulations or classifications that are too rough and ready. To claim, as has been done, that Strether in Henry James's *The Ambassadors* is "telling his own story," whereas the novel is written "in the third person," is as nonsensical as to claim that the sentence "Elizabeth saw him lie there, pale and lost in thought" is narrated, from the comma onwards, by the character Elizabeth; that would mean it is spoken by her. What this sentence does is to present Elizabeth's vision clearly: after all, she does see him lying down, whether or not she seeks to put this vision into words.

If we examine the current terms from this point of view (to use a problematic term), only the term *perspective* seems clear enough – almost. This label covers both the physical and the psychological points of perception. It does not cover the agent that is performing the action of narration, and it should not do so. Nevertheless, my own preference lies with the term focalization for two reasons. The first reason concerns tradition. Although the word "perspective" reflects adequately what is meant here, in the tradition of narrative theory it has come to indicate both the narrator and the vision. This ambiguity has affected the specific sense of the word. I also find its use in art history too different from the literary one, more specifically spatial-visual, to maintain it in a theory that can also be brought to bear on visual images but then not in that specific sense of "linear perspective."

There is yet another, more practical objection to this term. No noun can be derived from "perspective" that could indicate the subject of the action; nor is there a verb like "to perspectivize." In an agent-oriented theory such as this one, to describe the focalization in a story we must have terms from which subject and verb can be derived. These two arguments seemed to me to be weighty enough to justify my choice for a newer term for a concept that is not completely new. Focalization offers a number of additional, minor advantages as well. It is a term that looks technical. It is derived from photography and film; its technical nature is thus emphasized, even if the term is best abstracted from its specific visual slant. As any vision presented can have a strongly manipulative effect and is, consequently, very difficult to extract from the emotions, not only from those attributed to the focalizer and the character but also from those of the reader, a technical term will help us keep our attention on the technical side of such a means of manipulation. Technicality is just another tool, but a strategically useful one. It helps us to understand, not only follow our emotions. Considering patiently the different actions and agents involved helps in that attempt. For this reason, I now go briefly through the focalizer and its object, respectively.

Let me recall a few examples already discussed. When the inhabitants of Emecheta's allegorical country Shavi saw white people for the first time, they saw albinos: normal black people with a skin defect. In Mulisch's short story "What Happened to Sergeant Massuro?" (1977 [1972]) analysed in *Narratology* (72–8), we see with the eyes of the character who later also draws up a report of the events. The first symptoms of Massuro's strange disease are the phenomena the other man perceives. These phenomena communicate Massuro's condition to us; they tell us nothing about the way he feels about it. And in Barnes's *Nightwood* Felix so strongly focalizes that the woman he sees is triply framed, imprisoned in his vision without her knowing she is being seen at all, so as to be reduced to a status as object.

Finally, the sentence in *Madame Bovary* that sums up the no-exit situation of the couple's marriage demonstrates the difficulty, yet the necessity to assign focalization to different agents. This is a complex sentence, already discussed apropos of "Levels of Narration," which becomes even more complex when we consider focalization: "La conversation de Charles était plate comme un trottoir de rue, et les idées de tout le monde y défilaient … " (54) (Charles' conversation was flat as a sidewalk, a place of passages for the ideas of everyman). The sentence preceding this one attributes focalization to Emma. It is as if the passage of which this sentence is a part consists of Emma's musings about her disappointing marriage. Hence, this sentence, too, would logically render her view of her exasperatingly boring husband. The detailed vision, however, is more plausibly the external narrator's judgment, the direct object of its utterances, which we can now name "external focalizer," abbreviated as EF. While Emma could perhaps still be the agent who offers the metaphor of the sidewalk, the next part of the sentence can scarcely emerge from her mind. The reason is that, as the entire novel demonstrates, Emma is just as subject to cliché thinking as Charles or any other character in the novel. She would not be able to discern the platitude in terms of reiteration of the clichés surrounding the couple.

A special case of focalization and perhaps the best justification for the distinction I am making is *memory*. Memory is an act of vision, hence, a focalization of the past. But as an act, it is situated in the present of the event of memory. As is looking. It is most often sense-based: an image, a cinematic-like sequence, sounds, smells, all pertain to memory. But frequently, it is also a narrative act: elements come to cohere into a story, so that they can be remembered and possibly told. But as is well known, memories are untrustworthy, in relation to the "truth" of the fabula. And when put into words, they are elaborated. Only then can they connect to an audience: for example, a therapist, a judge, a political gathering. Hernández's metaphor of himself as a "*flâneur* of time" (quoted above) is a gripping evocation of memory. This points to a memory without a fabula, just focalization as such, as well as of the way visuality and time are connected to it. The sentence in the passage on how slowdown of the video camera does not lead to a still image further complicates this musing on memory and time. That passage can be seen as a theory of memory.

Hence, the story one remembers is never identical to the one experienced; the former is a focalization, the latter an event in the fabula retrospectively evoked. This discrepancy becomes dramatic and, indeed, incapacitating in the case of trauma. Traumatic events disrupt the capacity to comprehend and experience the events at the time of their occurrence. As a result, the traumatized person cannot remember them; instead, they recur in bits and pieces, in nightmares, and cannot be "worked through." The incapability that paralyses the traumatized person has been caused by some occurrence in the fabula, but must be situated on both story and text levels.

As a narratological figure, memory is also quite often the joint between time and space. Although these can never be separated, the bond between them can be given figuration – what Silverman called in the quote above, "perceptual form." Especially in stories set in former colonies, the memory evokes a past in which people were dislodged from their space by colonizers who occupied it, but also a past in which they did not yield. Going back – in retroversion – to the time in which the place was a different kind of space is a way of countering the effects of colonizing acts of focalization in the past. Mastering, looking from above, dividing up and controlling is an approach to space that ignores time as well as the density of its lived-in quality. The frequently used verb of *mapping* hints at that approach. In opposition to such ways of seeing space, providing a landscape with a history is a way of spatializing. But the reverse is also possible. Evocations of the horror of concentration camps add space to the memory to enhance the unliveable character of the memorized time. This idea of a historically meaningful, heavily political investment of space can help to interpret stories in which a narratological analysis reveals the intricate relationship between characters, time, and space.

Narrative is also an important element of the rhetoric of scholarship. The following case involves a term that is both an ordinary word – not metaphorical at all – and a concept deployed for cultural analysis. The example joins Emecheta's novel and the more general issue of rape as allegorical, as well as my argumentation for the choice of the term focalization. Since in this case the texts stem from an ancient culture – therefore, different from our own – the authors were careful not to project anachronistically contemporary norms onto the past. The issue is the questions of whether in the ancient Middle East something like "just war" was thinkable and whether rape could be an acceptable practice therein.

The author, biblical scholar Susan Niditch (1993), struggled with the difficulty that ethical norms differ according to time and place, and the language in which we write about other cultures is also time-and-place bound. In that context she raised the question whether "just war" – in the biblical framework, "holy war" – is possible and, if so, whether in such a war the practice we call rape can have a place. With this question as her stake, she wrote about the biblical book of Numbers:

> Of course, enslaving the enemy (20:11) and forcing its women into marriage are the terms of an oppressive regime and difficult to imagine under the heading of that which is just. (69)

What concerns me in the sentence is that, in the attempt to avoid anachronism, something is nevertheless carried over, a description of rape – equally anachronistic, by the way. The author wished to avoid that term because of its anachronism, and the concessive clause in which the description "oppressive regime" occurred was meant to help that avoidance. "Forcing its women into marriage" is Niditch's attempt to avoid the anachronism. She doesn't want to call the action rape, she argues, because, in the culture under discussion, it was not perceived as such. Even if the war cannot be called just, the taking of women is culturally acceptable, and therefore cannot be called rape. This is undeniably a sound argument. Except for one aspect.

Niditch replaces "rape" with "forcing into marriage"; elsewhere, the action is called wife stealing. As a cultural phenomenon, in some cultures it is acceptable and ordinary, and is known in anthropological and historical studies. I see Niditch's point that "rape" is an obscuring term that fails to address the cultural status of the event. Also, it seems pointless to accuse the biblical culture, three thousand years after the fact, of a violation of human rights and thus feel better about our own behaviour. Yet, the alternative is unacceptable to me. Rather, in the awareness and acknowledgment that the term is "ours" – and leads to a lot of disagreement in the culture I live in – I would like to take a closer look at the contested term "rape."

That word is more often used as a noun than as a verb – which is my first worry. Like "secret" in my earlier example, it is one of those nouns that imply a story. Rape – the action for which we use that term: sexually appropriating another subject without her or (as also happens) his consent – has different meanings in different times and cultures. Its meaning depends on the status of, in particular, women in relation to men, and the status of the individual subject in relation to the community and its juridical organization. It is thinkable that the action concerned is interpreted as rape by one part of the culture at stake, and not at all by another part. Cultures that differ from "ours" tend to look more homogeneous and more coherent at a distance than they probably are. That deceptive vision is, precisely, the basis of ethnocentrism.

A recent experience of realizing the importance of focalization made me wish to foreground this concept even more. Watching the five instalments of artist and filmmaker Steve McQueen's series of films for television (2020) hit me with this awareness all over again. The five films of considerable length, made for Amazon Prime, titled *Small Axe*, are set in 1980s Britain, but alas, pertain to the whole (mostly "Western") world and all times since then, and especially, with the current renewed need for the Black Lives Matter movement. A catchphrase for McQueen's brilliant films, the one aspect that binds them together, is the consistent focalization through Black people. It denaturalizes the common "look" at the world through the eyes of white people. Here, white viewers will feel alienated from that commonplace look and will be drawn to borrow that merciless black gaze.

Focalization plays its part in such constructions more forcefully than we tend to assume. To see how it does, therefore, I borrow a photographic or cinematic look. I assume that within each community, large or small, ancient or recent, far or close, differences increase as one's vision approaches. Rape implies an event, if not an entire story with a number of episodes. Forging a noun out of a verb – nominalization – makes the concept analysable, discussable. That is a gain. There is also a loss. What gets lost from sight is the active nature of the event, the narrative of action including the subjectivities of the agents involved. When the subject of action disappears, so does the responsibility for the action – with responsibility having a culture-specific meaning according to the status of the individual in it. Instead, the entire narrative remains an implication, skipped as it were, in the abbreviation that is the noun. The subject who uses the word is, say, the story's narrator. The subject whose vision is implied in the word is its focalizer. Then there are the actors. The process in which all these figures interact, the fabula, is dynamic: it brings about change. All this is lost when a noun is used instead of a verb that would necessitate the naming of these subjects. Please note that this argument is the same as the one I advanced for my choice of the term focalization.

These aspects can be brought back into view by a dynamizing analysis of the noun that takes it as a narrative. The narratological perspective of the term "rape" requires that we appoint a narrator. The subject of the action, the rapist, needs to be mentioned. Then, there is the subject to whose body the action is done, in whom it brings about change. Reflection on the nature and the extent of that change warrants an amount of attention not triggered by the noun. Then, this is the meaningful question: Who is the focalizer? Is it the rapist, who would be likely to refer to his action differently, or the raped one, the victim who experiences the action? Or is it the narrator, and if so, does this agent identify with either one of these two positions?

The noun doesn't tell, and I don't want to answer the question in any general way. The point is in raising it. The realization of this narrative duplicity seems more productive than the unreflected choice of one of the possible answers. That, though, is what Niditch does by adopting a description she considers more fitting for the ancient culture. She does this with the laudable intention to shed ethnocentrism. This is, however, a gesture of cultural relativism. That relativism is, in fact, condescending. For if we take other cultures as seriously as our own, then the phenomenon in question deserves at least recognition as an event with "a difference within," an internal divisiveness which the quick narratological analysis already clearly indicates.

The item replaced and displaced, obscured, is a story with several agents, a variability of interpretation, and a difference of experience. What is sex, or theft, or lawful appropriation for the one may still be a violation of subjective integrity for another. This plurality of focalization needs to be acknowledged, whether the act is culturally accepted or not. But who, then, is the culture? Such an analysis and recognition of the narratives and the subjective meanings they entail do, minimally, disturb the academic as well as the social dilemma between ethnocentrism and relativism as a binary opposition. And while at least acknowledging, not repressing the inevitable anachronism of cultural analysis, they also enable a comparative, inter-historical perspective on present-day occurrences of rape in, and as, war – including within the same region.

The complexities of narrative depend for their understanding and appreciation on the readers' capability to sense whose vision it is we are being presented with. This is why the distinction between levels of focalization is the tool by excellence to generate the literary or cinematic experience of narratives. The point of discerning those is to sensitize ourselves to – to get visual expertise, or get "literate" in – the subtleties of the space between individual and collective experiences, visions, and memories. In Bibliowicz's novel *Migas de pan* it is, of course, crucial to distinguish the son Samuel's anguished reflections about his father, sequestered in the present, from those transmitted to him by secondary memorization or "postmemory," through the stories told or withheld by Josué when Samuel was growing up in a house transformed into a museum. But such subtle transitions are not the preserve of the postmodern novel. The classical realist novel of the second half of the nineteenth century also excelled in the creation of such complex structures.

4

Transition: Media in Dialogue

1: Preliminary Remarks

As I suggested with the examples of films and other visual images discussed so far, there is no reason to limit narratological analysis to linguistic texts only. The narrativity of films is obvious, even though the manner in which best to analyse their specifically narrative aspects is not, or not always, so immediately clear. Film narratology is a rich and diverse field, to which many studies are devoted. In art history, however, narratology is not very popular. This is understandable, as art-historical interpretation has often relied on the narratives that the image allegedly "illustrates," thus subordinating visual to literary narrative. In old-master art, the genre of history painting is considered narrative because it invokes well-known stories from ancient history or mythology. Recognition is the basic skill in the interpretation of such paintings, and iconography the method. I have argued that this method, indispensable as it is, when applied too fast or too easily tends to encourage the leap from what we see to what we know, or think we know, skipping or speeding up the act of looking.

The primary reason why, in this transitional part, I focus especially on the visual, is that our current societies are so replete with images, from advertisement, publicity, propaganda, to "the news" on television, internet fora, but also internet art and museal display. Images are everywhere, and thus they have a great social-political impact. This establishes continuity with the first transition part of this book. Looking a bit more closely at the bond between narrativity and images does not only enrich our understanding of narrative, how it works, and what it can do, but also, mutually, our understanding and appreciation of visual images; hence, our "visual literacy," in other words, our skills in engaging with visual practices, with images as seriously and profoundly as with literature.

Although focalization is not by definition vision-based, it seems the obvious place to begin easing in some elements of a visual narratology that can be extended into a sense-based one. What has been said about any narrative holds for images as well: the concept of focalization refers to the story presented from a specific angle, with or without anchoring it in a figure presented in the image, and the concept of narrator to its (material) arrangement. Focalization acts as the steering wheel or magnifying glass on the events or fabula. Although its basis in the notion of perspective seems to make its transposition to the realm of the visual seem simple, such a transposition is not unproblematic.

I would like to suggest the idea of visual stories by citing not the innumerable readings of classical paintings as "word-for-word" translations of well-known biblical and historical narratives in the tradition of a flat application of iconography, but a case of the reverse relationship. In a wonderful book of short stories called *Silence Please!* (Neri 1996) eleven authors have published widely divergent narratives. These texts only have in common their inspiration in the visual work of the Spanish artist Juan Muñoz (1953–2001). The collection is the more significant as Muñoz's work is known as anti-narrative; by reputation, he is considered, rather, a poet of space. His installations of architectural structures, within which sculpted figures are grouped in such a way that they do not communicate with one another, invariably entices critics to call his work silent. The stories in the volume do not describe his work – which would be the converse of illustration. Nor do they talk about it or adopt the themes of it. Instead, they create stories that somehow emanate the same visual qualities as Muñoz's works: isolation, finesse, what the editors call " staged contingencies" (7); episodes in which "the sculpture is implicated" (8).

This is just one of innumerable examples of the inextricable integration of literary narratives invented from within a visual experience. In what follows I will argue, through a variety of cases, how this kind of integration is culturally powerful and cannot be reduced to theoretical models, however useful and productive those are for analysis. But my goal is to show how an analysis, on the condition that it stays in dialogue with the object, can help get a more adequate grip on the subtleties of the object; indeed, in order to learn *from* it, not *about* it.

2: Novel and Film, a Two-Way Street

As an entrance into the question of a truly visual story and its relation to what art historians call iconography, the following can be made most directly relevant for comparative analysis of novels and films based on these. Again, this is not a matter of "illustration" nor of "faithfulness." Translation, or as it is commonly called, adaptation of a novel into film, is not a one-to-one transposition of story elements into images but is a visual working through of the novel's most important aspects and their meanings. Focalization is primary among those, as the specification of characters, spaces, and times it produces. For instance, if a novel addresses political issues in a powerful way, the film, through totally different means, without following the visual indications offered in the novel, may still address the same issues with comparable power. This is especially relevant as well as challenging if a historical novel is updated, with its political charge, to a contemporary world. Examining if this is done successfully requires, on the part of the critic, a narratological analysis as well as an engagement with film as a visual medium.

The following offers a reflection on the relations between narratology and iconography, in view of that challenge. Through it, I hope to suggest ways to articulate criticism in this domain without endorsing the hierarchical subordination of visuality to language that has pestered the study of art. Why did I, and many critics, consider Steven Spielberg's film *The Color Purple* (1985) ideologically and artistically problematic, in spite of its obvious attractions to a large audience? I contend that this was so because the movie failed to present with the required subtlety, the iconographic basis of the confrontational ideological position that Walker's novel proposed as well as the narrative sources used to articulate that position. Ignoring iconography, it ignored the novel's embeddedness in, and response to, a cultural tradition that is deeply narrative.

Alice Walker's bestselling novel *The Color Purple* (1982) refers directly to the double tradition of abolitionist and of self-assertive literature, such as Harriet Beecher Stowe's *Uncle Tom's Cabin* and the tradition of slave narratives. For example, when *Color* addresses the problem of education it evokes both slave-narratives and *Tom*:

> "Why can't Tashi come to school?" she asked me. When I told her the Olinka don't believe in educating girls she said, quick as a flash, "They're like white people at home who don't want colored people to learn." (162)

The theme of learning is presented in *Tom* as well as in autobiographical slave narratives. Frederick Douglass acutely discusses it in his autobiography, and the very existence of the slave narrative as the exemplary genre of persuasive texts points to the function of writing and reading for emancipation. And today, with the Black Lives Matter movement unfortunately re-becoming urgent, in Steve McQueen's brilliant film *Education,* one of his five-part 2020 BBC series *Small Axe,* the issue comes up again as shamefully alive and kicking.

But while *Color* refers directly to *Tom* and indirectly to slave narratives, it does not merely repeat: it puts *Tom*'s religiosity in its historical place by juxtaposing it to elements of Black religious culture. And in so far as the characters in *Color* repeat the characters of *Tom,* they are critically feminist rewritings of them. The character Celie is a female Tom ("I ain't never struck a living thing," 43). Her attempt to spare her little sister Nettie from rape by their father by offering herself to him is her version of Tom's Christlike self-sacrifice. Nettie is the female George who lifts herself up from humiliation, and like him she travels to Africa. The almost lifelong separations between Celie and Nettie and between Celie and her children recall the plot around George, Eliza, and Eliza's mother and sister, reunited as in the comedy-based romance. And Celie's husband has much of Legree, Tom's cruel master, including the flicker of hope for conversion towards the end. Sophia with her strength and her sense of humour as a weapon incarnates the insubordinate Cassie, the proud slave who manages to save herself with Tom's help. All this is not a matter of visuality but of intertextuality.

But the allusions to *Tom* and to all that novel stood for, are subtler and more complex than just the cast of characters indicates. The language, events, and conversations all respond to the choices made by Beecher Stowe and show the limits of Stowe's choices as well as open up more radical possibilities. The novel is effective because it balances and intertwines critically the discourse of modern popular culture, the context of the double oppression of black women, and the antecedent of the particularly effective sentimental social novel. How can that critical engagement be visualized in a film? This was Spielberg's challenge.

We can now see that Spielberg's film simplifies and alters all these connections. Because of this, as a visual versioning of Walker's novel the film arguably yields to both racist and sexist tendencies, as the representation of the character of Sophia alone demonstrates. The film provides visual instances of those generic conventions of the social novel that relate the genre to sentimentality. Thus, on the level of external focalization, it visualizes sentimentality in bright colours, counter-light, soft focus, and picturesque settings. Those characteristics of the social novel which Walker uses polemically to represent critically the relationship between sexism and slavery are stripped of their critical content. They are merely repeated, endorsed without any subtlety, sense of humour, or critical perspective; most important, they are repeated without resonance with the other texts.

Those who reject the idea of a visual narratology could be led to argue that the audiovisual medium of film – and the popular style of Spielberg's film – made it impossible to work in Walker's critical allusions. In the framework of a visual narratology, I don't believe this is the case. McQueen's television series contradicts such a view, which is condescending towards "popular culture." Ignoring what made the novel critical resulted in the film being uncritical. The film now comes to support problematic ideological positions. Two examples will illustrate how Walker's attempt to connect racism and sexism is turned, in the film's visualization, into the very racism and sexism her novel critiqued through focalization.

If taken as a twentieth-century documentary view, Walker's representation of Africa is rather naive; what made it effective was not its realistic adequacy, which it did not have nor did it pursue, but its relationship with the combative pre-text, *Uncle Tom's Cabin*. Stripped of this relationship, it is open to imperialist recuperation. With Spielberg, Africa comes to stand under an enormous orange sun; thus, visually represented, it is insistently focalized as unreal. Reduced to a postcard, Africa cannot fulfil the function of object of melancholic longing as well as utopian desire that it has in Walker's novel through its intricate relationship with *Uncle Tom's Cabin*. The slave narratives and the critical response to contemporary taste that replaced realism in Walker's novel disappear from sight. We are left with kitsch, which, under Spielberg's benevolent and competent direction, easily picks up a connotation of Black folklore as seen through white stereotyping.

The presentation of Black sexism without the reference to slavery allows the distanciation that results in the too eagerly adopted view that Black people are more sexist than whites. The father-daughter rape that informed the novel from the start is hardly present in the film, and neither is the alternative the novel proposed: the erotic friendship between Celie and Shug, the wife and the mistress. That these themes have been sacrificed to reach a larger audience may be understandable, even if I don't think larger audiences are by definition intolerant. But these gender relations form the background for other elements that become overemphasized in the film. For example, the figure of Sophia, who recasts Beecher-Stowe's Cassie, Tom's more belligerent female alter ego, has changed dramatically between the novel and the film – and not for the better.

Without the intertextual relationship to *Tom* on the one hand, and the contemporary context of the questioning of gender relations on the other, Sophia's insubordination is an easy target for cheap comical visual effects. Spielberg introduces her as a gigantic woman, an overwhelming mother figure who is dragging her husband-to-be along through the fields like a child, when the latter is supposed to introduce his fiancée to his father. The scene is focalized from afar and from above and accelerated, all devices for comical effect. Thereby, allusion to Charlie Chaplin and silent comedy film overrules the allusion to Cassie and thus to *Uncle Tom's Cabin* as a whole. Spielberg's Sophia is irreversibly ridiculous from the start, and so are, then, her insubordination, her husband, and her revolt. Visual effect is used to neutralize the critical potential of the novel. Seen in this way, the film can be criticized on its own terms as a visual artefact while its flaws can be illuminated through comparison with its narrative pre-text. Yet this comparison respects the specificity of each medium.

So far this comparison is between a film and its precedent novel. The point of comparing novel and film, then, is not to make aesthetic assessments of "faithfulness" to the source text. Rather, taking novel and film as equally embedded in the culture in which they function, the comparison can help to articulate what they each, through their own narratological make-up, have to say to their audiences. Their relationship is an intertextual as well as an interdiscursive one. The question of the image in movement is that it is a priori visual, while the audio is essential. In cinema, the orientation of the takes, such as the filming from above, from a distance versus the close-up; the movement filmed either from afar or from within the group of moving figures; and similarly, the sound recording and editing that makes whispers understandable and group murmurs not: it all pertains to what film as a medium can handle in order to narrate.

Conversely, verbal narrative can deploy such cinematic devices, even when the idea of cinema did not yet exist at the time of writing. This question can be addressed by the examination of some features generally attributed to Flaubert's *Madame Bovary*: its visuality, noticeable in the predominance of description and its narratively arbitrary appearances; the sparing use of dialogue and the author's avowed aversion to that mode of direct discourse; and the replacement of dialogue by not only narration but also that ambiguous mode, free indirect discourse (FID). This mode con-fuses the categories of "Who speaks?" with that of "Who perceives?"; in other words, voice with focalization, the orientation and subjectivity of perception. Focalization includes not only seeing but also hearing. Because it facilitates a multiplication of subjectivities, FID fosters an identification between the protagonist and the storyteller or "imager."

These modes tend to narrate through moving images, allowing a dynamic between the proclaimed objectivity and a fundamental subjectivity – solidarity with the latter by means of the former. This subjectivity is not only the character's but, more complexly, that of the meeting of character and reader-viewer, a meeting staged by the focalizer. This has consequences that, for me, pertain to the political. I am not making a case for a feminist Flaubert, to revert to that example; nor for the author as socially committed. Whether he was the "idiot of the family" Sartre called him or the sympathizing but apocryphal "Madame Bovary, c'est moi" does not concern me. Any projection of intention onto the author would obscure or even prohibit anachronism, a mode I find indispensable in making sense of the artistic heritage of the past by throwing into relief its actuality.

When so many filmmakers have tried their hand at Flaubert's novel, it seems relevant to briefly indicate the importance of attention to visuality, especially in focalization, as a motor of narrative. Whereas the nineteenth-century novel can be characterized by an increasingly elaborate appeal to visual display and hence, by the deployment of complex structures of focalization – Flaubert is a striking example, but Zola no less – modernist literature is particularly visual. The passage quoted from Virginia Woolf's *The Waves* in *Narratology* (98) is a good case. The description of Robin when Felix first sees her, in *Nightwood*, already recalled several times, insists on the visuality by means of the comparison with paintings by the Douanier Rousseau. Modernism's interest in questions of knowledgeability or epistemology lends itself to an exploration of vision. In the *Nightwood* passage, the focalizer embodies the embedded focalizer, whose movement is crucial for the description of the still, sleeping woman, to work as a way of gaining a knowledge that is strictly one sided.

Finally, here is an example where many of the issues and concepts of the story-level come together in a convincing case of a visual story. At the occasion of the 2007 film *Atonement* made after Ian McEwan's novel, the question was raised in the press why so many of this author's novels ended up in cinematic form. The answer is easy to give as soon as one opens a novel by this author, such as, for example, *Enduring Love* (1997), a novel about a stalker and the ending of a relationship. This was also turned into a film (2004). The qualifier "enduring" clearly produces a double meaning, referring to the temporal qualifier of duration and to the progressive form of the verb "to endure" as "to suffer," referring to a focalizing qualification. "Love" is durable, and it can be suffered. With reference to the romantic tradition of idealized love, the title warns us of the downside of this conception of relationships.

On all levels – text, story, and fabula – the novel begins with an accident: a balloon is adrift and a rescuer falls to his death, seen by others. The opening paragraph of *Enduring Love* runs as follows:

The beginning is simple to mark. We were in sunlight under a turkey oak, partly protected from a strong, gusty wind. I was kneeling on the grass with a corkscrew in my hand, and Clarissa was passing me the bottle – a 1987 Daumas Gassac. This was the moment, this was the pinprick on the time map: I was stretching my hand. And as the cool neck and the black foil touched my palm, we heard a man's shout. We turned to look across the field and saw the danger. Next thing, I was running towards it. The transformation was absolute: I don't recall dropping the corkscrew, or getting to my feet, or making a decision, or hearing the caution Clarissa called after me. What idiocy, to be racing into this story and its labyrinths, sprinting away from our happiness among the fresh spring grasses and the oak. There was the shout again, and a child's cry, enfeebled by the wind that roared in the tall trees along the hedgerows. I ran faster. And there, suddenly, from different points around the field, four other men were converging on the scene, running like me.

On all levels, also, the novel is concerned with visuality as the motor of storytelling. While there is only one narrator uttering this sentence, it is easy to imagine the scene, the backdrop, and the cast of characters. The CN-Joe is, it seems, writing the film script already. The first sentence is a temporal indication, stipulating that the story is to begin. This is a metanarrative commentary on the narrative about to unfold. Then follows a starkly visual description, where light and the visual consequences of wind accompany a zoomed-in scene of two people about to begin a picnic. It is the description of a situation waiting to be interrupted. As indeed happens with the next sentence – "This was the moment, this was the pinprick on the time map" – that, again metanarratively, appears to position the story in time. Yet, it does nothing of the sort, not in real time that is; only qua temporal interruption of a situation that itself is only the product of descriptive discourse. If only for this reason already, the narrative is a fiction.

Verb forms do their temporal work. "We were" initiates a descriptive passage; "I was kneeling" and Clarissa "was passing" slow down the actions, ordinary as they would normally be. The description zooms in on the date and name of the wine, indicating a memory trace of great detail that suggests another kind of temporal stop, that of a traumatic event. "I was stretching" and the description of physical sensations continue this work of rhythmic change. The first event is one of perception, a focalization: "we heard a man's shout." Follows a verb of action – "running" – and another metanarrative commentary that further qualifies the story that follows as labyrinth.

With "The transformation was absolute" the narrator insists on the nature of the event and its decisive importance. Events take over from focalization, before embedding focalization in themselves. The negative formulations, "I don't recall dropping the corkscrew, or getting to my feet, or making a decision, or hearing the caution," tell both the actions undertaken and the repression of these in memory, as well as the acceleration of rhythm. The interruption of the peaceful, pastoral scene suggests a cinematic shot/reverse shot: "We turned to look across the field and saw the danger." The spectator sees the two figures, sees them turn, then sees what they see: the definite article that accompanies the sight suggests that danger is already determined as the one that will set this story in motion.

The acoustic environment is eminently suitable for cinematic translation. For example, "a child's cry, enfeebled by the wind" places audio focalization at a distance. The second paragraph continues this cinematic mode of storytelling: "I see us from three hundred feet up, through the eyes of the buzzard we had watched earlier, soaring, circling and dipping in the tumult of currents: five men running silently towards the centre of a hundred-acre field."

The image is all there. The reference to an earlier act of focalization – seeing the buzzard – also serves as a metaphor of danger. Solidarity with the child in the balloon and yet positioning embedded focalization ("I see us … through the eyes") introduces retroversion and psychological distance. A distance that also splits the CN from the CF and the actor, for Joe is telling this, seeing it but with the eyes of another creature, and he is one of the men running. Also, "silently" indicates the effect of distance and its cinematic nature. And so it continues. As the description was waiting to be interrupted, so this novel was waiting to be put into film. The story of this novel is not a film script but it is such a strongly visual and sensory vision of the events that the film director must have been unable to resist it.

3: Making and Thinking Images in Text

Conversely to the transformation of novels into films, the literary features that can be seen to trigger the desire for that transformation can also be noticed in relation not to cinema but to photography and painting. This question of "how to know," which is a question of epistemology, is the particular tenet of Proust's many musings about getting to meet, to (not) know, and get rid of Albertine. The following passage from Proust's *A la recherche* (1954 [1913]) blends this concern with vision with a foregrounding of focalization as a subjectivizing technique.

The passage demonstrates that the question "Who sees" is dramatically made meaningful by the complementary questions, "Who is being seen?," "Who is not seeing?," and "What kind of act of seeing is at stake?" The intermedial dialogue here concerns photography rather than cinema. Entering the room without announcing his presence, the narrator tells us, "I was there, or rather I was not yet there since she was not aware of my presence, and [...] she was absorbed in thoughts which she never allowed to be seen by me" (2.141).

The protagonist, a CN, is paying an unexpected visit to his grandmother, who, unbeknownst to him, is near her death. This is a critical examination of visual focalization. It is also a good example of what Kaja Silverman (1996) called "heteropathic identification" – identification based on going outside of the self, as opposed to idiopathic or "cannibalistic" identification, which absorbs and naturalizes the other within the self. Heteropathic identification is associated with a risk of alienation, but enables the subject to identify beyond the normative models prescribed by the cultural screen, and is thereby socially productive. This identification never stops appealing to the Proustian narrator-protagonist, even while it exposes him to obvious risks.

The narrator-protagonist is examining his own status as witness, the specific kind of focalization in which he is involved:

> Of myself – thanks to that privilege which does not last but which gives one, during the brief moment of return, the faculty of being suddenly the spectator of one's own absence – there was present only the witness, the observer, in travelling coat and hat, the stranger who does not belong to the house, the photographer who has called to take a photograph of places which one will never see again. The process that automatically occurred in my eyes when I caught sight of my grandmother was indeed a photograph. (2.141)

The voyeur is constantly in danger, since alienation robs him of his self when he is not interacting with the other. But if he talks about himself in the third person, it is to focalize himself as well as, through his gaze, the embedded view of his grandmother. The latter is not mentioned in this fragment. What is clearly at stake, here, is the outsider's vision, to which only an object such as a photograph can come close.

Proust's use of photography to articulate this theory of vision makes this passage an appropriate allegory for the relation between modernism, vision, and narrative focalization. The contemplation of the spectacle afforded by the other is a photographic act. Even the temporal brevity of the shutter's closing is invoked through "the brief moment" and "suddenly." The estrangement is foregrounded in the ascending series of "witness," "observer," whose entrance from the outside is clothed in his cloths, in "in travelling coat and hat," to "stranger," qualified by his un-belonging, up to the most alienated figure, the photographer. For a brief instant, the looking I/eye wavers between the disembodied retinal gaze of linear perspective and the colonizing mastery it affords, on the one hand, and on the other hand, the heteropathic identification that takes him out of himself with body and soul to become other. He becomes a spectre – both spectacle and phantom refer to "lost time." It is exactly what the subject inevitably is himself.

The passage gradually develops a more hostile, almost violent language, leading at the end of this worrying amplification to the description of the mental photograph that will always be with the narrator: "I saw, sitting on the sofa, beneath the lamp, red-faced, heavy and vulgar, sick, vacant, letting her slightly crazed eyes wander over a book, a dejected old woman whom I did not know" (2.143). The "truth" of photography is this stranger, this unknowable person, cut off from the familial, affective gaze by photography. Thus, Proust's story is a sharp analysis of the very focalization it deploys. However, the theory of this itself takes a visual, photographic form; this turns the literary writer into a visual philosopher. But precisely for that reason, he is unable to limit his vision to the medium of the still image. In the middle of the passage on the mental photograph of the grandmother we find this strange comparison, which both explains the photographic effect, extending it to the cinematic, and embodies it:

> But if, instead of our eyes, it should happen to be a purely physical object, a photographic plate, that has watched the action, then what we see, in the courtyard of the Institute, for example instead of the dignified emergence of an Academician who is trying to hail a cab, will be his tottering steps, his precautions to avoid falling on his back, the parabola of his fall, as though he were drunk or the ground covered in ice. (2.142)

The comparison mercilessly dramatizes what remains of the puppet that is the other, divested of the protection of perceptual and affective routine. The wondering at the photographic look also historicizes this particular act of focalization. What better caution could we hope to find, in one of literature's richest and most visual narratives, to underscore the relevance of a disabused, politically alert analysis of focalization?

The dynamics of focalization is at play in every visual text that contains traces of representational work, as seen and interpreted by the viewer, since it is precisely in those traces that the text becomes narrativized. In principle all texts contain such traces, but some display them more openly than others. Also, the traces do not always betray without the shadow of a doubt what it is precisely that they are the traces of. But traces are signs, or remnants, of something that came before, as the footprint tells of the person who was there; a much-used ploy in detective fiction, especially in films. Hence, the trace itself already carries narrativity. But it becomes truly fascinating when we notice, as above in Proust's comparison, that the intermedial dialogue is not only present in the resulting text or image, but is even theorized by the narrator.

4: Image Making and Thinking in Images

As a counterpart to the Proust example that made a live situation still, I want to add one more instance of a visual still image that, through narrativity, becomes a moving one, while technically it is simply a still image – a painting. That narrativity is not dependent on the pre-text, the ancient story the image is allegedly illustrating (the Biblical one of 2 Samuel 2–5), but is created by a visual artist who deploys, strictly visually, not only a narrative thrust but also, or including, a theory of narrative. This is a painting about which I have extensively written before, so I will keep the analysis here short. It is also an interesting case of an almost empirical analysis, in the sense that I have several times asked people in the museum questions about my questions and invariably got confirmation of what I saw.

Focalization is my central concept for reasons that have hopefully become clear. It is the most fitting mediator between narrative layers, but also between art and society, as well as between media. It is an act, performed by a subject or agent. It is an act performed in the present tense, even if it is embedded in a retrospective story. The great advantage of that present tense is that in the present you can still change your attitude, view, or prejudice. In the past you cannot. Therefore, if a whole story is written in the past tense you forget that the readers and viewers who borrow the focalization of the text are actually in this moment, capable of changing their opinion. This makes focalization a tool for manipulation but also for persuasion. However, focalization is also multiple.

The present consists of *multiple* focalizations. In Rembrandt's *Bathsheba at Her Bath* (Figure 30) we see that the woman figure crosses her legs. Now, try to do this. Try to cross your legs and put your feet the way she does. You cannot do it! It is physically impossible, because the foot is on the far side of her knee while the calf is on this side of her

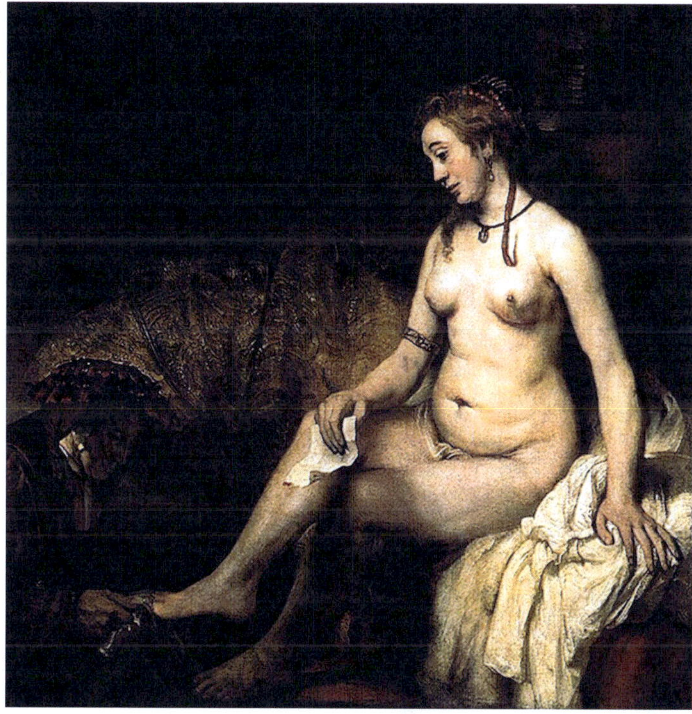

Figure 30.   Rembrandt, *Bathsheba at Her Bath* (1654). Oil on canvas, 1654, 798 x 800. Paris, Musée du Louvre.

knee. In my "empirical" research at the Louvre no one had seen it, and no one could imitate it in reality. But they all tried. Now, what does that mean? The impossibility is generally assumed to mean – if scholars notice it at all – that Rembrandt made a mistake, or a later copyist made a mistake. No, Rembrandt was no sloppy painter; nor is this painting a copy. In my view, Rembrandt is not making a mistake but a point; one about narrative, specifically about focalization, and about the act of looking. He does that through a doubling, thereby distorting the figure into a "disfigure." The spectator looks from the front and sees a nude. The figure is a bit shy so she looks sideways, but it is a nude. You get to see her body and you can find her beautiful or sexy and think, hum, I wish I had that body at my disposal.

Which is exactly what the other, barely visible character in the story, King David, is thinking. He is another focalizer. But there is also this other woman who is a servant and who is cleaning Bathsheba's foot –

that foot that is logically in the wrong place. Making her ready. In fact, she is making her ready for what amounts to royal rape. King David is about to rape Bathsheba. And so, this is a bad story, a story of abuse. Nonetheless, it is a story of appreciative focalization. But how can you make a story of abuse so that the spectators get it in their present, not to imitate the abuse but to reflect on it, while being in a position to appreciate the beauty? So what did Rembrandt do with the foot that doesn't match, the foot that is on the wrong side, which is not a mistake? I imagine he is making a pictorial collage of two paintings belonging to two different genres.

One is the nude that entices people to desire her. The other is the narrative – which is in the direction from her to the servant and the man who is spying from the roof. This is what is going to tell the story. It is going to end badly because she is going to be prepared like this, to be taken to the king to be raped. What she has in her hand is a letter. That letter has no direct bearing on the story, other than being an *allusion* to the letter that the king has sent to the head of the army to say, "Put her husband in the line of danger." The rape comes with a man-to-man violence that makes it possible to commit it and get away with it. In the biblical story Bathsheba never sees that letter. But with the crumpled letter and the melancholy look, she is already in a sort of subjection, dejection, and acceptance that her life is going to change. Her husband is going to die, and she is going to be taken by the king.

It is a completely different story from the one we see at first sight, of a nude woman presented for your pleasure. Except that you, the spectator who lives in the present, sees this nude body and can have appreciative or empathic responses to it. But precisely through your act of seeing, you are also compelled to acknowledge that other story, the one of abuse. At least you cannot help to see the story if you really look at the figure and recognize the oddity. Then you notice that, because of the foot directed to the left and behind where it should be, she is not there for you. Then you can conclude that she is basically trapped in that nasty narrative. So there are two stories in the painting, two "takes" if you see it as a film: one take from the front and one take from this side, in a montage that combines them so seamlessly that you don't immediately see it. That tells you that there are multiple focalizing positions with a single narrator.

This is a multilayered instance of narratology in practice. I was not joking when I wrote that I did empirical research in the Louvre. It is up to you whether you want to abuse Bathsheba, appropriate her, exploit her, or protect her against the danger that is about to happen. But you are made aware, you can even feel it, that there is not one but at least two images, stories; two genres even. It is also a play on the genre of narrative as an act of telling a story in which a fabula is inflected. The use of the letter as an allusion to the biblical narrative is not only an instance of intermediality but also, as an intertextual allusion, a ploy to alert viewers to that mediation within the narrative. That is, for a smart artist like Rembrandt, you can assume he must have had his tongue in his cheek. For a teacher, the question is, how do you get students to be sensitized to this; and for a museum tour guide, how do you get visitors interested in this strangeness?

As I mentioned, I do it sometimes in the Louvre where this painting hangs. I stand there and I see people look, and when I see them slightly puzzled, I often say, "Have you tried to do this: cross your legs and put your foot on the other side?" Oh, blast, yes! That is difficult, you can't do that. No, you cannot, and we start to talk. I do this because I find it so funny, but also gratifying; I see people become confused. I think that for a brief moment, on an unconscious level or maybe even on a conscious level they think Rembrandt made a mistake. Well, he was a good painter, so don't worry. Rembrandt doesn't make mistakes. Not of such magnitude. Do you see this woman? What would be her position if she wasn't directed in your direction, her body more compatible with her gaze? My view of Rembrandt is a construction in the present of looking. An anachronism if you like, but one we always necessarily commit when writing on art, because looking can only occur in the present, whereas an artwork in a museum is mostly primarily related to the past of its making. Working with this concept is taking yourself as a visitor-viewer seriously and taking responsibility for your interpretations, the narratives you construct.

This very practical instance of narratology in practice raises a question all empirical research must address, however: Is this an exploitation, even abuse of the museum's visitors? It could easily become so if, for example, I would laugh at visitors when they do their attempt, mock their inevitably clumsy attempts to cross their legs in the Bathsheba way. Against that risk I participate in the trials myself. But also, by asking that question, not only can I validate Rembrandt's work on a deeper level, but I also give something back to the visitors. In addition to giving them the pleasure of understanding, such an experience is a *social moment*. The important thing is that it establishes a relationship, a positive relationship with the artwork, with each other, the peers, with the teacher if a school class visit. Because you have this enjoyment together. I think fun, humour, joy are social moments that you feel intensely. But if you have that experience together, you are in a relationship, and that is good for the fabric of the social world.

Therefore, I think such an experience is very important: it de-intimidates. It de-intimidates because we are always a bit in veneration of artworks: "Oh god, this great artist, this master" – a *he* mostly – did something that I cannot do. But if you have this kind of joy of getting it or relating to it, standing there in the middle, then you are part of it and therefore you are no longer intimidated. This is for us all. It is part of our common legacy. For an artist who exhibits or sells work to a public institution, or who publishes their novels or stories, has given it to us. This gift is what art contributes to culture – our environment, for all. Focalization facilitates your stepping in: it *enables* you. That is a better word. It enables you to step in, so that you can be part of what gives joy, and, or through, understanding and sensuous participation. What you have is simultaneous participation with others and the artwork, so you are there together.

5: Merging Everything

Both Proust and Rembrandt can be said to offer reflections, in their own medium, of narrativity in their closest other medium. Both artists integrate reflections about that intermediality in a work that makes the ideas they think. Thus, both artists behave as narratologists practising their own and that other art. This final section of the second transitional part considers how the narratives already contain a practice of narratology within their narrative artworks. This brings the theory and its alleged object into that relationship of interlocution that I have advocated from the beginning. This is a form that is currently called, with a problematic term, "artistic research." In addition to philosophical problems with the term (see Vellodi 2019), I object to the implied one-sidedness: artists are asked to develop PhD projects, whereas academics remain out of reach for the concept. This fails to provoke them to deploy their own creativity more deeply and explicitly. For this reason, I prefer to call it, in a book currently in press, "image-thinking," a practice that leads to "thought images." I don't mean to reduce these artists' products to philosophical texts. Instead, I consider the theoretical underside of the images constructed, as enhancements of their powerful artworks. These are enriched with culturally relevant layers of meaning, which occur when the addressees, readers, or spectators open themselves up to their performances. This is a practice, and within the framework of the two books *Narratology* and *Narratology in Practice*, specifically a practice of narratology. To end this transition and ease into the short final part of the present book, I revisit a novel already discussed, now as an elaboration of the mutuality between making and thinking, words and images, past and present, and more. Indeed, *El dolor de los demás* (The Pain of Others) (Hernández 2018) integrates, merges, and mixes everything that can be fused together, turning confusion into con-fusion, in that new, positive sense in which – thanks to the hyphen – a potential lack of clarity morphs into a constructive, innovative, reveal-ing togetherness (con-) of merging (-fusion).

This novel is written in a minimalist style that creates the space, the environment, in which the events took place and where the people lived who suffered from them: a neighbourhood of a simple village in the countryside around the Southern Spanish city of Murcia, called *la huerta*: literally, the orchard. The style has short sentences, concrete evo-cations, personal encounters, elision of verbs, repetitions. Nevertheless, it is highly theoretical in effect, rich in intertextual and interdiscursive allusions and in encouraging stylistic devices, such as the time games, of which repetition, sometimes literal, sometimes with a difference, is the most prominent one. One repetition of the beginning sentence, but with a difference, is that misty event that is not quite true, as we already know by now (91).

The paragraph begins with a theoretical statement on memory: "Hice memoria, e intenté recordar esa noche," which, thanks to the differenti-ation in Spanish between two past tenses, is most adequately translated as "I performed an act of memory, and made an attempt to remember that night," if we wish to catch its theoretical tenor. For the literary ef-fect only, this translation would be a bit heavy-handed. Both verbs are in the form of the *pretérito*, the equivalent of the French *passé simple*. This verb form insists on the act as a one-time event in the past, of which the exact moment is not specified but the momentariness itself is. The rest of the short paragraph describes the content of the act of memory, which is visual ("obscurity"), tactile (feeling the fabric of the curtain), and auditive, but as a question: What was the first thing I heard? Or, to account for the verb tense: the first thing that reached my ear? I insist on the verb tense because it turns the verb itself into an expression of an *event*, in the narratological sense.

Then begins the very short following paragraph: "It was then that I heard my father's voice." Again, the tense is the *pretérito* whereas the verb of what he hears turns to the *imperfecto* of longer duration or rou-tine: the voice of my father reached me, while he was talking to my mother. These are ordinary effects of the Spanish language, but care-fully selected to distinguish events from states or situations. Compared to the first sentence of the novel, quoted above in the chapter on tem-porality, the important shifts are three. One is from the second-per-son to the first-person discourse. This can be seen as a shift from the dissociative "you" form, which can be interpreted as a sign of the traumatic state, to the "cured" state of grief; the grief he seeks, as the title suggests, to share with others.

> I paid attention and I managed to distinguish his words:
> – They have entered Rosario's home, they have killed Rosi and they have abducted Nicolás.
> This is how it all began. This is how this book must begin.

> [Presté atención y conseguí distinguir sus palabras:
> Han entrado en la casa de la Rosario, han matado a la Rosi y se han llevado al Nicolás.
> Así empezaba todo. Así debía comenzar este libro.] (91)

It is a bit strange that it takes up to page 91 to begin the book; but not stranger than Proust's statement, in the middle of his novel, that he decided to "have his novel" with that one girl he had singled out in the group of girls at the beach, a passage I have analysed in the theoretical volume (*Narratology* 120–4).

What seems theoretically relevant and, for readers willing to slow down and reflect, is the auxiliary verb "must," a verb of which the subject is the book, not the author. Preceding this passage, several moments have already occurred when the decision to write the novel is taken, then abandoned again or left dormant. And in fact, the hesitation lasts until the final paragraph. The entire novel, it turns out, is about how to put the words together: those you say out loud and those you write up, those you keep your entire life in your soul and those that take half a lifetime to arrive – to paraphrase the ending. This is the narration. Within it, as its content, is the question about how to remember, as an attempt to be specific with the focalization. But most importantly, he realizes that he can write this novel – stage the acts of narration, focalization, and action – only once he manages to share the pain of the others.

This process begins from the start, is elaborated at several moments, such as a year after the event, when he is incapable of reaching out to the brother of the victims, and later, when, already steeped in his doomed attempts to do the adequate research, he spends an afternoon with the murdered woman's best friend and feels that he is beginning to do what he set out to do: to feel the pain of others. This is also when the victim, Rosi, who, he now realizes, has always been the object, never the subject of the action (245), is seen as a shadow. He is now determined that this shadow must accede to visibility. This becomes possible through the concentrated look at a photograph in which Rosi stands, small and in the back, but at the centre of the image. What was earlier called the sea of mist of memory, its vagueness, is, finally, thanks to that best friend, a clear and defined image, with a history (291). Given that this woman is the victim of a violent act of her brother, combined with the metaphor of the shadow, this realization implies the coming-to-feminism of the protagonist.

The primary device of the intermediality of the (somewhat Proustian) search that this novel is consists of the protagonist's photographic imagination. This imagination increases in density as we move towards the end. When the "I" visits the graves of Rosi and Nicolás, it is through intense looking at the small photographs that are on the tombstones that he manages to grasp the complexity of the memory. The photo is also a moving image ("impossible to fixate," 292) and a shadow, when the image fades to black. When he sees his own reflection on the photo of Nicolás while still trying to come to terms with the question of whether his former best friend is a friend or a monster, he takes a sideward step. On the next page he calls what goes through him during that visit a "home video" [película doméstica], of which he briefly tells the content in images. Images of all kinds.

In the end, the reflection on memory, in visual thought, offers a "thought image" about photography and film as the indispensable tools or media to reach a memory. The entire search the novel as a practice of image-thinking yields, at the end, is this thought-image, which he needs in order to bind literature and life together. This is a con-fusion that is necessary to make art socially relevant. But these tools are no longer just media. They, too, are impacted by the *reflection*, in both senses of the word: mirroring and thinking together. The word's ambiguity helps us realize that thinking always also implies the subject doing the thinking, so that the old attempt to reach "objectivity" is necessarily qualified. In this way, the novel as a whole, of which the central fabula event remains multilayered, is about this theory of memory, vision, and the search, in image-thinking, to achieve it.

The practice that this novel stages, performs, achieves, and tells about, is undefinable. Although it is fundamentally a text, a linguistic narration, the generous reflections on vision, memory, language, places, and all this towards understanding and feeling the pain of others, make it difficult to pin down the linguistic text as literature (only) – unless we dare follow this narrator and accept that literature is a royal road towards an art that encompasses all the senses and merges the intellectual with the visual reflection into a sense-based understanding. Not only does the text mention the tactility of memory, for example, but the words, so auditive that you can actually hear the narration, also arouse a tactile – or rather, haptic – experience of them. When the protagonist tries to trace the itinerary of Nicolás towards the abyss into which he will throw himself, he feels a drawing appear on his GPS screen – there is no less-clumsy way of saying this (231). All through this novel we participate in a failed historical enactment, the failure of which opens up possibilities of cultural participation that will begin when the novel is finished. "[T]o repeat the past [in order to] let it vibrate in the present" [repetir el pasado, dejarlo vibrar en el presente] (232), finally, is the novel's lesson in historical awareness. But if I try to pin down the events that constitute this novel's fabula, I utterly fail.

The practices analysed in this transition part all engage the art form or medium of their own product and connect or integrate those with other forms or media. This engagement is the artistic shape of the intership I have proposed in the Introduction. The artists whose work I have discussed are clearly all intrigued by their "others": painters by writers, writers by photographers, filmmakers by the great literary heritage. But don't go and ask to check out if this is truly the case. They may not even be aware of that specific form of intership they are practising. As I have frequently argued, and again here in the first part of this book, it is the work of the author or artist to make the cultural object; the task of critics, analysts, students and scholars is to mediate between the resulting work and the public, readers, spectators, or other users or "engagers" so that they can benefit more profoundly, on more levels than one, from the complexities and subtleties and incentives to integrate enjoyment with thought. This is how narratology as cultural analysis can best serve its purpose.

Remarks and Sources

For the most relevant study of *A Thousand and One Days* for the perspective I presented here, see Khanna (2008). I have written more extensively on the film, from a different angle, specifically with the question of the narrator, "Who speaks?" in a book that is in press simultaneously with this one, titled *Image-Thinking* (2022). On the hyphen as a concept, see Tuin and Verhoeff (forthcoming). For more on the work of Ken Aptekar, see Bal (1999). For the debates on *the political*, as an alternative term to *politics*, I rely primarily on Chantal Mouffe's succinct essay from 2005. For a more elaborate discussion of the political of art, see the introduction to my book on Doris Salcedo, the first of a trilogy on the subject (2010).

The example of the merging of fairy tales and Auschwitz in Friedman's novel is further analysed in an article by Alphen (2006). I have developed the analysis presented here first on the basis of that article, then together with Alphen. There, it is combined with other instances in the theoretical reflection on the transmission of trauma, and the difficulty of understanding what exactly the trauma is, how it relates to but is also different from that of the parents, in the aftermath in which the next generation grows up. This text discusses the term "postmemory," proposed by Marianne Hirsch (1997), which Alphen considers problematic because the children of survivors don't really have *memories* of the holocaust. Moreover, since the trauma remains "stuck" in the present, the preposition "post-" is also not quite adequate; as I have argued, it barely ever is. Hirsch responds to this and other criticisms later (2008). For the most lucid explanation of trauma in relation to narrative, there is a fundamental article by Alphen (1999) that lays out, in a mere fourteen pages, how narratology and actual trauma can be studied together.

For more in-depth ideas on theatre, theatricality, and dialogue, I refer to the work of Maaike Bleeker. In two publications from 2008 Bleeker explains with both broad overviews and subtle finesse how theatre relates to the social-political world in which it functions. The ideas of Bakhtin are best accessible in the 1981 publication of four of his essays. For the most relevant and lucid commentary, brought to bear on literary, cinematic, and televisual texts, see Esther Peeren (2007). An earlier study of Bakhtin's work that has useful connections to the present book is by Hirschkop and Shepherd (1989). On depression and art in contemporary culture, see Ross (2006).

On Calvino's novel and Tan's videos relating to it, see van Alphen's analysis in his book *Art in Mind* (2005). On the novelistic work of Miguel Á. Hernández, Manuel Alberca (2020) wrote an excellent essay that introduces the work of this new star in Spanish writing to those who don't know it yet. For now, it exists only in Spanish. Both the television series *Picket Fences* (1992–6) and the film *Turbulence* (1997) have Lauren Holly as the female lead, who is central to the fabula in both.

Kaja Silverman is in my view the most important of humanities scholars bringing psychoanalysis to bear on literature and the arts. Her primary subject area is film studies. Her most illuminating book on that link is *Threshold* (1996), in which she theorizes the relationship between subjectivity and space, as part of what she calls an "ethics of vision." The book pairs clarity to complexity – both indispensable when discussing the ideas of a difficult writer like Lacan – and demonstrates the ideas she put forward in dialogue with very interesting artworks, photographs, and films. The passage quoted here is from a later book, *World Spectators* (2000).

Christensen's (1974–present) work with interruption can be seen against the background of Brian Massumi's famous phrase "the shock to thought" in his 2002 edited volume. I have followed Christensen's work for decades (e.g., Bal 2009) and consider her one of the very important artists working today.

On Cervantes's years in slavery, see Garcés (2002), a meticulously documented, gripping biography. I discuss the *Don Quijote* novel and installation at length in my forthcoming book on image-thinking (2022). For Proust I have used the edition in three volumes, on which I based my 1996 book *The Mottled Screen*. The translation I used is the one by Scott- Moncrieff. For Flaubert I have used the most complete edition, and various translation, always checked and adapted. I don't refer to page numbers but to chapters, to facilitate finding the passages in any edition.

Character is a notoriously difficult category to analyse with any form of discussable method. The most systematic approach remains Philippe Hamon's (1983) aptly titled book *Le personnel du roman*. This title suggests that characters are staff, helpers in the construction of the novel's world.

For a most incisive critique of ideas reigning in adaptation studies, especially the ineradicable but wrong-headed idea of "faithfulness," see Leitch (2003), who is the most widely known theorist of that field. The analysis of the painting *Bathsheba's Bath* is based on a much more extensive earlier one, in *Reading "Rembrandt"* (219–46), of which I also talked in the interviews with Lutters.

The most in-depth critique of the concept of "artistic research" is by Kamini Vellodi (2019), in a collective volume devoted to the issue from a philosophical, specifically Deleuzian, perspective. The spelling of the word "con-fused" or "con-fusion" with a hyphen, which turns a negatively connoted word into a positive, productive concept, was suggested to me by philosopher Kyoo Lee of CUNY, New York.

5

Fabula: Elements

1: Preliminary Remarks

The lingering question that *El dolor de los demás* (2018) put on the table is the issue of events. There is a singular, central event: the double family drama of murder and suicide. But as I have argued, all along the novel, the narration concerns many other, different events, whereas that central one remains elusive. Acting either like a traumatized, narratively incapacitated co-victim or like a bad detective, the narrator – and the "I" and "you" that are his pronouns – is searching but never really grasps what happened there. Meanwhile, though, his search, the search for who his best friend was, who he himself is, and, late in the novel, who the primary victim, the sister of the perpetrator, has been, constitutes another primary event, although "process" is more like it. And then, the exploration of the nature of memory, of images, constitutes a string of reflections that can perhaps in themselves be considered events. Above I have argued that the use of the *pretérito* is an indicator of the eventness of the act the verb designates. In English, the verb "happens" frequently foregrounds the event, the act, the punctuality, the momentariness. It is less easy than it may seem to decide what is an event. For Slavoj Žižek, who wrote a short book with the resounding title *Event* (2014), the first meaning of "event," of the six different ones he discusses, is *reframing*.

In *Narratology* I have laid out the analytical tools for the analysis of the fabula. I also contend there that the fabula logic has similarities to other realms of human logic, such as the structure of the sentence, rituals, and more. In this short final part, I will do little more than bringing in a few cultural objects – a.k.a. narratives – to question, undermine, and suspend the distinctions and categories that I have differentiated in theory. *El dolor* is a primary example of this. This doesn't mean the theory is wrong, nor that the artefacts are not quite narrative or even of dubious quality; on the contrary. The "sea of mist," as Hernández calls the ungraspable nature of the past, is still filled with stable elements, locations, objects, and characters, or as they are called here, actors, and changeable elements, the transformations of which produce events. Underlying this part is the conviction, mentioned already several times, that the "failure" of an analysis, the impossibility to come up with a clear and definite analysis, as long as, or better said, *because* the attempt is carried out with care and sharpness, is as useful, as a characterization of the text, as its technically successful completion would be.

But most useful, and most frequent, is something in-between: a difficulty of analysing and an uncertainty of the results. Those are the moments that the analysis and its tools become discussable, and hence, intersubjective, communicable. Together with the near certainties we also develop along the way, the analysis becomes exciting when others can recognize, but perhaps, and partly, disagree with the entire analysis.

These preliminary remarks are meant as hint and reassurance, as well as a statement of "theoretical relativism" that, like cultural relativism, is not the opposite of "theory-centrism" but a companion, or discussant, in our efforts to develop what is hinted at, and meanwhile resting reassured that disagreement is a positive thing to happen, according to the meaning of "the political" according to Mouffe, as explained at the end of the Introduction, which has been my guideline in this book.

2: Events

There have been rich debates on the event, in philosophy, semiotics and other fields. This book is not meant to participate in such debates, only to offer tools and demonstrate their potential productivity in analysis. Events are easiest to identify when seen as the transition from one state to another state, caused or experienced by actors. The word "transition" stresses that an event is a process, an alteration. Trying to establish which sentences in a text or images in a film, lines in a painting or drawing, present an event is the beginning of a fabula analysis. If events are transitions or changes, the question is, of what? What changes can be an actor, a state of the world of the fabula, or a frame? A change of frame entails all other possible changes. That is probably why Slavoj Žižek begins his book titled *Event* with frame change as his first conception of what an event is (10). A well-known change of frame is the traditional ending of detective fiction, where a parade of possible suspects has been examined and interrogated. At the end the master detective, let's say, Agatha Christie's Hercule Poirot, brings all the suspects together and tells his own story. Therein the least suspect actor suddenly becomes the major one, and indeed, the murderer. This frequently also entails a change of location: for example, from the entire estate to the library or the living room. That serves as a concrete frame change.

Among the other possible definitions of an event Žižek discusses is rupture; when something or someone breaks the normal routine (38). Also, the question of responsibility participates in determining not what constitutes an event but what kind of event it is. In rape cases this is often the issue at stake. Something happened, but between consensual sexual intercourse and unwanted violent rape, the event is either a pleasant, perhaps even routine one barely deserving the name "event," or a crime, potentially traumatizing for the one and possibly leading to a prison sentence for the other; hence, life changing for both. Did the rapist feel provoked by the woman, as he may claim, or was she completely overwhelmed? There is an event of unwanted sexual penetration, and days go by in court to determine what kind of event it was. This goes back to what I wrote on focalization regarding Niditch's reflection of "just war."

Events can be either a somewhat slow process, such as an actor dying of an illness, or a very sudden change, such as an accident. Instead of proposing a novel or film with clear, even spectacular events, I want to consider how we can bring fabula narratology to bear on a novel and a film where events are barely noticeable. In this section I consider especially the deployment of slowness in the presentation of events; the artists' attempts to blur the events, con-fusing them with actors, places, and other elements. I select these works for what we can see as a counter-structure; a reticence to bring up the kind of statement such as "and then this happened." And to make the distinction between events and their minimalist telling as clear as possible, for the novel I focus on the dramatic topic of death; for the film, Béla Tarr and Ágnes Hranitski's *Werckmeister Harmonies* (2000), on revolution. In both works, these events are unclear. This will be discussed only very briefly.

The event status of a death is undeniable. But in the telling of it, this remains to be seen. In Toni Morrison's second novel, *Sula* (1973), challenges to any search for punctuality of events make for a fascinating structure. The first sentence begins with "In that place" and ends on "there was once a neighbourhood." "There was once" sounds a bit like the typical fairy-tale beginning, "Once upon a time," but the following belies that ambiance, substituting a social setting that has ceased to exist. No "happily ever after." Irreversible destruction is more like it. After this prologue that posits the time and place, its structure is made up from years, starting with 1919, when Shadrack, a traumatized veteran from WWI, returns to his home town and founds the "National Suicide Day." The chapters are titled only with the dates, from 1919 to 1923, then a jump to 1927, followed by 1937, 1939, 1940, 1941, with another leap to 1965. Whereas Shadrack was said to be "for many years the only celebrant" of Suicide Day, in 1965 the town's population participate in the game. They end up being killed when they destroy a derelict building site for a tunnel that never got built: the tunnel collapses, the river rises, and they all drown. Except for Shadrack. No "happily ever after" indeed. Given the name of the day, one may wonder if the accident is in fact a collective suicide, since the promise of jobs, made decades before, was frustrated when the company abandoned the project, and the neighbourhood remained as poor as it had always been. Unlikely, but it seems important that the thought may occur to the reader.

But this Shadrack / suicide frame is just that: a frame that positions the actors in a location and a time. The events are many and often unclear. No triumph of the truth, as in Poirot's conclusions. It is in the nature of death and the people involved that the events take their questionable shape. There are some deaths that can be either manslaughter, murder, or accidents. And the death of the main character, Sula. She dies in a way that is as impossible as it is gripping. The end of the chapter "1940" described Sula's death as follows. Sula is ill and in a lot of pain, which occupies her thoughts and concentration completely. We never hear what illness she suffers from. Then, the two final paragraphs of the chapter go like this:

> While in this state of weary anticipation, she noticed that she was not breathing, that her heart had stopped completely. A crease of fear touched her breast, for any second there was sure to be a violent explosion in her brain, a gasping for breath. Then she realized, or rather she sensed, that there was not going to be any pain. She was not breathing because she didn't have to. Her body did not need oxygen. She was dead.
>
> Sula felt her face smiling. "Well, I'll be damned," she thought, "it didn't even hurt. Wait'll I tell Nel." (133)

Nel was her best friend during their girlhood. They had fallen out because Sula had made love with Nel's husband, who subsequently left his wife. Nel had just come to visit Sula at her sickbed, after ten years of estrangement. The visit is awkward, though; they remain estranged.

The content of that chapter ending is certainly an event: the death of the main character. A more radical transformation is hardly thinkable.

As an event it is overruled by focalization, however; an impossible one, yet not at all jarring with the rest of the novel. It seems summed up in the beginning of the passage: "she noticed that she was not breathing." If at the end she is dead and still continues to feel, smile, and think, we know that this is that impossibility that Foucault once mentioned: "One cannot say: I am dead." Sula's realization of being dead is as impossible as the statement is forceful, and even true: there may be pain in dying, but not in being dead. But the content of the thought is a final characterization of the character, who has been having clashes with Nel and all through the novel creates a fascinating, different kind of friendship than the one the good girl Nel is herself trained in by her neat mother. With the exception of the mass death at the end, all the deaths – suspect, ambivalent, or not – happen in Sula's family, with one exception.

Earlier on, in the chapter "1923," Sula's grandmother, the one-legged Eva, burns her only son to death, after hugging and rocking him warmly for quite some time. Then suddenly, unexpectedly, the event occurs:

> Eva stepped back from the bed and let the crutches rest under her arms. She rolled a bit of newspaper into a tight stick about six inches long, lit it and threw it onto the bed where the kerosene-soaked Plum lay in snug delight. Quickly, as the *whoosh* of flames engulfed him, she shut the door and made her slow and painful journey back to the top of the house. (49)

Although there is no explanation to answer the "why?" question, the description of the man called Plum as a thieving up-to-no-good man who spend his days sleeping must be a prospective hint of motivation. But that this is indeed an event; who is its actor; and what is the result: all that is clear. When it happens, no further attention to it is being paid. Later, Eva's daughter Hannah confronts her mother, asking: "What'd you kill Plum for, mamma?" (67). The answer is neither forthcoming nor clear when after a long passage on Eva's thinking, she tells only about how difficult it had been to have a boy and raise him. She ends on, "But I held him close first. Real close. Sweet Plum. My baby boy" (69). The narrator frames this in all uncertainty, including, for emphasis, a visual lack of clarity: "Eva couldn't see Hannah clearly for the tears, but she looked up at her anyway and said, by way of apology or explanation or perhaps just by way of neatness"; followed by the quote of the why question. Is this strange conversation between the killing mother and her daughter itself an event? That question is up for discussion – one of those productive ones, for which the narrator positing the uncertainty leads the way.

Burning to death happens again soon after, if we calculate time by text length, when we read only a few pages later that the same Hannah tries to light a fire in the yard, as the fifth of a series of "strange things" that form the content of this chapter ("or fourth, if you didn't count Sula's craziness" 72). The phrase "strange things" could be a designation of what can be considered events, but clearly the narrative stages and thus compels uncertainties about what an event is when it says,

> But before the second strange thing, there had been the wind, which was the first. (70)

That declaration is focalized externally, it seems, whereas the hesitation about fifth or fourth is explicitly focalized by Eva. But in none of these cases, the verb "to happen" accompanies the "strange thing." The strange thing in question is that she cannot find her comb and starts to search for it. Which is why she missed seeing the fire catching Hannah. Once the comb is found, her act of focalization constitutes an event in itself, which has consequences:

> She rolled up the window and it was then she saw Hannah burning. The flames from the yard fire were licking the blue cotton dress, making her dance. Eva knew there was time for nothing in this world than the time it took to get there and cover her daughter's body with her own. (72)

What the external narrator-focalizer attributes to Eva through the verb "she saw" is the event described as Eva's embedded focalization: "The flames from the yard fire were licking the blue cotton dress, making her dance." Both "licking" and "dance" are descriptions of what Eva sees, rendered quite affectless at that, even if right after seeing this strange spectacle – a "strange thing" if ever there was one – she does act upon realizing – hence, focalizing – that she must do something to save her daughter. Therefore, it is the seeing that constitutes the event.

She jumps out of the window, cutting herself and bleeding heavily. This must have been both difficult, one-legged as she is, and bold, even brave. She lands too far from Hannah to do anything. Neighbours help, and the ambulance comes. Hannah dies on the way, whereas Eva survives. A possible discussion could be, Is this a single event, Hannah's death by burning, of which we may wonder if it is suicide or an accident? Or is it four events: Eva's seeing it, Hannah burning, Eva jumping, and the ride to the hospital during which Hannah dies? The logic, here, consists of the uncertainties themselves, while the process that encompasses the transformations is nevertheless clear. The event according to Žižek's first definition of an event would be the change of frame of focalization within Eva: the change, that is, from frantically and with irritation searching for her comb – from total self-absorption – to risking her life in a dangerous and courageous attempt at rescuing her daughter. In Žižek's view, that change of frame, of the actor's state and place and action, constitutes the event, not the act itself.

A third instance of the event of death precedes this one, and again, it is the looking, the watching, that may well be the main event. For in this case, Nel's watching while Sula plays with a boy called Chicken Little will return later. During Nel's first visit after the break-up and the last one before Sula's death, it is recalled as the important act: watching. But then again, it is not certain: watching, or just seeing ? The event in question is the accidental death by drowning of the little boy that Sula had been swinging around. She was playing with him, to his delight. But then she let the boy's hand slip so that he flew through the air into the lake.

When he slipped from her hands and sailed away out over the water they could still hear his bubbly laughter:

> The water darkened and closed quickly over the place where Chicken Little sank. The pressure of his hard and tight little fingers was still in Sula's palms as she stood looking at the closed place in the water. They expected him to come back up, laughing. Both girls stared at the water. (50–1)

This event the precise nature of which remains unnamed, happens in chapter "1922" when the girls were twelve years old. The event confronts them with fear, of being seen, and with guilt, since they don't do anything, don't even report the accident, although the word "fear" does but "guilt" does not appear in the text. The key word is *staring*. The event, then, is not simply that the boy drowns but that they look, watch, impassibly. Again, an act of focalization constitutes the event, of which the death seems almost a side effect. No searches for the missing child, no grieving parents; just the affectless gazes of the girls.

Between these deaths, there are many small events, none of which seem dramatic enough to make a list of them. But then, what is dramatic is not dramatized at all. When it comes to Nel's husband Jude leaving her for Sula, who dumps him soon after, there is really no event being narrated. On page 95, Jude is thinking that Sula is an interesting woman who would be unmarried for a reason: "She stirred a man's mind maybe, but not his body." An asterisk marks the end of that section. The next one begins with Nel seeing that Jude had left his tie. So, he has left. Like Eva's missing comb, such unremarkable small, negative acts are the events. The departure is a major event that changes

Nel's life, that of her children, her relationship with Sula, and Jude's own life: in the fabula, however, it is simply a hiatus. After a short paragraph of an interior monologue of Nel addressed to Jude in case he'd come back for his tie, a blank line marks another hiatus, followed by a retrospective act of Nel watching again, this time the love-making of Jude and Sula that initiates the (again unmentioned) break-up.

Sula, then, is a narrative that undermines narrative structure by means of rigorously posting it. Events become "strange things," whereas murder, suicide, manslaughter, or accidental deaths are events that cannot be pinpointed. And so is adultery and subsequent spouse elopement. Instead, events such as we can notice them are the frame-changes within the characters. The chronology is simultaneously rigorous, thanks to the dates as chapter titles, and totally unclear, as the dramatic events slip away from narration. The first page of the novel posits the obedient narrative structure with temporal emphasis. As mentioned, the first words – "In that place" – are followed in the same sentence by "there was once a neighbourhood." Then the present asserts itself, after a brief description of the neighbourhood as it was in the past, when it says, "The beeches are gone now …" only to be followed by the future, both immediate and long term: "They are going to raze the Time and a Half Pool Hall … A steel ball will knock to dust Irene's Palace of Cosmetology …" And the second paragraph begins with "There will be nothing left of the Bottom." So the reader is warned: no happy ending can be expected. This prediction is realized when the final disaster happens, the job-promising tunnel collapses, and Shadrack's "suicide day" is finally realized. This is an event indeed.

The Black neighbourhood, doomed by its poor infertile soil and the cancelled construction of the tunnel, undergoes a few transformations, which can be taken to have been caused by events yet are depicted rather as a chronic state. When Sula is away, there are the usual disgruntlements, disputes, and violence, and a general discontent. When she is back, the united front of hatred for and contempt of her makes the community peaceful again. This is how her return is described:

> Sula stepped off the Cincinnati Flyer into the robin shit and began the long climb up in the Bottom. She was dressed in a manner that was as close to a movie star as anyone would ever see. A black crepe dress splashed with pink and yellow zinnias, foxtails, a black felt hat with the veil of net lowered over one eye. In her right hand was a black purse with a beaded clasp and in her left a red leather travelling case, so small, so charming – no one had seen anything like it ever before, including the major's wife and the music teacher, both of whom had been to Rome. (84)

If event there is, that would be summed up in the first sentence. This is not her return, but the transition is from the train to the dirty ground. That's hardly an event. And "the long climb" suggests a durational, uneventful walk. But then follows the admirative description of Sula's look, dress, and other attributes. And the specific remark that she looked "as close to a movie star as anyone would ever see" insists on the fact that the woman is a spectacle, rather than a woman. This insistence is repeated and brought closer to home just a sentence later with "no one had seen anything like it ever before," mentioning two high-prestige people who "have been to Rome." The passage seems a description that is focalized by an anonymous agent who sees for everyone living in the neighbourhood. Is this focalizer external or internal to the fabula? Even that remains unclear.

But what is the event: the return of the allegedly wicked Sula, or the changed attitudes? Hard to tell. Then, when Sula has died, everything turns nasty again. The rupture of the equilibrium consisting of common hatred causes two events: the change from unrest during her absence to peace after her return; and peace during her presence, ruptured and turned to routine social turmoil after her death. Clearly, in a novel the title of which consists only of the figure's given name, this important impact of her presence and absence attributes to her the primary role of an actor. Yet she barely does anything.

Events in Béla Tarr's *Werckmeister Harmonies* are even harder to identify. The two-hours-and-twenty-five-minutes-long film text consists of only thirty-nine takes, all slow and long, in black and white, with an insistence on centralizing the figures in the image. Set in a wintry decaying small town, a general lethargy is shaken up by the announced arrival of a "monster": a whale, brought by a circus led by a "prince." The whale, a bloated, rotting and blank-eyed carcass, appears only late in the film. The main figure – "character" is too psychological a term here – János Valuska, a typical "idiot" as Rancière (2013) characterizes him, does little more than wander the streets, always central in the frame. Valuska, with wild hair and sunken cheeks, a far cry from the movie-star type, is mainly just "being there," not really causing or undergoing events. The film shows, literally, in these long takes, the proximity of "normal" disorder and extreme, destructive madness.

The proximity of these two forms of madness is primarily presented in the contrast between individual and collective madness. The three potential events are the conflict between Mrs. Eszter, the wife of the musician who is in thrall of Werckmeister's legacy, and her husband; the disorderliness of the town, ready to explode; and the long-awaited arrival of the truck with the dead whale. This arrival does release the violence of the mob. They march to the hospital and begin to beat up the patients and smash the machinery. The arrival of the truck with the whale yields an image in which it is no longer just the "idiot" who centralizes the frame but a partition into four squares. Rancière analyses the quadruple frame as follows:

> … the gray shadow of the truck preceding the brightness of the facades its headlight illuminate, the black mass of the trailer, and the pale shadow of the space at back. (51)

As this description shows, the division of the frame is entirely based on nuances in the black and white (non-)colouring of the film. Could we consider this an event? As a literal change of frame, perhaps, it would qualify.

The moment the mob marches towards the hospital, with no slogans, expressions of anger, or other of the usual "explanations" of revolution, loses its motivation and so, perhaps even its eventness. In contrast, it is the moment when the march and the destructive action stop that constitutes the event. A naked old man, standing in a blinding white light, confronts the mob with the futility of what they are doing. After the movement forwards, the opposite, the decrescendo movement turns the mob into a procession of shadows, then a dispersal. The event of the mob march only seemed central. In fact, it is its demise that is the true event, in the frame-changing sense. At the end of the film we see János sit on a hospital bed, with dangling legs. Only when declared "mad" could he escape punishment for his participation in the riot.

3: Actors

For an analysis of the fabula, actors are regarded in terms of their relation to the sequences of events that they cause or undergo. These elements we call "actors" because they do something, in the sense of causing or undergoing events. They are not necessarily human. We don't need to remember La Fontaine's animal fables to realize that. But inanimate objects can cause events, too, and the collapsing of the half-built tunnel at the end of *Sula* even causes the major, concluding event of mass death. That semi-ruin we can consider an actor, collaborating with the rising water of the river to bring about the definitive destruction of the neighbourhood. This raises the question of its relation to the fabula. In this case, it brings it to closure in its resonance with the beginning, where the words "there once was a neighborhood" already predicts what is called the "anterior future": the moment or state when in the future nothing will be left.

For an analysis of actors as what Philippe Hamon (1983) has called "le personnel du roman" (the staff of the novel), the grouping of actors is a way of grasping what each of them is doing there, in the universe of the narrative's fabula. In some fabulas, there are many actors, some functional and some less so. In such cases it may be worthwhile to sort out the functional from the non-functional actors. But there are also novels or other narratives with very few or even a single actor. Most commonly, there is one main actor, surrounded by others who may be helpers or opponents during the search of the main actor (the subject) to achieve its goal, which is the acquisition of the object. Structurally, actors in the fabula are connected to one another through a pursuit of one or more primary characters. These primary ones who set the sequence of events in motion we call the "subject," a figure in pursuit of an object. The nature of the quest, the kind of actions it entails, is called the "function." Whether or not the subject can be successful depends on the "power," the figure(s) or circumstances that make success possible. The subject is on the receiving end of that power. Other figures, in their status as actors, can be grouped as "helpers" or "opponents." The actors grouped in such clusters share a technical name, which, derived from structuralist theory, is *actants*.

In Indian writer Anita Desai's second novel, *In Custody* (1984), the first sentence presents the main actor, as well as the actor who will turn out an opponent of sorts:

> His first feeling on turning around at the tap on his shoulder while he was buying cigarettes at the college canteen and seeing his old friend Murad was one of joy so that he gasped "Murad? You?" and the cigarettes fell from his hand in amazement, but this rapidly turned to anxiety when Murad gave a laugh, showing his betel-stained teeth beneath the small bristling moustache he still wore on his upper lip. (9)

The main actor is indicated only by the first word "his," and it will take quite some words before his name, Deven, is mentioned. All through the novel, the reader wonders when this man will be taken into the custody of the title. We expect a major event – perhaps a crime, an imprisonment, and a conviction. This never happens as an event. As it turns out, he is in custody from the first go. "Custody" is a descriptive term.

Living as a college teacher in Mirpore, a small town not too far from the capital Delhi where his former study friend Murad runs a small publishing house, Deven feels a prisoner in his everyday life, with his classes to teach, students and colleagues, a wife and a son. Who, of these people, will turn out functional actors? Deven has two interests, which he calls hobbies: poetry and Urdu, the language of the Muslim minority. He is bound to teach Hindi, though, because the department of Urdu is too small. He has written a book of poetry but never got it published. Murad persuades him to come to Delhi to meet, in view of an interview, Nur, an old man who is the major poet in Urdu and is getting on in age. The second chapter begins with the bus ride to Delhi, during which Deven muses:

> The bus soon left Mirpore behind. It came as a slight shock to Deven that one could so easily and quickly free oneself from what had come to seem to him not only the entire world since he had no existence outside it, but often a cruel trap, or prison, as well, an indestructible prison from which there was no escape. (19)

The title's idea of "custody" is beginning to be filled in here. Just as in *Sula*, in *El dolor*, and in older novels such as *Madame Bovary*, a small space with a limited community is more than a setting; it is the main characters' world and as such confining, close to a prison. Desai's novel makes that confining aspect explicit; it becomes the primary topic of the novel.

This imprisoning effect is the case for Emma Bovary, who, like Deven, is locked up in an unhappy marriage, whereas for Sula and Nel, it is simply their world. The "I" narrator of *El dolor* feels confined, too, but he can and does escape, to the "big city," the city of Murcia that remains more or less unnamed, and to other places, such as an American university, Madrid, and other places where he conducts his research. The actor in Desai's novel, in contrast, is embarking on a mission that will be another form of custody. Wherever he goes and whatever he tries, he remains imprisoned. The small town with its surrounding countryside from which he thinks he is escaping is presented as follows:

> Then, after he graduated and married and came to Mirpore to teach, it became for him the impassable desert that lay between him and the capital with its lost treasures of friendships, entertainment, attractions and opportunities. It turned into that strip of no-man's land that lies around a prison, threatening in its desolation. (24)

Words like "for him," followed by qualifications, and "lost treasures" dress the actor up into a character-focalizer. The interpretation of the countryside as "threatening" clutches the relationship between Deven and the environment, which is compared to but, in fact, becomes, for him at least, a prison.

This actor is defined by solitude, and this turns all the others into potential non-actants, from which the events, as far as there are any, may select those that matter to the subject-actant – here, Deven – in his pursuit of his object. The problem for this "little man," as he can be qualified, is that the object itself is unclear, even to him. Pushed by Murad, he undertakes to interview the great poet Nur whom he admires and whose poems he can even quote from memory. This will be his object: to interview the great man, to write the interview out for publication in Murad's journal, and thus to achieve something more than he has: a bit of renown and a proximity to the poetry he so loves, to the Urdu language. But the meeting is a disaster, any specific conversation made impossible by the large attendance the poet has around him all the time.

The opponents to Deven the subject-actant in pursuit of his object-goal, a meaningful interview, perhaps, he fantasizes, even a book on the poet, are not only the crowds around the old man, and the domestic dramas with his wives, but also Murad, who bosses him around and supports him with insufficient funds. His colleagues who help him to some funding to acquire a tape recorder but never engage in a consequential conversation with him also act as opponents. We can even see his own technical incompetence in making the recorder turn at the right moments, when among insignificant babbles the poet suddenly says something important or recites his own poems, as an opponent. When he returns home from one of the many bus trips to Delhi to find his son and take him for a walk, the change goes from his continuous nightmares to a paradoxical sense of contentment. In this utterly sombre novel, this seems a major event:

> The calm exhilaration of the evening and the walk gave him an unaccustomed peace of mind, contentment with things the way they were, and a certain modest, suburban wellbeing. (71)

The paradox is in the phrase "calm exhilaration" that connects excitement with calm. This descriptive phrase can perhaps be seen as a major event.

The sense of imprisonment continues wherever he is: at home when he is home, in the college when he is there, in Delhi, in the poet's house, where he realized that his imprisonment is broader; rather something like the human condition in general. He muses:

> Being an illustrious poet had drawn people to the zoo to come and stare at him but Nur had not escaped from his cage for all that – he was as trapped

> as Deven even if his cage was more prominent and attracted more atten-
> tion. Still, it was just a cage in a row of cages. Cage, cage. Trap, trap.
>
> Then, where was freedom to be found? Where was there fresh air to
> breath? (131)

His realization that the great poet is as trapped as he feels he is turns his condition into something else than his personal failure or his incapacity to change his life, however. His conceptual, existential struggle is not to be generalized into the human condition, but in the isolation of one who is caged, trapped, by others. The crowds who come to Nur's house are also human. But they play the part of visitors at the zoo, as Deven phrases it here.

The others as trap: its sounds like Jean-Paul Sartre's philosophical explorations of the human condition, best known through the often-quoted sentence "L'enfer, c'est les autres" [Hell is the others], in his 1944 existentialist play *Huis clos* (Behind closed doors, translated as *No Exit*). For Sartre, a philosopher who practised literature as another form of what I have called "image-thinking," this play was an enquiry into what makes humans human, which for him was freedom and responsibility, both extensively qualified. Desai's figure Deven, himself locked up in the ambition and illusion of achieving some modest degree of "greatness," for which neither his talents nor his habitat qualify, knows less and less what the others who are trying to help him – help he has asked, begged for – really "mean": helping him escape from his prison of mediocrity, or locking him up more firmly?

> Were these people really helping him to succeed in a unique and wonderful
> enterprise or simply locking him up more and more firmly in a barred trap?
> And was the trap set by Murad, by Siddiqui [a colleague who raises money
> for him], or by Nur and his wives? All he knew was that he who had set out
> to hunt Nur down was being hunted down himself, the prey. (143)

For those readers who are keen for events and a denouement, whether tragic or happy, this novel is countering that expectation. Yet it is fully narrative. From page to page, a narrator tells, a character-focalizer shows, and an actor is doing. What he is doing, all through the novel, is attempting not only to achieve his goal, the object, but to understand what in fact that object is.

Depending on the result of that search, the other actors are either helpers or opponents. And if the final sentence is "He ran, stopping only to pull a branch of thorns from under his foot," that symbolic gesture of self-help in the most mundane of non-actions counts as much as a denouement as Poirot's triumphs in the library when he arrests the killer. Just a few lines before, Deven uses the word from which the title of the novel was derived, but turns it into something precious: he feels he is the "custodian" of Nur's poetry. What that can possibly entail, after the total failure of the "unique and wonderful enterprise" is anyone's guess. Perhaps it is just the ambition, no longer for his own glory, but for the continuation of the poetry in Urdu.

Actors and their interrelationships can be considered, also; not only in film, of course, but even in still images, sculpture, photography, and installation art. In the first chapter I mentioned Mary Longman's sculpture with the telling title *Co-Dependents*, where a sensuality and sexual tension but also a tense relationship appears: "Anywhere couples are engaged in trust situations, there is bound to be tension," as McMaster (1996) writes in an essay on Longman's work. He calls it a "constant push/pull in its dynamic and aggressive balletic form. Their performative act exudes tension. Their ambivalent desire creates a co-dependency" (24–5). The point here is not to fixate the meaning of this relationship but to acknowledge that there are two actors, that they are doing something, and hence, that a potential event, even perhaps a story, is being shown, announced, or suggested.

Longman is also keen on installation art, and this is another helpful side path for considering actors, especially non-human, non-animate ones. McMaster connects that artistic inclination to the wish to recall orality, the basis of Aboriginal cultures. What makes installation relevant for narratology is that there is a dynamic openness. "Objects can be constantly rearranged wherein meaning becomes ever more dynamic, and arguably, reflects the idea of orality," writes McMaster (1996). Thereby, "the practice of creating installation art becomes a strategic alternative for the continuity of ideas, not just objects" (11). This view put me on the track of narrativity in installation, along with the actor-status of objects. Since in an installation, the arrangement of the objects provisionally determines the relationships among them, the dynamic nature of the installation, the place in which it stands, and the way the objects confront, face, look at one another: it all produces the potential of a narrative, which it is up to the visitor to make. The objects here are actors without events, because they stand still. But with the participation of the visitor, events can erupt any time, and when the artist, necessarily adapting to the space with each instalment, rearranges the objects, the narrative changes, sometimes quite significantly.

Installation, as does oftentimes, sculpture, stages the intense participation of the viewer as a narratee, the addressee of the narrative. Art historian Claire Bishop (2005) articulates this as follows:

> Installation art … differs from traditional media (sculpture, painting, pho-
> tography, video) in that it addresses the viewer directly as a literal presence
> in the space. Rather than imagining the viewer as a pair of disembodied
> eyes that survey the work from a distance, installation art presupposes an
> *embodied* viewer whose sense of touch, smell and sound are as heightened
> as their sense of vision. That insistence on the literal presence of the viewer
> is arguably the key characteristic of installation art. (6, emphasis in text)

This emphatic presence of and co-making by the visitor is a useful reminder that narrative, like all cultural texts, can only function – hence,
exists as such – if it addresses itself to others: readers, viewers, or other
"engagers."

Finally, the one-main-actor narrative can equally well contain a lot of
events. The recently released film *Radioactive*, a very well-made "biopic"
by the Iranian-French graphic novelist and filmmaker Marjane Satrapi
(2020), offers new possibilities. Satrapi is widely known for her *Persepolis*, a comic – not very comical – on her childhood in Iran. This basis
of her reputation is a useful reminder that films, with their frames that
are in fact still images in quick succession, have something fundamental in common with graphic novels and comics. The 2020 film presents
the life of Maria Skłodowska Curie and is based on a graphic novel by
Lauren Redniss. Two aspects make this film, which is unambiguously
narrative, remarkable beyond the conventions of the genre. The main
character Marie Curie – a role model of a woman who, against the grain
of anti-feminist prejudice, became a world-famous scientist, inventor of
radioactivity together with her husband, Frenchman Pierre Curie – is
presented as devoted to her work more than to anything or anyone else.
She is super serious, but not very engaging.

Not that she is nasty. But as a character she does not solicit identification at all, in spite of the admiration we may have for her achievements.
She is a bit harsh in her ambition. When, soon after the birth of her second daughter, Marie and Pierre together win the Nobel Prize for their
discovery, Pierre goes alone to Stockholm. When he returns, Marie is
furious and makes a scene, alleging that it is unacceptable that he went
on his own, however strongly he asserts that he has made it crystal
clear to the audience that they did the work together and that the prize
is for both of them. Because she didn't want to go and couldn't so soon
after birth-giving, her anger fit is unreasonable, spoiling Pierre's pleasure in the distinction.

As an actor in the narratological sense of the fabula, Madame Curie (played by Rosamund Pike) carries the plot beautifully, which
means the cinematic narrator is expertly put to work. She is the overall

focalizer, too, and only in interaction with her do other characters see things. Whether the main actor shows the radiation, or the digits and calculation, or her anger at her husband Pierre (played by Sam Riley) when he says "we" and she rejects that plural pronoun, this barely ever smiling figure is not very appealing. But her actions are. When the department head refuses to grant her a larger and better equipped laboratory, she doesn't refrain from showing her anger and even gets up and leaves in the middle of a solemn event. In the next section I will briefly revert to this film. For now, let me just wind up by alleging that all the other characters are either helpers or opponents, sometimes moving the opponent status to helper status, such as Pierre, whom Marie really loves, and her children, who are a burden but also treasured, even if the affective bond is barely ever shown. They become helpers when they keep the ambitious scientist's affective deficit balanced.

The opposite also happens. Paul Langevin, a fellow scientist working in the same laboratory, helps Marie get over Pierre's accidental death. He comforts her, praises her even in the exact same words as Pierre had done, and, predictably, they become lovers. Until Paul's wife confronts Marie, makes a scene in the street for everyone to hear, slapping her and treating her as a "dirty Pole," and the husband follows his wife home, leaving Marie. A more general hostility towards her ensues, and once she is even scolded as a "dirty Jew" – none too emphatically, but still, we are already in the early thirties. In fact, thinking about who is a helper and who is an opponent is an instructive way of interpreting the film. The change from one status to the other of the secondary actors is as important for a sense of the fabula as is Marie's status as the main actor.

These shifts are all based on the actors' connection to or view of the main actor. But what makes this film particularly effective is the red thread, or rather, two red threads: the feminist versus sexist opposition, within which some actors go along with Marie and the majority does not; and the value and danger of the Curies' invention. The struggle Marie has to go through to be accepted in the all-male community in which she is bound to work is one of the ways in which this historical costume drama historicizes the life of this scientific star. The ambivalences compel us to think and rethink our preconception that in the past sexism was so much worse than it is now. According to this film, yes and no. The evaluation of the value of the discovery is a highly controversial one. Curing and causing cancer, fighting wars: both appear, are thematized, and again, the answers are inconclusive. In promoting these uncertainties, the film takes full advantage of its medium.

4: Time

In the case of a "bio-pic" or a biography, whether historical or fictional, a duration of decades is to be expected, during which the character develops. But narrative episodes tend to have shorter durations, and thus, they present fragments of a life, not the entire, continuous life story. Time, duration, development, and crisis can be very varied. The first realization when reading a novel or watching a film is the genre-bound characteristic: a life, an episode such as a quarrel or a love affair, and everything in between.

Comparable to *Sula* but also in a very different way and with different effects, *Radioactive* makes consistent use of dates. In Morrison's novel, the dates that are the chapter titles are rigorously chronological, even if three times a big hole in the chronology occurs. But whereas the beginning posits past, present, and future as time frames and almost even as actors, *Sula* does not deviate from the basic chronology. It seems that Morrison wanted to implement the realization that in spite of apparent major changes in the socio-political situation of African-Americans, the mass death at the end does not, not at all, predict a radically better future. Chronology, its relentless continuity, underlies the events, such as there are.

In *Radioactive* the dates are mentioned also in a rhythm that suggests chapters, with the places where these things happen. And the life history of Sula and her surviving childhood mate Nel draws a sketch of a period that refuses to go away. As we see, in a different manner in *Radioactive*, the consequences of the life history of the subject-actor also refuse to go away. In pairing these two narrative artworks I am almost tempted to set up a "second-person narrative" situation between the two. But I'll keep to the fabula-temporality. The beginning of the film is "Paris, 1934." We see the main actor falling, a servant hurrying to her aid, and the next image is a perfectly linear view of a hospital corridor through which she is being driven on a stretcher. Nothing, at this point, indicates the irony that she is riding on her own invention, nor that due to a childhood trauma, she cannot enter hospitals. Later we realize that the fainting spell of the main actor and the rush to the hospital is the prelude to her death, which the ending says occurred in 1934 indeed. This seems to make all the other dates reminiscences, or does it? The following date is forty years earlier: "Paris, 1893." Here the character begins to appear controversial, deviant from the common pattern: too demanding, not a man, Polish … three features that make the actor's pursuit – her passion for science and her desire to achieve important things in that domain – nearly hopeless.

She attends a performance by American actress and dancer Loie Fuller, whose colourful, whirling long skirts have made her a near-abstract artist earning great acclaim in Paris, where she frequently performed at the Folies Bergères. This historical appearance serves many different purposes to bind the actors together, and date that togetherness. Pierre and Marie, who had briefly met in the street, now engage more deeply in conversation, involved as both are in their passion for science. Pierre's remark that Fuller is interested in the movement of flames is centrally relevant for the development of the fabula. In the history of cinema, Fuller stands for exuberantly moving imagery and is one of the first artists appearing in (artificially added) colour images. For Marie Curie this evening is when she meets Pierre seriously enough that something can, so to speak, flame up between them. Science and fiction go hand in hand. This becomes even more prominent as a con-fusion when Fuller's home turns out to be the location for spiritistic séances, which fascinate Pierre and occasions some fierce discussions between the two.

When, still in this 1893 chapter, Pierre takes Marie to a hospital, she turns around and runs away. It seems strange. This is followed by memories of Marie as a child attending to her mother's illness and, as becomes clear later, hospitalization and death. While this memory explains her intense aversion to hospitals, it is also the recurring earlier moment in the film. Her mother asks her to cure her with a kiss. "Did you feel that?" the mother asks. The little girl says no, but after trying it once more, she says she did feel it this time, and this turns the world into a new direction. The kiss to her sick mother and the mother's suggestive question already predict the child's growing interest in science as a way to change the world. Her lifelong suspicious attitude towards spiritism, including Pierre's interest in it, also goes back to this experience. She is suspicious of it, but cannot entirely reject it. Much later she actually does ask the leader of the spiritism's place to make Pierre, who has died, appear for her. The fine line between science and fantasy remains fine, and in place; unstable, but ineradicable.

The same can be said of the gender distinction and Marie's behavioural issues, which it entails. When she gets an opportunity to present her/their finding to a large audience of (all-male) scientists, she says, unhampered by politeness, "You have fundamentally misunderstood the atom." Soon, we assume without knowing the timeline – at any rate, sometime later – Pierre is appointed professor the same day that Marie is confirmed in her second pregnancy. Of course, Marie's joy is mitigated by the question, Why Pierre and not me? But other obstacles to recognition follow, paradoxically, by means of recognition of a different order. A dancer uses their theory to formulate her work, the séances abuse it; all kinds of silly applications make us, with hindsight, shiver: radioactive matches, radioactive cigarettes, radioactive perfumes …

The next chapter is "Cleveland 1957," and the subject, a young boy who has cancer, is the first guinea pig to be treated with radioactivity. This first occurs more than twenty years after Marie's death. The film never tells if the boy is cured or not. Then we get "Stockholm 1903," when Pierre begins to feel sick and to understand the danger of their invention. Of course, for a contemporary audience of the film, this is not surprising. But we will see that the point of the film's temporality lies elsewhere. In the sequence "Hiroshima 1945" a man watches a boy who plays with a paper airplane. He throws it into the air, and the man's facial expression changes from pleasure to worry when the small paper toy imperceptibly morphs into a bomb, and a violent explosion follows. This moment will recur. In "Nevada 1961" nuclear testing has catastrophic effects. Pierre dies in a carriage accident in 1904, dragged along by the straps of the horses. Marie feels how strong their bond was ("I can't do anything without him"), and when Paul Langevin tries to comfort her, she is the one who kisses him first, similar to her meeting with Pierre. She causes a scandal by publishing an interview about women and sex. The public, or the mob, turns against her. "Go home," they shout. When, in 1910, Marie is the first woman to receive the Nobel Prize twice, this time not in physics but in chemistry, she is asked not to come to Stockholm, for the hosts fear the scandal will follow her and contaminate their purely scientific event. Of course, she does go, and is acclaimed by Swedish women in what looks like an early feminist manifestation. One woman stands up, another follows, more follow, and soon even the men, somewhat reluctantly, join in that standing ovation.

Then we jump to the moment "Chernobyl 1986." The present draws near, and Marie is long dead. By now we are already fully aware that these memories are not, cannot be, Marie's but must be our own. The point of the temporality becomes clearer. I personally remember school lessons about Hiroshima, reading Marguerite Duras's screenplay and novel and seeing Alain Resnais's 1959 film *Hiroshima mon amour* in mid-adolescence. This was part of my awakening political awareness. Soon I was going to participate in rallies against the Vietnam War. But I was an adult, on a research fellowship in the United States, when the Chernobyl disaster happened, the consequences of which are still ongoing. The widening of experiences and memories is a central element of this film and its complex durational structure, which makes it impossible to construct Curie's life and work as a linear biography. And if we don't get that yet, the sequence set during World War I when her eldest daughter Irène (played by Anya Taylor-Joy) finally manages to persuade her mother to let go of her hospital phobia when she says to her, "It's time to make this war your war," the widening ripple effect becomes inevitably visible. Irène later also won a Noble Prize, also with her partner, Frédéric Joliot, for the invention of artificial radiation. This appeal to that merging of professional scientific ambition and empathy for the suffering soldiers will bring Marie to do what her daughter says she must. She sets out to design mobile X-ray machines and goes on to raise money for their production and deployment, as well as the production of ambulances, which saved a lot of lives and pointless amputations. Still her usual blunt self, she says to the unwilling minister, "This is my last fight, and I will win it."

The time structure, full of leaps to the future, constitutes a temporal ripple effect. This is not rendered by a chronology of the future, but on the contrary, by a disorderly set of leaps that suggest this is neither an actor-bound development nor a punctual crisis, but an ongoing result of a more general (scientific) development that morphs into an ongoing crisis, if such a paradox is possible; thus making that distinction between development and crisis in fabula analysis hard to sustain. The leaps, here, are like the holes in the chronology of *Sula*. They have methodological implications that are useful for the practice of narratology. They point to the limited relevance of an analysis that would easily turn too rigidly structuralist. But without such an "attempt at a method" – to recycle Greimas's modest subtitle of his break-through book on semantic analysis – we might not have realized how the things we – and especially scientists – do, poignantly and strongly refuse to go away. This, in retrospect, might illuminate Sula's impossible musings after death I quoted above.

The insight we can gain from these temporal effects can then be brought to bear on other cases in this volume. This is how the mosaic works to become a constellation. The narrative style of Flaubert, who creates extensive descriptive sequences for routine (non-)events and rushes through crises such as, most prominently, Emma's suicide, makes a distinction between development and crisis not only irrelevant but also impossible to establish. Perhaps, we must then conclude, that is the point, precisely. Something similar can be alleged for Desai's *In Custody*, in which transitions are frequently simply skipped. Deven is now in Delhi, then in Mirpore, but how and why specifically at that time is seldom made explicit. The ninth chapter begins with an evocation of something that seems a film running wild in acceleration:

Then began a period when events moved at such a pace and images and sensations packed themselves in so closely that Deven quite lost the

> earlier vision of the shining horizon and the empty road, hurled as he was
> upon the flying horse of a merry-go-round that turned upon its axle with
> such rattling speed that he could decipher no one image, follow no single
> sequence and was merely aware of the rush of things as they sped by, now
> mounting by stages, now descending, in circles around him, leaving him
> giddy, somewhat sick, and almost giggling with exhilaration. (147)

The "film" in which the subject-actor is not acting but being whirled around consists of one element: excessive speed. Right after this passage that we cannot place in time, Deven, it turns out, is in Murad's office and about to begin that unfortunate interview for which so much had to be done – from buying insufficiently financed recording equipment to finding (as it turns out later, renting) a quieter place – and much more.

How it all happened is not systematically told. But this cinematic passage is all "about" speed, and the loss of grip on what happens, so the lack of clear transitions is consistent with the sensations the actor goes through. After this, and the somewhat unpleasant confrontation with Murad – who enacts the actant-power, as well as frequently shifting between helper and opponent – a long passage retrospectively narrates, with Deven as the focalizer, all that precedes, and that had produced the accelerated cinema passage. Where *Sula* and *Radioactive*, each in their own way, foreground an enduring continuity and consequently, a lack of denouement, *In Custody*'s mad or at least maddening passage destroys all hope of linearity and hence, of a happy ending, even if it talks about many events and a shining horizon.

A temporal effect in *Small Axe* that is heavy with implication is neither slowed down nor speeded up but, we can say, real-time enduring. In all films, there are sequences in which something everyday-like seems to go on too long. The duration is real; there is no technical manipulation. In *Education*, in which a brilliant but rebellious Black youngster is sent to a "special school" where the kids don't get any serious teaching, a totally indifferent teacher plays an entire song with lousy guitar music. Do we need to hear and see the entire song? Yes, says McQueen's narrator, we need to experience the utterly futility of the lazy teacher and the boredom of the educationally doomed children. Another film of this series, *Lovers Rock* consists almost in its entirety of a rock party where young men and women are trying to meet the other of their lives. A party that confines, and confines the viewer almost just as much. Duration, here, is a weapon, or the bars of a prison, in situations in which so little "small axes" are possible. In another film of this series, *Alex Wheatle*, the young man, a future novelist, is thrown on the floor in one of many acts of violence. We see his head and the catatonic look in his eyes. The close-up shot is very slowly zoomed in, until his head almost reaches the edge of the screen. Then, equally slowly, the zooming-out places the head where the sequence began. There is no movement in the figure's head; only the camera moves, ever so slowly. Here, again, what matters is the sense of real-time duration, a durationality that resonates with the enduringness of the racism.

The works discussed in this section have different ways of destroying the illusion of narrative as something that we can follow patiently. But then, have we seen other cases where fabula temporality is as obvious as from "Once upon a time" to "happily ever after"? Yet the narrativity of these texts is never in doubt. What is in doubt, instead, is the belief that a method can ever exceed its status as Greimas's "attempt." This is not a non-result nor an un-truth but the truth about narrative art, narrative communication, and cultural life. Narrative is "about" life, but in itself it is "live." This is at issue in the final section.

5: Location

In *Sula*, the ironically named place "The Bottom" is the Black neighbourhood in which the story is set in its entirety. It is located on top of a hill and is called its nickname because, being totally infertile, it is the shabby, poor neighbourhood where, in the novel's ironic use of the derogatory term, "the Blacks" live. The bottom, not in the geographical but in the social sense. The ten years that Sula is away are not narrated at all. She is gone, then she is back. In this respect this novel can be compared to *El dolor*, which is also confined to one place, *la huerta*. Both places are confining suburban areas, which turns the story into one that is inevitably focalized from within. And we can add *In Custody* to this characterization. Whether or not the primary focalizer is fabula-internal and perceptible, as in *El dolor*, or anonymous yet also fabula-internal, as is the most likely scenario in *Sula*, or so consistently central that his identity as a focalizer doesn't even matter, as in Desai's novel, makes only a small difference for the inflection of the events by a subjectivity that steers our view. What does matter, and this explains why "location" is a relevant category of fabula analysis, is the relationship not only among actors but also between actor and place.

For this short final section, therefore, I want to connect two ideas brought up earlier. One is the narrative efficacy of setting fabulas in confining small spaces. This can be a provincial town or a single room, a sense of being "in custody" to an actual prison. The advantage is the easy structuring of actors into actants and the relationships among them. Such places are frequently negatively connoted, and as such they take on an actantial significance: they become actants-opponents. The second idea is the sense that the addressee of the narrative can be "appointed" a participant, the actant-helper who makes the fabula live. In that function, the place participates, and facilitates the addressee's role to enable the narrative to effectuate its affects and effects. Then, just as the confining space but in the opposite direction, the places become the setting of the events, which in this case are different according to who that visiting participant is.

Although she devotes an entire chapter to the dispersal of the (formerly unified) subject, Bishop's definition in the quotation above about installation art, remains subject-centred. This seems to me reasonable as long as that subject is not considered as the full human being but as the functional subject whose goal, or actant-object, is to be a participant in, in the sense of actively, including physically, being part of the installation. The goal, in other words, is the relationship. The dispersal of the subject in this sense is at stake in the installations of the Spanish artist Concha Jerez (born 1941), in which her "image-thinking" brings up what one of her exhibition titles called "ideas instaladas" (installed ideas). True to the continual revisioning of concepts that is the backbone of Jerez's art, however, she does not allow us to catch her out in defining her concept "installed ideas" definitively. She defines *installation* differently in different moments. Thus, she makes the installation form itself "live."

To understand Jerez's vision of installation art as relevant for fabula analysis, allow me to quote three of her statements about this, her favourite, artistic genre. In one description she says that she sees it as "a unique work generated from a concept and/or from a visual narrative created by the artist in a specific place. A complete interaction is established in it between the elements introduced and the space considered as a total work" (Maderuelo 1987, 8). That specificity of place is what connects her installations to the narratives we read, watch, and see all around us. This comment by Jerez adds to Bishop's definition the idea of uniqueness that is bound up with Jerez's empowerment of the space, in reciprocation with the artist as well as, later, the visitors.

Unique does not refer to an evaluation of the artwork but to the impossibility of separating, distinguishing, time from space, as well as to the transformation of each installed object according to where it is located. It is unique in that it cannot remain the same when the objects are moved to and installed in another place. This makes it impossible for

Jerez's installations to travel. Each deployment of (sometimes) the same objects in a different space creates a different work, for no two spaces are identical. This attributes to places a powerful actantial participatory function.

Jerez was even more emphatic about this in another interview, in which she gave expression to the art-space reciprocation specifically:

> For me an installation is something that requires a place for it to be developed. This place is part of the work. I do not consider a work that appears in different places in the same form, without a close relationship with the space, to be an installation. To my way of thinking, the installation is associated with the place as a support and part of the narrative. In each emplacement the work changes radically because the space is part of it, it is a living element. (Murría 2018, 26)

The word *support* denotes more than the floor, pedestal, paper, or canvas. As a thought-image the word *support* resonates with its social use as "helpful," "making possible": a friendly relationship. Opposed as this is to the hostility that Emma Bovary experiences within the confined space of the village, it is also a relationship, for which a place is indispensable. The central point is the importance, liveness, and participation of the place. It is no longer just an environment into which the viewer is admitted but a full participant in the process that art constitutes or sets in motion. The sensation of this participation of the space also changes the visitors. A respect for the specificity and the liveness of the space transforms their sense of mastery over an allegedly neutral space. This spatial aspect cannot be reduced to architectural, physical space. Participation presupposes a dialogue, of which the space is one of the "speakers."

In her text for the catalogue for the exhibition *Del lugar al no-lugar* (from place to no-place) (2001), Jerez further nuances her view of installation. Now she adds hearing:

> I HEAR it in the interaction with spatial measurements, such as those that involve the fullness/emptiness and the emptiness/silence present in the visual reality and its measurement through concepts of time.

But hearing is always participating, whether or not sound or music are installed as well as objects, images, or other elements that carry ideas. In this last fragment, synaesthesia rules. The spatial measurements have, or make, an acoustic specificity. Full or empty involve, also, the tactile sense of being in that space. Then, she turns emptiness and silence into a visual element. Time comes in to further vitalize the place. Time is, here, couched in the present tense.

This, in turn, connects back to cinematic narratives, as well as to the question of social relevance. I would like to invoke a highly synesthetic moment in the essay film I recently made (2020). As mentioned above, I had been invited to make an "essay" film as an experiment exploring what such a genre could be and how it relates to narrative. The inviting group is called Narrative Media Lab, which agreed very precisely with my own attempt to make narratology relevant beyond literature, and beyond art alone. We agreed I'd come for the first week of March, and we barely made it through the filming and a first-draft edit when the week was up, and the next thing I knew was the coronavirus lockdown. Both the timing and the choice of topic make this an apt provisional endpiece for a book that binds narratology to practice and that offers a plea for the social-political relevance of narrative.

No Conclusion

This book does not warrant a conclusion; not one, at least, that would bind together all the threads of the arguments. Instead of closure, I want to open up narratology even further than I have done all along this text; even though the return to the beginning might suggest otherwise. Inspired by Wolf's novel and Malani's video-shadow play, and by the threatening condition of the world, I decided, in early January, to make the figure of Cassandra central to the film *It's about Time!* (2020). This was an attempt to enlist a fictional character on behalf of an argumentative film; an essay film.

But an essay film, like any essay, wrote Adorno, is defined as thought "alive," that is partial in the two senses of the word: subjective and fragmented. These two meanings characterize the partiality this book has laid out. Thinking as social, performative, and always unfinished; as dialogic. Through the mythical figure of Cassandra, who could foresee the future but was cursed to never be believed, I tried to "figure," make a figural shape for the thoughts on the indifference of people towards the imminent ecological disaster of the world. Not coincidentally, the reason she was cursed was her refusal to be coerced into sex with Apollo; an early case of #MeToo. Sexual harassment on the work floor is of all times, it seems. In the combination of thought as partial in the two senses and narrative fiction that assists that thinking, we can probe the relevance of narrative as political, in the sense of activating.

To honour Adorno's inflection of the essay as form, mentioned above, among other motivations, I gave the present book a form I have called a mosaic. To make my case for the practical relevance of narratology I decided to give this book, as well as the essay film, the formless form of short fragments, without a clear order, logic, binary, or hierarchy. My hope is that the analyses, short and somewhat longer, that constitute the bulk of the book will persuade readers, by means of their concreteness, of "the point" of narratological analysis, whether or not the texts are meant to be narratives or not.

I bring this film briefly in at this point because of a moment, about halfway into it, where Cassandra addresses the place as such, on her way to a reflection on time. Against the backdrop of multiple reflections of a stained-glass window, she sits down for a moment before moving on. This is in an intermediate place, on a stairwell, when she is on her way to her next encounter, which is like a "lesson" in time-thinking.

I quote a brief passage from the script, which is a combination of quotations from Wolf's novel and my own thought on the central issue: of time, timeliness, and urgency.

> Cassandra enters her parents' Palace. She looks around, sighs, and mutters:
> Cassandra: I learned that protest begins with this silence in which more than one takes part.
> Cassandra is dressed casually. She carefully steps down the stairs:
> A palace of silence ... I learned a lot by observing the various types of silence. Only much later did I learn silence myself; what a useful weapon.
> What would artists make of this silent palace?

She then walks into a white-cube-type gallery space, where a video on a contemporary Spanish sculptural installation is being projected, wall filling. Her reflections on this sculpture engage the multiple icons from past art and the frightening huge head of the "Soplador" who is breathing these traditions in and out. That monstrous head is a self-portrait of the artist Lidó Rico.

Cassandra's passage from her parents' quarters in the palace to the modernist space through the silence of the palace is indispensable for the connection between the place and the sculpture that multiplies and reverses time. The location of this brief moment of reflection on silence on a stairwell, as a three-dimensional threshold, makes the short scene synaesthetic, in the way Jerez describes installation art. Hearing is the primary sensation – hearing silence. Maybe this is the moment I had better stay silent, rather than ending on a conclusion that might suggest a closure. Instead, this book is meant to open up practices of narratological analysis, to be done by everyone in their own way, on one condition: to keep them discussable.

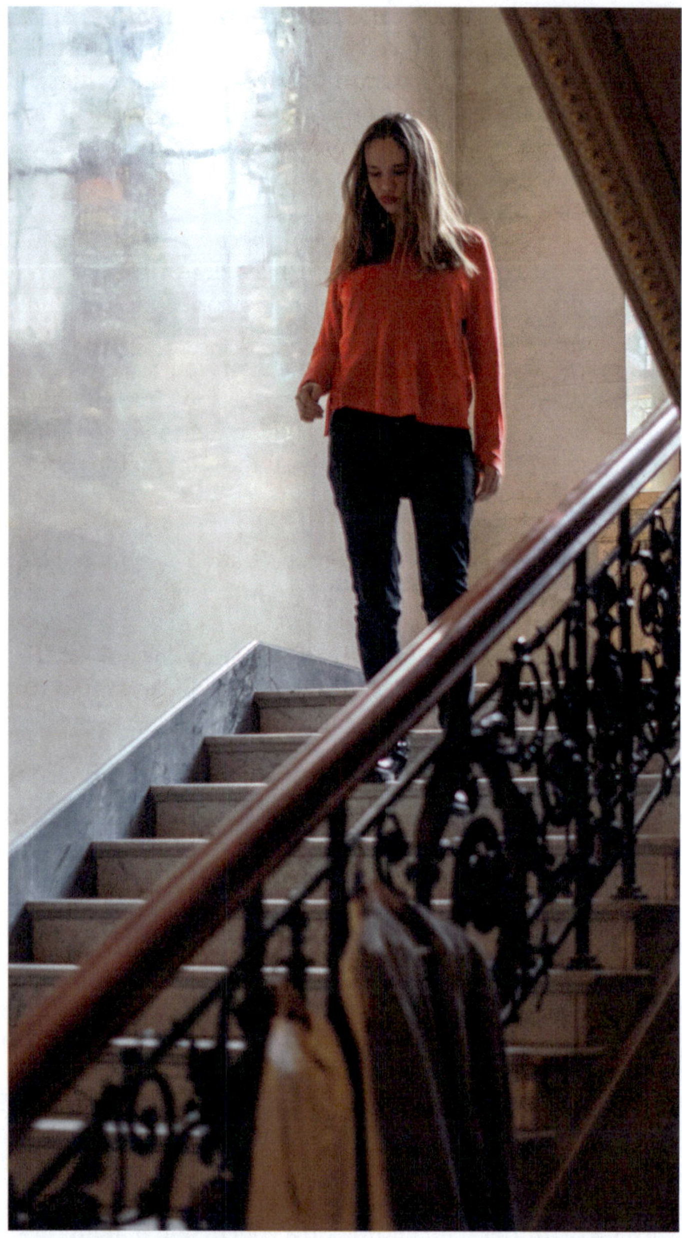

Figure 31.   Cassandra (Magdalena Żak) on her way to a new episode in her lessons in time-thinking. Location: Muzeum Sztuki w Łodzi, Pałac Herbsta. Photo: Alicia Devaux.

Remarks and Sources

The philosophical musings of Slavoj Žižek in his short book *Event* (2014) on the event propose six different conceptions of what an event is. The first of these is "reframing." The others are close to this one or derived from it. Among other philosophical works on the event I only mention Alain Badiou (2005), who integrates reflections on the event with ethics. For an accessible introduction, see Norris (2009).

On framing as an analytical concept, I have written a chapter in the book on "travelling concepts" cited earlier (2002). There, I take Culler's "Author's Preface" in his book from 1981 as my starting point, wherein he decisively substitutes the concept of framing for the problematic one of context, with all the convincing arguments in half a page. Culler's work is invariably useful for its generous, communicative clarity combined with a refusal of unwarranted simplicity. From *Structuralist Poetics* (1975) to his later *The Literary in Theory* (2007), which contains the best overview of the issues of the concept of performativity, and beyond, for difficult concepts and theories, I recommend to always start with his work to clarify challenging theoretical ideas. To give one example, Culler's (2007) critique of the concept "omniscient narrator" persuasively indicts the metaphysical ideology that underlies it (see 183–204).

On the impossibility to think or speak when dead, Denis Hollier (1988) has written a useful article on Foucault's "theo-necrology," as Hollier calls it. The issues of death and representation are entangled in the complex areas between epistemology and ethics. For a short discussion, see Bal and Williams Gamaker (2013).

For the concept of *actant* and the elaboration of the six actants, see *Narratology* (165–77). The theory was best elaborated by A.J. Greimas (1983), a book that is modestly and instructively subtitled "an attempt at a method," a subtitle which is to be taken seriously. This method is not dogmatic but tentative. The practice of this theory is demonstrated in a useful concrete analysis of a short story in a later book (1988). Limited as it is, with fabula structure as the primary topic, the theory and the practice remain very helpful for the practice of narratological analysis of the fabula, with the text and story levels temporarily in the background. As an overall method, it would be too narrow.

On the early use of colour in cinema, including Loie Fuller's famous *Fire Dance*, see Gunning et al. (2015). This beautiful book demonstrates that the early cinema's fascination with movement comes with an early interest in colour as an indispensable, even if fantasmatic element of the moving image. On the keen interest in movement, including travel, in early cinema, see Verhoeff (2006).

Graphic novels and comics are not discussed in this book. There is no particular reason for this, other than lack of space and sufficient knowledge. The ideas of, for example, Laura Mulvey (2006) on film frames as basically still images would work very well in connection to Scott McCloud (2010), a remarkable study of the comic in the form of a comic. This book can be considered a narratology of the comic.

I have recently been involved in studying Concha Jerez's work, especially her installations, which come so close to my concept of image-thinking that I got a lot of inspiration from it. Her exhibition was commented on and published in a book with DVD (Jerez 2007). This I have listed under the pieces of the mosaic. See Maderuelo (1987, 8). The second quote is from Murría (2018, 26). The third one is in Jerez (2001, 125).

The analysis of the painting *Bathsheba's Bath* is based on an earlier more extensive one, in *Reading "Rembrandt,"* (2006 [1991], 219–46) of which I talked in the interviews with Lutters on teaching. The "mistake" of the foot ending up on the wrong side compared to the crossing of the knee, I have termed there a *disfigure*.

The most in-depth critique of the concept of *artistic research* is by Kamini Vellodi (2019), in a collective volume devoted to the issue from a philosophical, specifically Deleuzian, perspective. For more on the essay film and my attempt to make one, see my article in *Text Matters* (2020c). On Lidó Rico's sculptural installation, and on another Spanish sculpture that appears in the film *It's about Time*, I wrote analyses in a short book on the contemporary (2020b). I also wrote a more extensive study of Lidó Rico's art (2021).

References

Multiple titles by single authors are listed in reversed-chronological order. This keeps the focus on the present or recent past.

Theoretical and Critical Writings

Adorno, Theodor W. 1991 [1954–8]. "The Essay as Form." In *Notes to Literature*, vol.1, translated by Shierry Weber Nicholson, 3–23. New York: Columbia University Press.

Alberca, Manuel. 2020. "Miguel Ángel Hernández: el tríptico del arte o la vida." *Cuadernos Hispanoamericanos* 838 (30 April).

Alphen, Ernst van. 2017. "Attention for Distraction: Modernity, Modernism and Perception." *Text Matters* 7 (7): 87–97.

– 2008. "Affective Operations of Art and Literature." *RES: Journal of Anthropology and Aesthetics* 53/54 (Spring/Autumn): 20–30.

– 2006. "Second-Generation Testimony, Transmission of Trauma, and Postmemory." *Poetics Today* 27 (2): 473–88.

– 2005. *Art in Mind: How Contemporary Images Shape Thought*. Chicago: University of Chicago Press.

– 1999. "Symptoms of Discursivity: Experience, Memory, Trauma." In *Acts of Memory: Cultural Recall in the Present*, edited by Mieke Bal, Jonathan Crewe, and Leo Spitzer, 24–38. Hanover, NH: University of New England Press.

Alphen, Ernst van, and Tomáš Jirsa (eds.). 2019. *How to Do Things with Affects: Affective Triggers in Aesthetic Forms and Cultural Practices*. Leiden: Brill Press.

Badiou, Alain. 2005. *Being and Event*. Translated by Oliver Feltham. New York: Continuum.

Bakhtin, Mikhail. 1981 [1934]. *The Dialogic Imagination: Four Essays by M.M. Bakhtin*. Edited by Michael Holquist. Translated by Caryl Emerson and Michael Holquist. Austin, TX: University of Texas Press.

Bal, Mieke. 2022. *Image-Thinking: Art Making as Cultural Analysis*. Edinburgh: Edinburgh University Press.

– 2021 "Thinking, Seeing, Taking Away: Lidó Rico's Strategies of Activating Sculpture" / "Pensar, ver, quitar: las estrategias de Lidó Rico para activar la escultura." In *Lidó Rico, Tu vuelo, mis alas*, 6–53. Murcia: Sala Verónicas.

– 2020a. "Challenging and Saving the Author, for Creativity | Sfidare e salvare l'autore, per creatività." In *Vesper. Rivista di architettura, arti e teoria | Journal of Architecture, Arts & Theory* 2, Materia-autore | Author-Matter, Quodlibet, Macerata primavera-estate (Spring-Summer): 132–49.

– 2020b. *Exhibition-ism: Temporal Togetherness*. Berlin: Sternberg Press.

– 2020c. "It's about Time: Trying an Essay Film." *Text Matters* 10 (issue "Literature Goes Pop"): 27–48.

– 2019. *Don Quijote: Sad Countenances*. Edited by Niklas Salmose. Växjö, Sweden: Trolltrumma. Bilingual edition English-Spanish: 2020. *Don Quijote: Tristes figuras; Don Quijote: Sad Countenances*. Murcia: Cendeac (Ad Litteram).

– 2017a. *Emma & Edvard Looking Sideways: Loneliness and the Cinematic*. Oslo: Munch Museum / Brussels: Mercatorfonds; Yale University Press.

– 2017b. "Intership: Anachronism between Loyalty and the Case." In *The Oxford Handbook of Adaptation Studies*, edited by Thomas Leitch, 179–96. New York and Oxford: Oxford University Press.

– 2016. *In Medias Res: Inside Nalini Malani's Shadow Plays*. Ostfildern, Germany: Hatje Cantz.

– 2011a. "A Thousand and One Voices." In *Confronting Universalities: Aesthetics and Politics under the Sign of Globalisation*, edited by Mads Anders Baggesgaard and Jakob Ladegaard, 269–304. Aarhus, Denmark: Aarhus University Press.

– 2011b. "*Mektoub*: When Art Meets History, Philosophy, and Linguistics." In *Case Studies in Interdisciplinary Research*, edited by Allen F. Repko, Williams H. Newell, and Rick Szostak, 91–122. Thousand Oaks, CA: SAGE.

– 2010. *Of What One Cannot Speak: Doris Salcedo's Political Art*. Chicago, IL: The University of Chicago Press.

– 2009. *Fragments of Matter: Jeannette Christensen*. Bergen: Bergen National Academy of the Arts.

– 2008. "Phantom Sentences." In *Phantom Sentences: Essays in Linguistics and Literature Presented to Ann Banfield*, edited by Robert S. Kawashima, Gilles Philippe, and Thelma Sowley, 17–42. Bern: Peter Lang.

– 2006 [1991]. *Reading "Rembrandt": Beyond the Word-Image Opposition*. Cambridge, UK, and New York: Cambridge University Press. 2nd edition (paperback) 1994; reprint Amsterdam: Amsterdam University Press.

– 2002. *Travelling Concepts in the Humanities: A Rough Guide*. Toronto: University of Toronto Press.

– 2001. *Louise Bourgeois'* Spider: *The Architecture of Art-Writing*. Chicago, IL: University of Chicago Press.

– 1999. *Quoting Caravaggio: Contemporary Art, Preposterous History*. Chicago, IL: University of Chicago Press.

– 1988. *Death and Dissymmetry: The Politics of Coherence in the Book of Judges*. Chicago, IL: University of Chicago Press.

Bal, Mieke, Jonathan Crewe, and Leo Spitzer, eds. 1999. *Acts of Memory: Cultural Recall in the Present*. Hanover, NH: University Press of New England.

Bal, Mieke, and Michelle Williams Gamaker. 2013. "Scenography of Death: Figuration, Focalization, and Finding Out." *Performance Research* 18 (3): 179–86.

Banfield, Ann. 1982. *Unspeakable Sentences: Narration and Representation in the Language of Fiction*. Boston: Routledge & Kegan Paul.

Barthes, Roland. 1967. "The Death of the Author." Translated by Stephen Heath. In *Image-Music-Text*, 142–7. New York: Hill and Wang.

Benjamin, Walter. 1999 [1927–40]. *The Arcades Project*. Translated by Howard Eiland and Kevin McLaughlin. Harvard, MA: Harvard University Press.

Bishop, Claire. 2005. *Installation Art*. London: Tate Publishing.

Bleeker, Maaike. 2008. "Being Angela Merkel." In *The Rhetoric of Sincerity*. Edited by Ernst van Alphen, Mieke Bal, and Carel Smith, 247–62. Stanford: Stanford University Press.

– 2008. *Visuality in the Theatre: The Locus of Looking*. Basingstoke: Palgrave Macmillan.

Bollas, Christopher. 1987. *The Shadow of the Object: Psychoanalysis of the Unthought Known*. New York: Columbia University Press.

Booth, Wayne C. 1961. *The Rhetoric of Fiction*. Chicago: The University of Chicago Press.

Chatman, Seymour. 1990. *Coming to Terms: The Rhetoric of Narrative in Fiction and Film*. Ithaca: Cornell University Press.

Crary, Jonathan. 1999. *Suspensions of Perception: Attention, Spectacle, and Modern Culture*. Cambridge, MA: MIT.

Culler, Jonathan. 2007. *The Literary in Theory*. Stanford, CA: Stanford University Press.

– 2004. "Omniscience." *Narrative* 12, no. 1 (January): 22–34.

– 1981. *The Pursuit of Signs: Semiotics, Literature, Deconstruction*. Ithaca: Cornell University Press.

– 1975. *Structuralist Poetics: Structuralism, Linguistics, and the Study of Literature*. Ithaca: Cornell University Press.

Dällenbach, Lucien. 1989 [1977]. *The Mirror in the Text*. Translated by Jeremy Whiteley with Emma Hughes. Chicago: University of Chicago Press.

Doolan, Paul. 2013. "Maria Dermoût and 'Unremembering' Lost Time." *Canadian Journal of Netherlandic Studies* 34 (2): 1–28.

Elleström, Lars. 2021. "The Modalities of Media II: An Expanded Model for Understanding Intermedial Relations." In *Beyond Media Borders*, vol. 1, 3–91.

– 2013. "Adaptation within the Field of Media Transformations." In *Adaptation Studies: New Challenges, New Directions*, edited by Jørgen Bruhn, Anne Gjelsvik, and Eirik Frisvold Hanssen, 113–32. London and New York: Bloomsbury Academic.

Elleström, Lars, ed. 2021. *Beyond Media Borders: Intermedial Relations among Multimodal Media*, vols. 1 and 2. Basingstoke: Palgrave Macmillan.

Foucault, Michel. 1979. "What Is an Author?" In *Textual Strategies: Perspectives in Post-Structuralist Criticism*, edited by Josué V. Harari, translated by Donald Bouchard and Sherry Simon, 141–60. Ithaca: Cornell University Press.

Freud, Sigmund. 1982 [1900]. *The Interpretation of Dreams*. Translated and edited by James Strachey. New York: Avon Books.

Fuchs, Martin. 2001. "Textualizing Culture: Hermeneutics of Distanciation." In *Travelling Concepts*, edited by Joyce Goggin and Sonja Neef, 55–66. Amsterdam: ASCA Press.

Garcés, María Antonia. 2002. *Cervantes in Algiers: A Captive's Tale*. Nashville, TN: Vanderbilt University Press.

Geertz, Clifford. 1984. "Anti Anti-Relativism." In *American Anthropologist* 86: 263–78. Reprinted in *Relativism: Interpretation and Confrontation*, edited by Michael Krause, 12–34. Notre Dame: University of Notre Dame Press.

– 1983. *Local Knowledge: Further Essays in Interpretive Anthropology*. New York: Basic Books.

Genette, Gérard. 1972. *Discours du récit*. Vol. 3 of *Figures*. Paris: Editions du Seuil. (Eng. *Narrative Discourse: An Essay in Method*. Translated by Jane E. Lewin. Ithaca and London: Cornell University Press 1980).

Greimas, Algirdas Julien. 1988 [1976]. *Maupassant: The Semiotics of Text, Practical Lessons*. Translated by Paul Perron. Amsterdam and Philadelphia: J. Benjamins, Publishers and Co.

– 1983 [1966]. *Structural Semantics: An Attempt at a Method*. Translated by Daniele McDowell, Ronald Schleifer, and Alan Velie. Lincoln: University of Nebraska Press.

Gunning, Tom, Giovanna Fossati, Joshua Yumibe, Jonathon Rosen. 2015. *Fantasia of Color in Early Cinema*. Amsterdam: Eye Film Museum / Amsterdam University Press.

Hamon, Philippe. 1983. *Le Personnel du roman*. Geneva: Droz.

Hansen, Miriam Bratu. 1996. "Schindler's List Is Not Shoah: The Second Commandment, Popular Modernism, and Public Memory." *Critical Inquiry* 22 (2): 292–312.

Herman, David. 2003. *Narrative Theory and the Cognitive Sciences*. Stanford, CA: CSLI Publications.

– 2002. *Story Logic: Problems and Possibilities of Narrative*. Lincoln, NE: University of Nebraska Press.

Hernández, Miguel Á. 2020. *El Arte a contratiempo. Historia, obsolescencia, estéticas migratorias.* Madrid: AKAL.

Hirsch, Marianne. 2008. "The Generation of Postmemory." In *Poetics Today* 29 (1): 103–28.

– 1997. *Family Frames: Photography, Narrative, and Postmemory.* Cambridge: Harvard University Press.

Hirschkop, Ken, and David Shepherd. 1989. *Bakhtin and Cultural Theory.* Manchester: Manchester University Press.

Hollier, Denis. 1988. "The Word of God: 'I Am Dead.'" *October* 44 (Spring): 75–88.

Jerez, Concha. 2001. "From Place to Non-place." In *Concha Jerez. Lekutik ezlekura - del lugar al no-lugar*, 125–9. San Sebastián: Koldo Mitxelena Kulturunea.

Khanna, Ranjana. 2008. *Algeria Cuts: Women and Representation, from 1830 to the Present.* Durham, NC: Duke University Press.

Leitch, Thomas. 2003. "Twelve Fallacies in Contemporary Adaptation Theory." *Criticism* 45 (2): 149–71.

Lutters, Jeroen. 2018. *The Trade of the Teacher: Visual Thinking with Mieke Bal.* Interviews by Jeroen Lutters. Amsterdam: Valiz.

Maderuelo, Javier. 1987. "Todo está en la realidad." Interview with Concha Jerez in *Concha Jerez: In Quotidianitatis Memoriam.* Kassel: Hall K 18.

Marx, William. 2020. *Vivre dans la bibliothèque du monde.* Paris: Collège de France – Fayard.

Massumi, Brian, ed. 2002. *A Shock to Thought: Expression after Deleuze and Guattari.* New York: Routledge.

McCloud, Scott. 2010. *Understanding Comics: The Invisible Art.* New York: Morrow.

McMaster, Gerald. 2017. "Under Indigenous Eyes: This Summer's Major European Exhibitions Revealed the Critical Spirit of Global Indigeneity." *Art in America*, October: 64–71.

– 1996. "Little Traces in My Mind." In *Mary Longman: Traces*, 7–28. Kamloops: Kamloops Art Gallery.

Mouffe, Chantal. 2005. *On the Political.* New York and London: Routledge.

Müller, Günther. 1968. *Morphologische Poetik: Gesammelte Aufsätze.* Edited by Elena Müller. Tübingen: Niemeyer.

Mulvey, Laura. 2006. *Death 24x a Second: Stillness and the Moving Image.* London: Reaktion.

Murría, Alicia. 2018 [1998]. "Ideas, Spaces, Fissures in the Work of Concha Jerez." In *Concha Jerez. Interferencias*, 20–37. Las Palmas: Centro Atlántico de Arte Moderno.

Negrete, Fernanda. 2020. *The Aesthetic Clinic: Feminine Sublimation in Contemporary Writing, Psychoanalysis, and Art.* Albany, NY: SUNY Press.

Newell, William H., ed. 1998. *Interdisciplinarity: Essays from the Literature.* New York: The College Entrance Examination Board.

Norris, Christopher. 2009. *Badiou's Being and Event: A Reader's Guide*. London, Continuum.

Pascal, Blaise. 1910 [1660]. *Pascal, Blaise: Thoughts, Letters, and Minor Works*. Edited by Charles William Eliot. The Harvard Classics, vol. 48. New York: PF Collier & Son.

Patron, Sylvie, ed. 2020. *Optional-Narrator Theory: Principles, Perspectives, Proposals*. Lincoln: University of Nebraska Press.

Peeren, Esther. 2007. *Intersubjectivities and Popular Culture: Bakhtin and Beyond*. Stanford, CA: Stanford University Press.

Perniola, Mario. 1995. *Enigmas: The Egyptian Moment in Art and Society*. Translated by Christopher Woodall. London: Verso.

Pollock, Griselda. 2018. *Charlotte Salomon and the Theatre of Memory*. New Haven: Yale University Press.

Rancière, Jacques. 2013. *Béla Tarr: The Time After*. Translated by Erik Beranek. Minneapolis, MN: Univocal.

Ross, Christine. 2006. *The Aesthetics of Disengagement: Contemporary Art and Depression*. Minneapolis, Minnesota: University of Minnesota Press.

Rothberg, Michael. 2009. *Multidirectional Memory: Remembering the Holocaust in the Age of Decolonization*. Stanford: Stanford University Press.

Silverman, Kaja. 2000. *World Spectators*. Stanford: Stanford University Press.

– 1996. *The Threshold of the Visible World*. New York: Routledge.

Sontag, Susan. 2003. *Regarding the Pain of Others*. New York: Picado/Farrar, Straus and Giroux.

Stoler, Ann Laura. 2002. *Carnal Knowledge and Imperial Power: Race and the Intimate in Colonial Rule*. Berkeley: University of California Press.

Tuin, Iris van der, and Nanna Verhoeff. (forthcoming 2021). *Critical Concepts for the Creative Humanities*. London: Rowman & Littlefield International.

Vellodi, Kamini. 2019. "Thought beyond Research: A Deleuzian Critique of Artistic Research." In *Aberrant Nuptials: Deleuze and Artistic Research 2*, edited by Paulo de Assis and Paolo Giudici, 215–33. Leuven: Leuven University Press.

Verhoeff, Nanna. 2016. "A Tale of Two Times: Augmented Reality as Archival Laboratory." In *Exposing the Film Apparatus: The Film Archive as a Research Laboratory*, edited by Giovanna Fossati and Annie van den Oever, 357–428. Framing Film. Amsterdam: Amsterdam University Press.

– 2006. *The West in Early Cinema: After the Beginning*. Amsterdam: Amsterdam University Press

Verstraten, Peter. 2009. *Film Narratology*. Translated by Stefan van de Lecq. Toronto: The University of Toronto Press.

White, Hayden. 1978. "The Forms of Wildness: Archeology of an Idea." In *Tropics of Discourse*, 150–82. Baltimore: Johns Hopkins University Press.

– 1973. *Metahistory: The Historical Imagination in Nineteenth-Century Europe*. Baltimore: Johns Hopkins University Press.

Žižek, Slavoj. 2014. *Event*. London: Penguin Books.

The Pieces of the Mosaic

Written Texts

Barnes, Djuna. 1936. *Nightwood*. London and Boston: Faber and Faber.

Bibliowicz, Azriel. 2013. *Migas de pan*. Mexico: Alfaguara.

Borges, Jorge Luis. 1983. "The Garden of Forking Paths." In *Labyrinths: Selected Stories & Other Writings*, edited by Donald A. Yates and James E. Irby, 19–29. New York: Modern Library.

– 1962 [1939]. "Pierre Menard, Author of the Quixote." In *Labyrinths*, translated by Anthony Bonner, 62–71. Harmondsworth: Penguin.

Brontë, Emily. 2009 [1847]. *Wuthering Heights*. New York: Harper & Row.

Butor, Michel. 1957. *La modification*. Paris: Minuit.

Calvino, Italo. 1974 [1972]. *Invisible Cities*. Translated by William Weaver. New York and London: Harvest Harcourt Brace Jovanovich.

Cervantes, Miguel de Saavedra. 1950 [1605; 1615]. *The Adventures of Don Quixote*. Translated by J.M. Cohen. Harmondsworth: Penguin Books Ltd. (quoted here); Spanish: 2016. *Don Quijote de la Mancha*. Translated into modern Castilian by Andrés Trapiello. Barcelona: Ediciones Destino.

Colette, Sidonie Gabrielle. 1977 [1933]. *La chatte*. Paris: Hachette, Le Livre de poche.

Cruz, Sor Juana Inés de la. 1955. "Loa para el auto sacramental *El Divino Narciso*." In *Obras completas de Sor Juana Inés de la Cruz*, vol. 3, Autos y Loas, edited by Alfonso Méndez Plancarte, 3–21. México: Fondo de Cultura Económica.

Dermoût, Maria. 1984 [1958]. *The Ten Thousand Things*. Translated by Hans Koning. New York: Simon & Schuster, Inc.

Desai, Anita. 1984. *In Custody*. New York: Harper & Row.

Dickens, Charles. 2003 [1860]. *Great Expectations*. Penguin Classics. Harmondsworth, Middlesex: Penguin.

Emecheta, Buci. 1985 [1983]. *The Rape of Shavi*. London: Fontana.

Flaubert, Gustave. 1971 [1857]. *Madame Bovary*. Vol. 1 of *Oeuvres completes de Gustave Flaubert, Tome 1*. Paris: Club de l'Honnête Homme.

Friedman, Carl. 1994. *Nightfather* [*Tralievader* 1991]. Translated by Arnold Pomerans and Erica Pomerans. New York: Persea.

Hernández, Miguel Ángel. 2018. *El dolor de los demás*. Barcelona: Anagrama.

Keller, Evelyn Fox. 1992. *Secrets of Life, Secrets of Death*. New York: Routledge.

– 1984. *Reflections on Gender and Science*. New Haven: Yale University Press.

Lahiri, Jhumpa. 2012 [2003]. *The Namesake*. London: Fourth Estate.

McEwan, Ian. 1997. *Enduring Love*. London: Jonathan Cape.

Morrison, Toni. 1984 [1973]. *Sula*. London: Triad/Panther Books.

Mulisch, Harry. 1977 [1972]. "What Happened to Sergeant Massuro?" In *Verzamelde verhalen*, 455–78. Amsterdam: Athenaeum, Polak & van Gennep.

Müller, Heiner. 1977. *Hamletmachine. Performing Arts Journal* 4 (3) (nr 12): 141–46.

Neri, Louise, ed. 1996. *Silence Please! Stories after the Works of Juan Muñoz.* Dublin: Irish Museum of Modern Art/Scalo.

Niditch, Susan. 1993. "War, Women and Defilement in Numbers 31." *Semeia* 61: 59–75.

Proust, Marcel. 1981 [1922–33]. *Remembrance of Things Past.* Translated by C.K. Scott-Moncrieff and Terence Kilmartin. London: Penguin Books.

– 1954 [1913]. *A la recherche du temps perdu.* 3 vols. Edited by Pierre Clarac and Léon Ferré. Paris: Gallimard, Pléiade.

Verweg, Hanna. 1984. "Anamnesis." In *De Volkskrant.*

Walker, Alice. 1982. *The Color Purple.* New York: Harcourt, Brace, Jovanovich.

Wolf, Christa. 1984 [1983]. *Cassandra.* Translated by Jan van Heurck. New York: Farrar-Straus-Giroux.

Visual Texts

Aptekar, Ken. 1996. *I'm Six Years Old and Hiding behind My Hands*, oil on wood, 16 panels, with sandblasted glass plates bolted an inch before the paint. 120 x 120 inches.

Bal, Mieke. 2020. *It's about Time! Reflections on Urgency*, video essay (32 min.).

– 2019. *Don Quijote: Sad Countenances*, 16-channel video installation, 33 photographs.

Bal, Mieke, and Michelle Williams Gamaker. 2012–14. *Madame B*, feature film and installations (versions in 19-, 13-, and 5-channels).

Bourgeois, Louise. 1997. *Spider*, steel and mixed media, 175 x 262 x 204 inches. Photograph: Marcus Schneider. Courtesy Cheim & Read, New York.

Butler, Robert. 1997. *Turbulence*, feature film.

Chabrol, Claude. 1991. *Madame Bovary*, feature film.

Christensen, Jeannette. 1974–present. *Woman Interrupted*, polaroid photographs and videos.

Colorbitor (Rumanian artist collective). 2013. *The Cronovizor* (app).

Coppola, Francis Ford. 1972. *The Godfather*, feature film.

Deren, Maya. 1946. *Ritual in Transfigured Time*, feature film.

– 1944. *At Land*, feature film.

Itárritu, Alejandro González. 2006. *Babel*, feature film.

– 2003. *21 Grams*, feature film.

– 2001. *Amores Perros*, feature film.

Janssens, Ann Veronica. 1994. *Corps noir*, sculpture, Black Perspex hemisphere, 50 cm diameter, 25 cm depth. Photo: Marc Dommage.

Jerez, Concha. 2007. *Ideas instaladas*, edited by José Iges and Alberto Flores. Madrid: Librería Gulliver.

Kelley, David E. 1992–6. *Picket Fences*, television drama series.

Longman, Mary. 1996. *Co-Dependents*, wood, leather, copper, 214 x 153 x 55 cm. Collection of Aboriginal Achievement Foundation.

Lynch, David. 1986. *Blue Velvet*, feature film.

Malani, Nalini. 2012. *In Search of Vanished Blood*, six-channel video/shadow play with five reverse painted rotating Mylar cylinders, 4 rpm, sound, 11 minutes.

McQueen, Steve. 2020. *Small Axe*, television series of five films.

Michell, Roger. 2004. *Enduring Love*, feature film.

Munch, Edvard. 1898–1900. *Red Virginia Creeper*, oil on canvas, 119.5 x 121 cm. Oslo, Munch Museum.

Pawlikowski, Pawel. 2013. *Ida*, feature film.

Rembrandt van Rijn. 1654. *Bathsheba at Her Bath*, oil on canvas, 798 x 800. Paris, Musée du Louvre.

Satrapi, Marjane. 2020. *Radioactive*, feature film.

Spielberg, Steven. 1993. *Schindler's List*, feature film.

– 1985. *The Color Purple*, feature film.

Tan, Fiona. 1999. *Facing Forward*, installation film.

– 1998. *Linnaeus' Flower Clock*, installation film.

Tarr, Béla, and Ágnes Hranitski. 2000. *Werckmeister Harmonies*, feature film.

Theuws, Roos. 2014. *Kitab Al Manazir*, three-channel video installation (black-and-white).

– 2012. *Fences & Pools*, two-channel video installation.

Verheul, Thom. 1992. *Denial*, documentary film.

Index of Names and Titles

Acker, Kathy, 89–90
Addams, Charles, 43–4
Addams Family, The. See Addams, Charles
Adorno, Theodor W., 192
Aeschylus, 110
Africa, 43, 133, 148–9
Agamemnon (*Oresteia*), 110
A la recherche du temps perdu (Proust), 125–6, 130–1, 153
Alberca, Manuel, 165
Alberti, Leon Battista, 67
Alex Wheatle (McQueen), 188–9
Allegory of Painting (Boucher), 92
Alphen, Ernst van, 73, 122, 164–5
Ambassadors, The (James), 138
"Anamnesis" (Verweg), 88–91
Apollo, 109, 192
Aptekar, Ken, 92–8
Arabian Nights, 75, 101
Arcades Project, The (Benjamin), 108
Art in Mind (Alphen), 165
Ashima (*The Namesake*), 5–6
At Land (Deren), 114–15, 164
Atonement (McEwan), 151
Auschwitz, 83, 164
Austen, Jane (*Emma*), 24, 164

Bacon, Francis, 55
Bakhtin, Mikhail, 15, 89–91, 126, 129, 165
Balzac, Honoré de, 37
Banfield, Ann, 71
Barnes, Djuna, 57
Barthes, Roland, 24–5, 40, 71
Bathsheba at Her Bath (Rembrandt), viii, 156–9, 166, 196
Beecher Stowe, Harriet, 147–8
Beloved (Morrison), 103, 175
Benjamin, Walter, 108
Bible, Hebrew, 18, 21
Bibliowicz, Azriel, 107, 113, 144
Bishop, Claire, 181–2, 190
Black Lives Matter, 143, 147
Bleeker, Maaike, 165
Blue Velvet (Lynch), 41
Bollas, Christopher, 53, 73, 111–13
Booth, Wayne C., 27, 72
Borges, Jorge Luis, 38, 40, 46–8, 96, 114
Boucher, François, 93–8
Bourgeois, Louise, 47–54, 114
Brigitte (Verheul), 135–6
Brontë, Emily, 74
Butler, Robert (*Turbulence*), 126, 165
Butor, Michel, 45–6

Calvino, Italo, 103, 130
Caravaggio, 50, 73
Cassandra, viii, 32–6, 109, 192–4
Cassandra (Wolf), 32–6, 71,
    109–12, 192
Cat, The (Colette), 64
Cervantes, Miguel de (Saavedra), 37,
    40, 89, 92, 123, 166
Chabrol, Claude, 65
Chaplin, Charlie, 150
*Charlotte Salomon and the Theatre of
    Memory* (Pollock), 73
Chatman, Seymour, 28
Chomsky, Marvin J., 62
Christensen, Jeannette, 39,
    120–4, 165–6
Christie, Agatha, 168
Cinema Suitcase, 76
Close, Glenn, 45
Clytemnestra (*Oresteia*), 110
Co-Dependents (Longman),
    16–17, 181
Colette, Sidonie-Gabrielle, 64
Colorbitor, 134–5
Color Purple, The (Spielberg),
    45, 147–8
Color Purple, The (Walker), 45, 147–8
Conrad, Joseph, 34
Coppola, Francis Ford, 126
Corps noir (Janssens), 66–70
Crary, Jonathan, 122
Cree (Aboriginal people), 72
Cronovizor (Colorbitor), 134–5
Cruz, Sor Juana Ines de la, 90
Culler, Jonathan, 72, 195
Curie, Maria Skłodowska
    (Madame), 182–6

Dällenbach, Lucien, 72
Danka (*Schindler's List*), 31–3, 63
Darwin, Charles, 54
David, King, 157–8

Dean, Nelly (*Wuthering Heights*), 74
Death and Dissymmetry (Bal), 71
"Death of the Author, The"
    (Barthes), 24–5, 27, 40
Deleuze, Gilles, Deleuzian, 48,
    58–9, 124
Denial (Verheul), 135–6
Deren, Maya, vii, 114–16
Dermoût, Maria, 57, 72
Derrida, Jacques, 15
Desai, Anita, 177–81, 187–8
Dickens, Charles, 37, 137
Don Quijote, 37, 66, 72, 123
Don Quixote, 37, 89, 90, 123
Doolan, Paul, 72
Dostoevsky, Fyodor, 37
Douglass, Frederick, 147
Duras, Marguerite, 102, 186

Education (McQueen),
    148, 188
El dolor de los demás (Hernández),
    105–14, 161–4, 167–8, 178, 189
Elleström, Lars, 71
El Narciso Divino (Cruz), 90
Emecheta, Buchi, 132–3, 139–41
Emma (Jane Austen), 24
Emma & Edvard (Bal), 71
Enduring Love (McEwan), 151–3

Facing Forward (Tan), vii, 103–5
Felix in Exile (Kentridge), 102
Fences & Pools (Theuws), viii, 119–20
Figures III (Genette), xiii
Flaubert, Gustave, 24, 57–8, 66,
    91, 99, 100, 122, 129, 131, 150–1,
    166, 189
Foucault, Michel, 24–8, 32, 40, 71,
    171, 195
Frears, Stephen, 45
Freud, Sigmund, 51, 53, 73
Friedman, Carl, 82–9

Fuchs, Martin, 71
Fuller, Loie (Satrapi), 185, 195

Garcés, María Antonia, 166
Garcia Márquez, Gabriel, 102
"Garden of Forking Paths, The"
    (Borges), 46–8
Geertz, Clifford, 18–21
Genette, Gérard, xiii
Germaine, Thomas, 65
Godfather, The (Copola), 126
Goeth, Amon (*Schindler's List*),
    30, 63
Gogol (*The Namesake*), 4–6
Great Expectations (Dickens), 137–8
Greimas, Algirdas Julian,
    187, 189, 195

Hals, Frans, 122
Hamletmachine (Müller), 34, 71
Hamon, Philippe, 166, 177
Hansen, Miriam Bratu, 71
Heredia, José-Maria de, xiv
Herman, David, 71, 99
Hernández Navarro, Miguel Á., 73,
    140, 161–4, 167–8
Hiroshima mon amour (Duras), 186
Hiroshima mon amour (Resnais), 186
Hirsch, Marianne, 73, 165
Hirschkop and Shepherd, 165
Holly, Lauren, 165
Homer, 109
Huis clos (Sartre), 180

Ida (Pawlikowski), vii, 7–14, 15
Ideas instaladas (Jerez), 190
Illiad (Homer), 109
*I'm Six Years Old and Hiding behind
    My Hands* (Aptekar), vii, 91–8
In Custody (Desai), 177–81, 187–9,
    189–9
In Medias Res, 71–2

In Search of Vanished Blood (Malani),
    vii, 32–6, 71
*Interpretation of Dreams,
    The* (Freud), 53
"Invisible Cities" (Calvino), 102–4
Itárritu, Alejandro González, 102
It's about Time! Reflections on Urgency
    (Bal), 192–4

James, Henry, 138
Janssens, Ann Veronica, vii, 66–70
Jephtah's daughter, 20–1
Jerez, Concha, 190–3, 196
Jirsa, Tomáš, 73
Judges, Book of (Hebrew Bible),
    18–21, 64, 71, 90

Keller, Evelyn Fox, 54–6, 73
Kentridge, William, 102
Khanna, Ranjana, 164
Kitab Al Manazir (Theuws), viii,
    118–19
Kublai Khan ("Invisible Cities"), 103
Kulesza, Agata (*Ida*), 9

Laclos, Choderlos de, 45
Lahiri, Jhumpa, 4–7
La jalousie (Robbe-Grillet), 40
La modification (Butor), 456
L'après-midi de Monsieur Andesmas
    (Duras), 102
Lee, Kyoo, 166
Leitch, Thomas, 166
Le personnel du roman
    (Hamon), 166, 177
Liaisons dangereuses (Laclos), 45
Linnaeus' Flower Clock (Tan),
    vii, 103–5
Local Knowledge (Geertz), 18–21
Łódź Film School, 111
Longman, Mary, vii, 16–17, 72, 181
Louvre, Musée du, 157–9

Lovers Rock (McQueen), 188
Lutters, Jeroen, 70, 84, 166, 196
Lynch, David, 41

Madame B (Bal & Williams
    Gamaker), 58–61
Madame Bovary (Chabrol), 65
Madame Bovary (Flaubert), 24, 58–9,
    65, 128–30, 140, 150, 178
Malani, Nalini, 32–6, 71–2
Malkovich, John, 45
Marx, William, xiv, 19
McEwan, Ian, 151–3
McMaster, Gerald, 16, 72, 181
McQueen, Steve, 143, 149, 188
Metahistory (White), 40, 73
Migas de pan (Bibliowicz),
    107, 113, 144
mise en abyme, 72, 88, 95
Montanier, Mathieu, vii, 39
Morrison, Toni, 103, 169–75
Mouffe, Chantal, 23, 70, 164, 168
Mulisch, Harry, 139–40
Müller, Günther, xiii
Müller, Heiner, 34, 36, 71
Munch, Edvard, vii, 41–4, 56, 67
Muñoz, Juan, 146
Murcia, 161, 178

Namesake, The, 4–8
National Gallery of Art (Washington,
    DC), 92
Negrete, Fernanda, 73
Newell, William H., 71
Niditch, Susan, 141–2, 144, 169
Night Father (Friedman), 82–6
Nightwood (Barnes), 57, 133, 140, 151
Numbers, Book of, 142

One Hundred Years of Solitude (García
    Marquez), 102
Oresteia (Aeschylus), 110

Pakula, Alan J., 62
Pascal, Blaise, 68
Patron, Sylvie, 72
Pawlikowski, Pawel (*Ida*), 7
Peeren, Esther, 109, 165
Pensées (Pascal), 68
Perniola, Mario, 73
Persepolis (Satrapi), 182
Picket Fences, 126, 165
"Pierre Menard, Author of the
    Quixote" (Borges), 38, 96
Poirot, Hercule (Christie), 168
Pollock, Griselda, 73
Proust, Marcel, 91, 125–6, 132, 153–8,
    160, 166
Puzo, Mario, 126

Quoting Caravaggio (Bal), 73

Radioactive (Satrapi), 182–6, 188
Rancière, Jacques, 175–6
Rape of Shavi, The (Emecheta),
    132–3, 139
Reading "Rembrandt" (Bal), 71
Recherche. See *A la recherche du temps
    perdu* (Proust)
Red Virginia Creeper (Munch), vii,
    41–50
Regarding the Pain of Others
    (Sontag), 105
Rembrandt, viii, 50, 156–60, 166
Resnais, Alain, 186
Revelations, Book of, 120
Ritual in Transfigured Time (Deren),
    114–18
Robbe-Grillet, Alain, 40, 45
Ross, Christine, 165
Rothberg, Michael, 72
Rousseau, Douanier (*Nightwood*), 151

Santa Claus (*Turbulence*), 126
Sartre, Jean-Paul, 151, 180

Satrapi, Marjane, 182–6
Scheherazade (*Arabian Nights, A Thousand and One Nights*), 75
Schindler's List, vii, 29–32, 56, 62
Shadow of the Object: Psychoanalysis and the Unthought Known, The (Bollas), 112
Silence Please!, 146
Silverman, Kaja, 112, 141, 154, 165
Small Axe (McQueen), 143, 148, 188
Snow White, 129
Sontag, Susan, 105
Sophie's Choice, 62
Spider (Bourgeois), vii, 47–54, 66
Spielberg, Steven, vii, viii, 29–32, 62, 148–50
Stoler, Ann Laura, 75
Sula (Morrison), 169–75, 176, 178, 184, 187, 188, 189

Tan, Fiona, vii, 103–5
Tarr, Béla, and Ágnes Hranitski, 169, 175–6
Ten Thousand Things, The (Dermoût), 57
Theuws, Roos, viii, 118–20
Thousand and One Days, A (Cinema Suitcase), 7, 76–82, 164
Thousand and One Nights, A, 75–7, 164
Tolstoy, Lev, 37
Trzebuchowska, Agata (*Ida*), 9
Tuin, Iris van der, 164
Turbulence (Butler), 126

Uncle Tom's Cabin (Beecher Stowe), 147–50

Vellodi, Kamini, 160, 165–6, 196
Verheul, Thom, 135–6
Verhoeff, Nanna, 73, 134–5, 164, 195
Vermeer, Johannes, 121–3
Verstraten, Peter, 64
Verweg, Hanna, 88
Vitruvius, 53

Walker, Alice, 148
Wanda, Aunt (*Ida*), 9–12
Waves, The (Woolf), 151
Werckmeister Harmonies (Tarr and Hranitski), 175–6
"What Happened to Sergeant Massuro?" (Mulish), 139–40
"What Is an Author?" (Foucault), 24–5
White, Hayden, 3, 38–40, 72, 127–8
Williams Gamaker, Michelle, 58, 195
Wolf, Christa, 34
Woman Interrupted (Christensen), viii, 121–4
Woman Interrupted at Her Music (Vermeer), 121
Woolf, Virginia, 151
Wuthering Heights (Brontë), 74

Żal, Łukasz (*Ida*), 8
Žižek, Slavoj, 167, 168, 173, 195
Zola, Émile, 129, 151

Index of Terms and Concepts

abstraction, abstract, 16, 32–5, 66,
  69–70, 88, 185
achrony, 116
actant, 177, 190, 195; helper, 177, 190;
  opponent, 177, 190; power, 188;
  subject, 179
activating, 70, 192
activist, 70
adaptation, 147, 166
aesthetics, aesthetic, 8, 56, 59, 61, 77,
  117, 122, 124–5, 150
affect, 7, 13, 53, 58–62, 73
allegory, allegorical, 47, 50, 90, 132–3,
  139, 141, 154
allusion, 16, 44–5, 108, 115–16, 123,
  150, 158–9
alter (MPS), 136
anachronism, anachronistic, 40, 73,
  96, 100, 141–4, 151, 159
antagonism, 23
anteriority stories, 50–4
anthropology, anthropological,
  x, 16, 18, 21
anthropomorphism, 16, 49, 125
anti-Islamism, 127
anti-Semitism, 127
architecture, 50–1, 53
archive, archival, 104–5, 134

Aristotelian poetics, 46
Aristotelian unity, 78
art history, 49, 120, 139, 145
artistic research, 160, 166, 196
augmented reality, viii, 134
authority, 25–8, 31, 40, 87
authorship, 25–7, 31–2, 40, 71
autobiography, autobiographical, 90,
  92–5, 107, 147
autonomy, xi, 35–6, 121

baroque, 67–9, 73, 90, 92, 97
becoming (Deleuze), 112–13, 124
Bildungsroman, 107
binary opposition, 127–8, 144
biography, 24, 26, 166, 184, 186

"camp," 82–5, 91, 101, 113
censorship, 26
character–effect, 131
character-narrator (CN), 32
character-plot knot, 47, 73
chronology, 184
close-up, 11, 31, 43, 63, 122, 150, 189
collage, 158
comparison, comparative, 28, 64–5,
  83, 144, 146, 150–1, 155, 156
competition, 54, 73

concubine, 18–21
confusion, 5, 14, 70, 83–4, 123, 161
con-fusion, 83–4, 91, 109, 114, 161,
    163, 166, 185
constellation, x, xiv, 73, 109, 112–15,
    116, 187
contemporary, 20, 35–40, 58, 61, 82,
    90–2, 100, 103, 105, 141, 147–9, 165,
    186, 193, 196
crisis (fabula), 114, 184, 187
critique, 56–9, 61, 65, 72, 123, 128,
    130, 166, 195
crystals of time, 47–8
cultural analysis, x–xi, 14, 22–3, 49,
    70–1, 141, 144, 164

deixis, deictic, 46–7, 70, 129–31
delimitation, 56
depression, depressed, 100, 135, 165
description, 56–63, 129–31,
    133, 137, 175
development (fabula), 63, 184, 187
dialogue, xi, 15, 35, 47–8, 59, 73, 89,
    114, 146, 150, 165, 191
disagreement, xii, 142, 168
disfigure, 157, 196
distinction, distinguishing, xi, 3–7,
    13–15, 19, 22–3 *et passim*
doublets, 63
drama, xii, 18, 86, 167
duration, 46, 70, 151, 161, 184, 188–9

ellipsis, 117
embedding, embedded, 10, 37, 44,
    64–5, 68, 74–5 *et passim*
empirical research, 157–9
emplotment, 40, 73
enduring, 121, 151, 188
essay, 110–12, 192
essay film, 111, 192–3
ethnocentrism, ethnocentric, 18, 21,
    142, 144

ethnography, ethnographic,
    18, 104

failure (of an analysis), 103,
    110, 164, 168
faithfulness, faithful (in
    adaptations), 150, 166
fiction, 8, 13, 15, 22, 28, 35, 59, 73,
    103, 138
figuration, 16, 43, 141
figurative, 44, 47
film narratology, 145
flâneur, 108, 140
focalisation, xiii–xiv
formalist, formal, 15
frame, framing, 57, 132, 133–4, 140,
    167, 168–9, 176, 195
frame narratives, 75
free indirect discourse (FID), 14, 66,
    68, 72, 150
freeze-frame, 115
futurality, futural, 103, 115

Garden, Biblical story of the, 49–50
gender, gendering, 54, 88, 149, 185
grief, 18, 57, 81, 105, 107, 162

heterochrony, 100–2, 113,
    117, 124
heterogeneity, heterogeneous, 89–90,
    93, 101–2, 126, 129–30
heteroglossia, 89
heteropathy, 48–9, 53, 154
historical present, 106
history, historical, 7, 8, 13, 63, 98,
    99–100, 123
holocaust, 62, 98, 113, 165
hors-champ, 42, 61
hyphen, 82–3, 92, 161, 164

iconography, iconographic, 41, 44,
    50, 145, 147

identification, identificatory, 62–3, 81, 91, 150, 182; heteropathic, 154–5; idiopathic, 154
ideology, xiv, 22, 26, 56, 126, 195
illusionism, 67; anti-, 97
illustration, illustrative, 32, 44, 50, 146–7
image-thinking, 72, 160, 163, 164, 166, 180, 190, 196
imagination, 6, 22, 34–6, 38, 49; photographic, 163
immersion, immersive, 66, 69
implied author, 27–8, 72
individualism, individualistic, 31–2, 48
in medias res, 3, 35, 71–2
installation, 32, 37, 52, 69, 121–3, 166, 181–2, 190–3
intention, authorial, 25–6, 151
interculturality, intercultural, 5, 76–7, 132
interdisciplinarity, 14, 16, 21, 22, 66, 71–3, 91
interdiscursivity, 36, 89–90, 150
interference, 66–9; text, 74
interior monologue, 46, 174
intermediality, xi, 3–4, 58, 111, 125–6, 156, 159, 160, 163
interpretation, x, xii, 25–7, 41–4, 88, 96, 133, 144–5, 178
interpretive community, xii
interruption, 118–24, 152–3, 165
intership, inter-ship, 14–21, 41, 42, 71–3, 164
intersubjectivity, xi–xii, 23, 25, 28, 70
intertextuality, 36, 89, 115, 148, 150, 159
intimacy, 48, 75, 79, 81, 107
irony, ironic, 5, 37, 89, 91, 95, 98

linearity, linear, 41, 53, 67, 98, 101, 110, 119, 139, 155, 186; anti-, non-, 67, 100, 114
loa, 90
loyalty, loyal, 59, 61, 100

manipulation, xiv, 64, 127, 139, 156, 188
marriage, arranged, 80
marriage forms, 21
material, materiality, x, 15, 16, 25, 35, 66–7, 134, 146
media transfer, 109
medium-specificity, 76
memory, 34, 53, 57, 72–3, 95, 101, 103, 108, 112–13, 140–1, 152–3; acts of, 6, 103, 161–7; multidirectional, multidirectionality, 6–8; multitemporal, multitemporality, 6
metanarrative, 88, 91, 96, 98, 152,
metaphor, 6, 16, 48–53, 55–6, 89, 103, 116, 126, 129, 138, 153, 163; literalizing, 47
migration, 4–6, 78–9, 101, 124; migratory, 78, 82, 102, 124
mirror, 38, 63, 66–8
mirror image, 66, 88
mirror text, 91, 95–6, 98
mise en abyme, 72. *See also* mirror image; mirror text
misogyny, 125
mosaic, x, xiv, 14, 23, 90, 105, 113, 116, 187, 193, 196
motivation, 56–63, 129, 137, 171, 176
multilingualism. *See* heteroglossia
multiple personality syndrome (MPS), 136
multi-temporality, 7, 101, 117

narratee, 34, 88, 181
narration, 8, 18, 28 *et passim*; second-person, 45–51, 54–8, 61, 104, 109, 161, 184

narrative text, ix, xiii, 4, 8, 24, 26–8, 54, 72, 76, 91, 98
narrator, 24, 26–9 *et passim*; embedded, 74, 88, 93; external, 14, 20, 37, 47, 56, 93, 129; non-perceptible (np), 36, 56; perceptible (p), 36; pictorial, 43, 57; primary, 45, 74, 76–80, 82–3, 86–9, 91, 95–7, 110
neoliberalism, neoliberal, 26
nominalization, 143
nostalgia, 57
nude, 157–8

objectification, 129
objectivity, objective, 8, 32, 72, 101–2, 129, 163
ostentatious self-definition by negation (White), 127–8

participation, participatory, 37, 51, 57, 69, 160, 164, 181, 191
passé simple (fr.), 130, 161
pastness, 103, 106
patrilocal, 20–1
performance, 117–18, 124, 185
performativity, performative, 43, 66, 69, 81–2, 181, 192
perspective, 41, 43, 67, 138–9, 146; linear, 119, 139, 155
phantom rides, 62
photography, photographic, 118, 126, 132, 139, 153–5, 163, 182
photographic imagination. *See* imagination
plot, 3, 7, 47, 73, 148, 182
plurality, 32, 81, 90, 107, 144
point of view, xiii, 138–9
political, 22–3, 25–8, 70, 76, 81, 117, 132, 141, 151, 164
politics, 22–3, 79–81, 164
post-, 101, 105, 165

postmemory, 144, 165
postmodernism, postmodern, 49, 61–2, 69, 91–6, 103, 125–6, 130, 144
predictability, predictable, 126–7
pre-posterous, 59, 73, 92, 96, 124
present (tense), 54, 61, 94, 95, 106, 108, 110–11, 114, 156–9, 192
present (time), 6, 34, 50, 51–3, 59, 69, 79, 83, 93, 95, 101, 106, 112, 134, 164
pretérito (sp.), 161, 167
pre-text, 149–50, 156
projection, 20, 25, 141
prostitute, 18–19, 21
psychoanalysis, psychoanalytical, 51, 165

quotation, 34–6, 40, 89, 92; poetics of, 35

racism, 127, 132, 149, 189
rape, 20–1, 132–3, 136, 141–4, 149, 158, 169
realism, realist, realistic, 57–8, 62, 74, 118, 125–6, 136–8, 149
recognition, 44, 114, 126–7, 144–5, 185
reference, 18, 95, 105, 131
reflection, 11, 22, 35, 38, 66, 68, 70, 95, 103–4, 108, 143, 163, 165, 193
relativism: cultural, 144, 168; theoretical, 168
re-painter (Aptekar), 92
repetition, 35, 59, 63, 82, 108, 113–14, 127
reversibility, 46
rhythm, xiii, 100, 116–23, 153, 184

second-person, 58, 61, 106, 109, 161
secret, 54–6, 73, 142
self-reflection, self-reflexive, 38, 66, 70, 108

semantics, semantic, 43–5, 72
semiotics, semiotic, 69, 71, 86, 88
sentimentality, sentimentalizing, sentimental, 11, 148
sequential, 41, 102–4, 134, 179
sexism, 125, 127, 148–9, 183
sexual violence, 132, 136
slave narrative, 147–9
slow-down, 108, 118–24, 131, 140
slowness, 69, 118–20, 123, 169
sound, 10, 32–5, 59, 65, 108, 121, 150
sound narrator, 65
speech act, 87
speed, 80, 188
still, stillness, 121–4, 131–2, 140
structure, structural, 18, 21, 46, 48, 56, 74–8, 93–6
suture, 29, 31, 56, 62
syntax, syntactic, 41–2, 44–5, 72

theatricality, theatrical, 89, 121, 165
theoretical object, 51, 70, 118
theory of the novel, xii–xiii, 131

thought-image, 47, 72, 160, 163
tragedy, 62–3, 77, 110, 114
trauma, traumatic, 21, 83, 108–9, 114, 123, 136, 141, 162, 164
truth, 32, 37, 38–40, 81, 112, 133, 140, 155, 189
truth claim, 37

"unthought known" (Bollas), 53

vanishing point, 67, 69
version, 28, 109, 148
versioning, 109
video-shadow play (Malani), 32, 36, 72, 192
virginity, virgin, 19–21
virilocal, 20–1
visuality, visual, 14, 51, 108, 113, 119, 140, 147–8, 150–2
voyeurism, 11, 40, 105, 154

witness, witnessing, 11, 37, 40, 61, 74, 154–5
wobbly, 59–61